FINANCIAL GATEKEEPERS

YASUYUKI FUCHITA
ROBERT E. LITAN
Editors

FINANCIAL GATEKEEPERS

Can They Protect Investors?

NOMURA INSTITUTE OF CAPITAL MARKETS RESEARCH
Tokyo

BROOKINGS INSTITUTION PRESS
Washington, D.C.

Copyright © 2006
THE BROOKINGS INSTITUTION
NOMURA INSTITUTE OF CAPITAL MARKETS RESEARCH

All rights reserved. No part of this publication may be reproduced or transmitted in any form or by any means without permission in writing from the Brookings Institution Press.

Financial Gatekeepers: Can They Protect Investors? may be ordered from:
BROOKINGS INSTITUTION PRESS, c/o HFS
P.O. Box 50370, Baltimore, MD 21211-4370
Tel.: 800/537-5487; 410/516-6956; Fax: 410/516-6998
Internet: www.brookings.edu

Library of Congress Cataloging-in-Publication data
Financial gatekeepers : can they protect investors? / Yasuyuki Fuchita and Robert E. Litan, editors.
   p.   cm.
Includes bibliographical references and index.
ISBN-13: 978-0-8157-2981-5 (pbk. : alk. paper)
ISBN-10: 0-8157-2981-2 (pbk. : alk. paper)
1. Financial statements—United States. 2. Financial statements—Japan. 3. Corporations—United States—Accounting. 4. Corporations—Japan—Accounting. 5. Disclosure of information—United States. 6. Disclosure of information—Japan. I. Fuchita, Yasuyuki, 1958– . II. Litan, Robert E., 1950– .
HF5681.B2F4622 2006
657'.30973—dc22   200601285

9 8 7 6 5 4 3 2 1

Typeset in Adobe Garamond

Composition by R. Lynn Rivenbark
Macon, Georgia

Contents

	Preface	vii
1	Introduction *Yasuyuki Fuchita and Robert E. Litan*	1
2	Financial Gatekeepers in Japan *Yasuyuki Fuchita* Comment by Paul Stevens 55	13
3	How and Why Credit Rating Agencies Are Not Like Other Gatekeepers *Frank Partnoy* Comment by Justin Pettit 100	59
4	Maintaining the Value and Viability of Auditors as Gatekeepers under SOX: An Auditing Master Proposal *Zoe-Vonna Palmrose* Comment by Peter Wallison 136	103

| 5 | Analyzing the Analysts after the Global Settlement | 139 |

Leslie Boni
Comment by George Perry 172

| 6 | Conclusion | 177 |

John Coffee

| Contributors | 191 |
| Index | 193 |

Preface

THE BROOKINGS INSTITUTION and the Nomura Institute of Capital Markets Research have joined in a new collaborative project, headed by Robert Litan, Brookings senior fellow, and Yasuyuki Fuchita, director of the Nomura Institute of Capital Markets Research, to conduct research in selected topics of financial market structure and regulation.

In October 2004 an introductory seminar was held at Brookings on the subject of the financial services industry in the aftermath of the Gramm-Leach-Bliley (GLB) Financial Modernization Act. The papers and a summary of that seminar are available on the web page of the Tokyo Club Foundation for Global Studies (www.tcf.or.jp/seminars/2004/20041005.html), which is underwriting this annual forum and publication of a conference volume.

This current volume is the result of a meeting on September 28, 2005, at the Brookings Institution that focused on the role of financial gatekeepers. All of the papers and discussion comments represent the views of the authors and not necessarily the views of the staff members, officers, or trustees of the Brookings Institution or the Nomura Institute.

The manuscript was edited by Eileen Hughes. Jesse Gurman provided research assistance. Eric Haven checked for factual accuracy, and Shannon Leahy organized the conference and provided administrative assistance.

FINANCIAL GATEKEEPERS

YASUYUKI FUCHITA
ROBERT E. LITAN

Introduction

THE SUCCESSIVE BANKRUPTCIES of Enron and WorldCom—once two of the leading U.S. high-technology companies—in the early part of this decade shook the economic and political establishment, in the United States and elsewhere around the world. Officials, investors, and ordinary citizens had simple questions. How could it have happened? Why wasn't the public alerted earlier to problems in those firms and in other large companies that also failed?

In the United States, reaction was swift—almost remarkably so. Within a year of Enron's failure, Congress had passed and President George W. Bush had signed what probably was the most sweeping reform of the nation's laws governing corporate disclosure ever enacted: the Sarbanes-Oxley Act (since commonly referred to as SOX). Among other changes, SOX creates a new system and a new body—the Public Company Accounting Oversight Board (PCAOB)—for regulating the accounting industry; requires chief executive officers of public companies to certify the reliability of their financial statements; and toughens penalties for corporate fraud and other misdeeds. The New York Stock Exchange quickly followed with new registration requirements, among them the requirement that the majority of public company board seats be filled by "independent directors," which generally excludes individuals currently or previously employed by the company and those related to them. And the New York State Attorney General's Office launched a series of investigations into the financial services industry, forcing a variety of sweeping changes. Among the more important of these inquiries was one into misleading research reports issued by many of Wall Street's leading investment banks—and more broadly into the conflicts that compensation systems at those banks created for the analysts who worked for them. That investigation, in particular, resulted in the Global Settlement, which prohibits the compensation of analysts from being based, in part or in whole, on the financial performance of the investment banking operations of the companies for which they work. The settlement also requires the ten investment bank defendants to fund and report stock research by independent third-party analysts.

There is much irony, of course, in these developments. Only a few short years before the scandals in the United States broke, U.S. officials and corporate leaders were busy criticizing Asian economies for the lack of transparency in their business sectors. But, as it turned out, the United States has not been alone in suffering through disclosure problems and associated corporate failures. Europe and Japan have also had their share of the same difficulties and in response have adopted or at least considered similar reforms.

At bottom, the broad theory behind SOX and other related reforms is that corporate managers cannot be trusted and so require much closer oversight, by multiple parties: boards of directors, their accountants, and third-party equity analysts. In turn, each of the "financial overseers" or "gatekeepers," in particular, must be more closely watched by government or quasi-official bodies.

How is all this new oversight, especially the regimes governing financial gatekeepers, working? What changes, if any, should be made? Should policies relating to other gatekeepers that were untouched by the post-scandal wave of reforms—credit rating agencies, in particular—be modified? Are the answers for the United States different from those for Japan? To address such questions, on September 28, 2005, the Brookings Institution and the Tokyo Club Foundation for Global Studies convened their second annual conference on financial issues of mutual interest to American and Japanese audiences.[1]

This book incorporates the papers presented and the remarks of discussants made at the conference. The authors and the discussants are leading experts in their fields, and we are privileged to include their views in this volume. In addition, the book closes with the luncheon remarks of one of the world's leading experts in corporate securities law, John Coffee of Columbia Law School.

---

1. For the conference agenda, see "After the Horses Have Left the Barn: The Future Role of Financial Gatekeepers" (www.brookings.edu). The Tokyo Club Foundation for Global Studies was established by Nomura Securities Co., Ltd., in 1987 as a nonprofit organization for promoting studies in the management of the global economy.

INTRODUCTION 3

If there is a common theme running through the chapters it is that the reform efforts, in both the United States and Japan, still are very much works in progress. The measures addressing accountants and analysts, at least in the United States, can be improved, while the rules governing the certification of nationally recognized credit rating agencies should be loosened to make the field more competitive.

ALTHOUGH BOTH American and Japanese readers of this volume are likely to be aware that Japan has had its own share of corporate accounting scandals related to nonperforming corporate loans and the fifteen-year slump in stock prices, American readers in particular may not know that Japanese authorities have responded by looking to the United States for solutions. In significant respects, Japan now has its own SOX-like regime for improving the effectiveness of its financial gatekeepers. In chapter 2, Yasuyuki Fuchita, of the Nomura Institute of Capital Markets Research, examines the Japanese system and offers a systematic way for thinking about financial gatekeepers generally.

Fuchita begins by observing that in the early years after the country's stock market "bubble" popped, Japanese corporations and banks, with the assent of their accountants, downplayed the decline in their assets, believing that the situation was temporary and soon would correct itself. Only as the decade of the 1990s wore on and asset values stayed depressed did it become more evident that some accountants had looked the other way while their clients manipulated their financial statements. The first stunning example of this was the disclosure in November 1997 that Yamaichi Securities, one of Japan's "Big Four" securities firms, had huge off–balance sheet debts and could no longer continue operating.

The Japanese government and its political system had long been geared to maintaining "order" in the financial system rather than exposing its difficulties, so when reform came, it was slow. In 1999, the Ministry of Finance set up a working group to consider ways to make external auditors more independent and to improve the system of supervising them. In 2000 the group responded with a series of incremental suggestions. Fuchita observes that more radical reforms came only after Enron. Following the enactment of the Sarbanes-Oxley Act in the United States in the summer of 2002, the Japanese Diet enacted amendments to the Certified Public Accountants Law, which roughly mirrored SOX in several respects, including the mandatory rotation of auditor staff; the prohibition of non-auditing work for audit clients; and the creation of the Certified Public Accountants and Auditing Oversight Board (CPAAOB), a new body to oversee auditors that is similar to the PCAOB in the United States.

Fuchita notes that the new measures did not end the reporting scandals; to the contrary, they may have helped lead to the discovery of several more, such as the revelation in October 2004 that Seibu Railway had falsified its reports. Meanwhile, other reforms continued, such as new reporting guidelines issued by the Financial Services Agency (FSA). Fuchita offers a useful comparison of the U.S. and Japanese reforms, outlining common elements and differences in accounting and its oversight in the two countries. Among the more important differences, he argues, is that there are far fewer independent accountants per listed firm in Japan than in the United States or, for that matter, in other economies. In addition, the time allowed for audits is shorter, and that is one reason that accountants' fees are lower in Japan than in other countries. As a result, although in the United States and Japan the formal rules governing reporting and accounting are similar, there remain large differences in the way the rules are actually enforced.

With respect to credit rating agencies, Fuchita observes that whereas rating services began as a business in the United States, credit ratings were introduced in Japan only recently, in 1992, as a new requirement for issuing a bond. The result, however, has been the same in the two countries: only a limited number of agencies are designated as those whose ratings "count" for some regulatory purpose, although the ratings market is not as concentrated in Japan as in the United States. Nonetheless, Japanese and U.S. ratings agencies confront similar problems (which are surveyed in chapter 3 by Frank Partnoy): lags or lack of timeliness in changing ratings when they need to be changed (illustrated by the celebrated bankruptcy of and bond default by Mycal, Japan's fourth-largest supermarket) and a bias toward issuers. Fuchita urges Japanese authorities to abolish the rating agency designation process or, as a fallback, to subject the agencies to registration and regulation by the FSA. At the time of the conference, similar ideas were being considered in the United States.

Fuchita also highlights a number of key differences between equity research analysts in the United States and Japan. Among the more significant is that equities, directly or through mutual funds (or investment trusts), account for a far lower share of household financial assets in Japan than in the United States. As a result, research analysts have never assumed the same public importance and notoriety in Japan as in the United States. Nonetheless, Japanese law prohibits securities companies from issuing misleading reports, while the Japanese Securities Dealers Association (JSDA) oversees analysts. The Financial Services Agency, in turn, oversees the JSDA. As in the United States, there have been a number of scandals involving analysts' reports, and the JSDA has been prompted by the FSA to tighten its rules in order to establish firewalls within securities firms between their equity research and their underwriting departments.

Fuchita concludes his survey of the three gatekeepers—accountants, credit rating agencies, and equity analysts—by offering a useful framework for regulating all three. In particular, he suggests that the need for regulation depends on both the influence each has on securities trading and the need for uniformity in the information being reported. Using those criteria, he suggests that accounting therefore requires the most oversight because investors are likely to place the most trust in accountants' attestations and because all companies must report financial information according to a uniform, common convention (generally accepted accounting principles). Analysts are at the other extreme. Since investors are likely to give less attention to their views, analysts should be free to say what they think. However regulation is designed, Fuchita argues that it ought not to artificially constrain competition among the firms performing each gatekeeping function.

CREDIT RATING AGENCIES are little known—and perhaps less understood—but nonetheless important parts of the financial systems of developed economies, especially in the United States. Credit rating agencies assign alphabetical ratings to new and existing issues of debt. For all practical purposes, corporations cannot issue debt—and financial institutions cannot issue various debt-like instruments, such as asset-backed securities—without having a credit rating.

In chapter 3, Frank Partnoy of the University of San Diego Law School addresses a puzzle: namely, that although credit rating agencies have performed no better than the other financial gatekeepers that are the subject of this book, their market value has soared. A major answer to the second part of the puzzle is that government regulators have conferred oligopoly status on a select few credit rating agencies by designating them "nationally recognized statistical rating organizations" (NRSROs) and thereby allowing them to earn supranormal profits, which are then capitalized in the market value of their shares. Partnoy also attributes their rising profits to the growth of new and increasingly complex instruments that must be rated, especially credit derivatives, which now generate a substantial portion of the agencies' revenues and profits. Indeed, he devotes a significant part of his chapter to explaining these instruments and their risks, especially collateralized debt obligations (CDOs), which are structured, leveraged transactions backed by one or more classes of fixed-income assets. In the mid-1990s, CDOs were backed primarily by high-yield corporate bonds; today, they are backed by a much wider assortment of fixed-income assets, including other CDOs.

As for the first half of the puzzle—the agencies' imperfect performance—Partnoy suggests two explanations. One is that the agencies face conflicts of interest that arguably are more severe than those of other gatekeepers, since the agencies not only are paid by issuers but also often give unsolicited ratings that, in Partnoy's view, have the effect of pressuring issuers to pay them, perhaps for better ratings. That was not always the case; in earlier times, investors paid ratings agencies.

But investors lost their appetite for ratings during and after the stock market crash of 1929, when agencies failed to anticipate the accompanying sharp decline in bond prices as well. Beginning in the 1970s and continuing into the present, the SEC and other agencies nonetheless have established various rules (such as the rule that money market funds buy only Treasury debt or highly rated commercial paper) that depend on NRSRO ratings. Partnoy broadly describes the multitude of these rules, which have now practically cemented the quasi-oligopoly status of the three major NRSROs.

Another explanation regarding their extraordinary profitability and perhaps their lackluster performance is that the agencies have been shielded from civil and criminal liability for mistakes—or, worse, for malfeasance—by having so far successfully invoked the protection of the free speech clause in the First Amendment of the Constitution. Partnoy outlines legal arguments that contest that view, but until the courts make clear that the NRSROs do not enjoy First Amendment protection, their effective immunity from lawsuits will remain intact.

Partnoy concludes by reviewing various proposals that he and others have advanced in recent years for bringing greater competition to the credit rating function. Some analysts have proposed eliminating the NRSRO designation altogether, while others want it more liberally construed or applied. At the time of the conference, Congress was considering legislation that would require the agencies to register with the SEC and then disclose material facts, much as other public corporations are now required to do. Partnoy describes a proposal that he has been advocating since 1999, one that substitutes market-based measures (based on interest rate differentials between various kinds of securities) for credit ratings in the numerous regulations that now depend on NRSRO ratings.

It is unclear whether any significant reform is in the offing. In the meantime, scholars, investors, and policymakers will continue to live with another paradox: that while rating agencies historically have not been a good guide to risk and market participants know it, parties increasingly rely on the ratings. Partnoy suggests that this paradox will continue as long as the law requires the NRSRO designation and allows only a few organizations to receive it.

SINCE ACCOUNTING FIRM failures were the "real world" triggers for SOX and related reforms, it is appropriate to focus, as Zoe-Vonna Palmrose of the University of Southern California–Los Angeles does in chapter 4, on the impact of those reforms on the accounting profession.

The gatekeeping function that auditors perform is a legal one. In the United States, securities laws require public companies to have their financial statements certified by independent public accountants. Historically, the Securities and

Exchange Commission (SEC), along with state regulators and the profession's self-regulatory body, the American Institute of Certified Public Accountants (AICPA), oversaw auditors. SOX fundamentally changed that oversight structure by vesting regulatory oversight of the profession in a new, independent entity, the Public Company Accounting Oversight Board, although technically the PCAOB itself is overseen by the SEC. SOX gives the PCAOB authority to set auditing standards (which used to be set by the AICPA); to inspect auditors for compliance with those standards; and to impose sanctions against wayward auditors. SOX also imposed additional requirements and duties on the auditors themselves, obligating them to report on public company managers' assessment of their company's internal controls over financial reporting (so-called section 404 obligations). As a result, auditors are even more highly regulated than they were before SOX.

And all the while, auditors remain subject to civil liability for negligence, as they were before the recent scandals and reforms. Elsewhere, tort law serves a dual function: it deters actors against negligent actions, and it also compensates parties injured by negligence. Yet liability law cannot realistically compensate for any more than a fraction of the losses suffered by stakeholders when a major public company fails. Nor, because the company's market capitalization usually would far exceed the combined net worth of its audit firm and the firm's partners, could the audit firm typically cover damages awarded (through trial or settlement) for the firm's negligence in failing to discover or disclose problems with the company (in the event that the limited liability shield of the firm was "pierced" in a legal action). Moreover, auditors cannot obtain insurance against their negligence, if they can obtain any at all, that will cover all of the losses that injured parties may suffer. For that reason, legal liability serves primarily a deterrent rather than compensatory function, at least with respect to auditors.

Palmrose points out that although auditors are subject to liability for financial misstatements by a client, some of that risk is not of their own making. The accounting standards that govern financial reporting by public companies are sometimes unclear and difficult to audit; thus they can actually facilitate misstatements. Indeed, Palmrose argues, auditors can conduct a "perfect audit" and nonetheless be held liable for client misstatements. Furthermore, even the best internal controls cannot eliminate fraud, which more often than not triggers lawsuits against not only the company that commits fraud but its auditor.

In short, auditors are subject to liability arising out of their engagement with a client—or what Palmrose calls "engagement risk"—even if objectively they have done nothing wrong. Palmrose presents data indicating the rising liability costs confronted by auditors, not only the costs from suits that already have been resolved or settled but also the potentially much greater costs from the "mega" liability cases now in the legal pipeline, flowing largely from the poor stock market performance of the 2000–02 period. It is the apparently random nature of the way that juries sometimes award enormous damages in such cases that drives auditors to settle rather than put the future fate of their firm on the line in a trial. Meanwhile, not surprisingly, audit firms have been trying to reduce their future financial risk by rejecting clients whom they believe to pose unacceptable engagement risk at the outset and by substantially raising fees for those clients whom they seek and with whom they accept engagement.

But even higher fees cannot fund all of the costs that can arise out of negligence actions and pose a potentially catastrophic financial risk for auditors in the future. Accordingly, Palmrose urges the PCAOB—the auditors' new regulator—to bear at least some of the responsibility for sound auditing itself, but in a novel fashion. In particular, recognizing that the oversight board was intentionally structured not to have accounting expertise so as to avoid even the appearance of conflict, none of the board members can have been a practicing certified public accountant within the five years before their appointment. Palmrose therefore urges the board to establish an auditing master's office, which would be independent of the board.

The office would be responsible for assessing auditor compliance with accounting and auditing standards and would stand ready to provide its opinion in court actions in which auditors are charged with negligence in carrying out their audits. The defendants in such cases (the audit firms) would have the option of asking for the office to furnish its opinion to the court. In cases in which the office's report would tend to exonerate the audit firm, not only would the firm be expected to call for the report but also, presumably, the report would accelerate settlement of the case to the benefit of the firm. When the report is not favorable, the defendant would not ask for it, but then the court (or jury) would be entitled to draw a negative inference from that fact. All in all, Palmrose argues, the office's reports would reduce some of the randomness in jury trials on auditor liability and thereby help make the legal system a more effective instrument of deterrence than it now is. The establishment of the office also would enhance, albeit indirectly, the expertise of the PCAOB.

STOCK MARKET ANALYSTS are financial gatekeepers only in the loosest sense of the term. In fact, no public company needs to have outside analysts reporting on its financial prospects, although the more analysts that cover a company, the more liquid the company's stock is likely to be on public markets. In addition, some retail stock investors pay attention to the views of stock analysts. Or, at least, the investment banks that employ analysts must believe that investors do; otherwise, why would the banks continue to pay the analysts?

In fact, stock market analysts initially were not one of the main targets of federal reform efforts in the wake of the Enron and WorldCom collapses, but they soon came to the attention of Eliot Spitzer, the attorney general of the state of New York. Spitzer's aggressive investigation eventually prodded the Securities and Exchange Commission and the National Association of Securities Dealers (NASD) to reach the Global Settlement agreement with ten of the largest U.S. investment banks, which radically changed the way that analysts are paid and provide recommendations to investors. Spitzer's investigation focused only on the so-called "sell-side" analysts—those who were employed by investment banks that also underwrote (or sold) the same stocks that the analysts covered (and recommended). Of particular interest to Spitzer and eventually the SEC was the question of whether analysts issued excessively optimistic investment recommendations because their compensation arrangements gave them incentives to do so.

Spitzer's investigation uncovered several important facts; one was that the compensation of many analysts did indeed depend on the success of their investment banking counterparts. That fact was widely known among institutional investors, who therefore tended to discount analysts' recommendations, but presumably it was not known or sufficiently appreciated by many retail investors. More disturbing were the numerous internal e-mails that Spitzer's office obtained through formal discovery, in which various analysts privately scorned the same companies whose stocks they were recommending to the public.

Spitzer's discoveries almost certainly account for the decisions by the investment banks to accept the Global Settlement in 2003. The agreement prohibited basing analysts' compensation on the performance of the investment banking operations of their employers and subjected the ten defendants to nearly $1.4 billion in total penalties. The penalties are to fund investor education and research for a ten-year period by independent analysts, whose recommendations must be provided along with those made the banks' own analysts. In addition, the settlement required the banks' analysts to disclose their historical recommendations, and it prohibited their research departments from benefiting from revenue derived from the firms' investment banking activities. All of the requirements were designed to remove conflicts that presumably biased analysts' investment recommendations while improving the amount of information made available to investors.

In chapter 5, Leslie Boni of the University of New Mexico and UNX, Inc., reports her findings from a comprehensive study of how the agreement affected analysts' recommendations through September 2004, thirteen months after it became effective. In principle, if the settlement were achieving its objectives, the recommendations of analysts employed by the ten defendant institutions presumably would have been more accurate or worthy of investors' attention than was the case prior to the settlement. Boni outlines a series of statistical tests of the validity of that hypothesis.

Boni assembled a data set on recommendations from recognized sources and divided the analysts' recommendations into three broad categories, "high," "medium," and "low," which are roughly equivalent to "buy," "hold," and "sell" recommendations. Among her many findings:

—Since analysts' research budgets can no longer benefit from investment banking revenues, one would expect that the banks' analysts would cover fewer stocks. On average, that reduction appears to have occurred, although the number of stocks covered by three of the banks increased after settlement.

—As already noted, one would presume that analysts would be less enthusiastic in their stock recommendations after the settlement. On average, such a change was not evident, at least through the end of Boni's study period. The share of recommendations in the "high" category actually increased substantially from 2003 to 2004, while the share of recommendations in the lowest category actually declined.

—Did analysts' recommendations enable investors systematically to outperform "the market," and did they do so before and after the settlement? Boni finds that in both periods, the stocks recommended most highly in fact did outperform the market, but surprisingly, investors could have done even better by buying the stocks in the *lowest* category, or those stocks that the analysts typically would have recommended that investors *sell*. Furthermore, there is no evidence that the Global Settlement has improved the investment value of the highest recommendations.

Given these and other findings reported in the chapter, Boni implicitly questions the value of the Global Settlement. But more than that, she offers concrete suggestions for improved disclosure going forward. In addition to disclosing past recommendations on specific stocks, as analysts were required to do by the New York Stock Exchange (NYSE) and the National Association of Securities Dealers even before the Global Settlement, Boni suggests that analysts and their employers disclose on an ongoing basis their *aggregate* performance across all stocks. Regulators could compile that information, which all firms, not just those subject to the Global Settlement, would then disclose on their websites. Boni doubts that the firms would do so voluntarily.

CHAPTER 6 CONCLUDES this volume with an even broader look at gatekeepers, by John Coffee of Columbia Law School. Coffee begins by offering both a narrow and a broad definition of the term "gatekeeper," noting that under either definition gatekeepers can be deterred from socially undesirable conduct more easily than their clients because they derive relatively little gain from such activity and suffer a disproportionate loss if discovered and punished. Coffee argues that gatekeeping should be encouraged because it cost-effectively encourages clients to comply with the law.

He then outlines different types of gatekeepers: the traditional ones that are the subject of this volume and a new breed, including the "lead plaintiff" in class action lawsuits; "nominated advisers" in alternative investment markets (which tend to be unregulated); and intermediated research or "marriage brokers," who find objective analysts to cover companies.

In Coffee's view, gatekeeping has become more important and has attracted more public attention because of the rising number of public company finance restatements. In turn, restatements matter. Coffee suggests that restatements cause companies to lose about 10 percent of their market capitalization on average. The most common reason for restatements is that revenue was initially overstated. In earlier times, firms had, if anything, an incentive to understate their revenues or to defer revenue recognition by establishing "rainy day reserves" to smooth out earnings. In the 1990s, however, the management of some companies began to recognize revenue prematurely. Coffee attributes the shift to the rising use of equity, stock options in particular, in CEO compensation agreements. When compensation is substantially, if not largely, tied to stock values, then some unscrupulous managers will choose to recognize revenues prematurely since doing so enhances the value of the company's stock and thereby the managers' compensation.

Securities analysts also grew more optimistic during the 1990s. In part, Coffee suggests, the change occurred because analysts' careers tended to progress more rapidly if analysts were more optimistic. In addition, analysts tended to be most optimistic about the stocks that were underwritten by their employers. Coffee concludes by arguing that auditors became less effective gatekeepers during the 1990s because the Private Securities Litigation Reform Act of 1995 made it more difficult to lodge suits against them.

IN SUM, the corporate accounting scandals that rocked the United States corporate landscape in the late 1990s and early part of the next decade have led to major changes in the way various financial gatekeepers are governed. Although only a few years have passed since these changes were introduced, analysts are already debating their effectiveness and necessity. If the authors of the chapters in this volume are right, the recent reforms are unlikely to be the last word on this important subject.

YASUYUKI FUCHITA 2

Financial Gatekeepers in Japan

ACCOUNTANTS, ANALYSTS, AND credit rating agencies function as gatekeepers to financial markets by providing information on investment products to investors. When these financial gatekeepers face conflicts of interest or engage in inappropriate behavior, investors' decisionmaking process is distorted and their interests are put in jeopardy.

Despite a mandate to protect investors, securities regulators have not clearly defined the role of financial gatekeepers and they rarely regulate gatekeepers' activities in the same way that they regulate those of broker-dealers and investment advisers to avoid securities fraud. The collapse of Enron and a series of other corporate scandals have called into question this relatively lenient treatment of financial gatekeepers.

Accountants have been accused not simply of being aware of accounting irregularities but even of aiding and abetting the perpetrators. Arthur Andersen, Enron's auditor, is suspected of putting higher priority on carrying out its more lucrative consultancy work for the company than on ensuring that the company's accounts were in order. Similarly, some securities analysts are suspected of succumbing to explicit or implicit pressure to write rosy reports for (potential) corporate clients in order to win investment banking business. The temptation for such bias is exacerbated by the fact that often analysts' compensation depends on the performance of their firm's investment banking department. Investors who trust the objectivity of an analyst's report may suffer big losses when the reality of the client's situation is exposed in the market.

Credit rating agencies also have come in for considerable criticism, in this case for maintaining investment grade ratings on a company until just before the company collapses, as they did, for example, with Enron. It has been suggested that rating agencies' dependence on fees for rating corporate debt issues conflicts with their obligation to provide investors with timely and accurate information on a company's status.

The Role of Financial Gatekeepers in the United States

Although the collapse of Enron in 2001 and the ensuing corporate scandal highlighted the problems with financial gatekeepers and led to specific reforms, all of these problems had been identified previously. In particular, the issue of biased reporting by equity analysts working for investment banks had been discussed frequently since 2000 and the bursting of the dotcom bubble. Similarly, the Securities and Exchange Commission (SEC) raised the question of how best to regulate credit rating agencies on several occasions since 1992, issuing a "concept release" in 1994 and a rule proposal in 1997. And as early as June 2000 the SEC proposed a rule prohibiting accounting firms from soliciting consultancy work from their audit clients, reflecting the regulator's concern that accounting firms' efforts to diversify operations by expanding their consulting services might affect the independence and objectivity of their audits.

Two factors intensified concerns about financial gatekeepers in the late 1990s. First, the number of private households investing in mutual funds and shares increased during the previous ten years. That meant that more market participants depended on information provided by financial gatekeepers to value securities and that misjudgments by financial gatekeepers affected a growing number of investors. Second, the potential for conflicts of interest among gatekeepers also increased. Both companies and investment banks cherished increasing hopes that the growth in the number of retail investors would increase the short-term impact of analysts' reports on share prices. Similarly, securities companies saw their revenues from investment banking grow faster than their revenues from brokerage.

At the same time, credit rating agencies continued to replace a business model that relied on revenues from subscriptions to their data services by a model that relied on fees from corporate clients. Similarly, income from consultancy work has come be the major source of income at many accounting firms, not just Arthur Andersen.

The general reason for these increasing conflicts of interest is that as financial gatekeepers have found it increasingly difficult to persuade customers to pay for information services, they have come to rely more on fees from issuers.

The Role of Financial Gatekeepers in Japan

In recent years Japan has also seen growing interest in the role of accountants, credit rating agencies, and analysts, as well as some regulatory reforms. Three factors spurred these changes. First, the bad debt problem and stock market slump starting in 1990 led to calls for reform of the country's debt and equity markets overall. Financial gatekeepers emerged as a focus of reform because they failed to warn investors about companies that collapsed during the burst of Japan's asset bubble. Second, the controversy that followed the collapse of Enron in the United States spread to Japan. Third, Japan has also had its fair share of accounting scandals in recent years. The gradual adoption by Japan of reforms similar to the ones that the United States adopted after Enron therefore is not simply a reaction to problems that arose in the United States; Japan had indigenous reasons to reform the regulation of its financial gatekeepers.

Let us first take a brief look at Japan's bad debt problem and stock market slump. When a number of companies (including some major ones) collapsed as the asset boom of the late 1980s turned to a bust in the 1990s, the two main issues were whether the risks to these companies had been identified by external auditors and properly reflected in advance in financial statements, and whether analysts and credit rating agencies had given investors sufficient warning.

Banks were accused of either underestimating their bad debts or misrepresenting their capital adequacy ratios, and the stringency of external auditors was called into question. The Financial Services Agency (FSA), the agency responsible for regulating banks and their auditors, was also criticized for accepting better-looking disclosure prepared by the banks and audited by the accountant.

While issues about financial gatekeepers in Japan came to light in the course of dealing with the country's bad debt problem, ensuring proper behavior on the part of financial gatekeepers is essential to avoiding a recurrence of the nonperforming loan (NPL) situation. Because the scale and duration of the bad loan problem are seen as a consequence of Japan's overreliance on banks, it is necessary to increase the role of securities markets in the economic system. In an economy that relies excessively on the banking system, economic changes will have an exaggerated effect on banks' balance sheets and lead to bad debt problems. In June 2001, soon after it came to power, the Koizumi government made assigning securities markets a more important role one pillar of its economic reform program.

Improving investor protection also is an objective of this program, and reforming the rules governing gatekeepers is one of its most important elements.

In the United States, securities markets have traditionally played a major role in the economy, and the recent increase in retail investor participation in securities markets fueled the debate about the role of financial gatekeepers. In Japan, on the other hand, reform of the rules governing the role of financial gatekeepers, which has been relatively minor in the bank-dominated financial system, is one means the government is using to revitalize securities markets. The fact that Japan's financial system has been dominated by the banks may have been one reason why it took so long to recognize the importance of financial gatekeepers.

Although the debate in Japan about reforming financial gatekeepers has been influenced by Japan's particular situation, that in itself was not enough to lead to calls for specific measures right away. What changed Japan's view was the debate in the United States that followed the collapse of Enron. Even though Japan had experienced similar incidents involving financial gatekeepers, albeit with some differences of degree and nature, the need to reform the rules governing their role was not seen as a priority. But the measures adopted in the United States in response to Enron had a big impact on Japan and helped to speed up the reforms already under way there.

In addition, the discovery in October 2004 that Seibu Railway, a leading company listed on the First Section of the Tokyo Stock Exchange, had falsified its securities filing and that the former management of Kanebo, another well-known company in the First Section, had perpetrated a major reporting fraud helped to accelerate improvements in internal controls, corporate governance, and auditing procedures. Japan's reforms were thereby brought more into line with the reforms recently adopted in the United States.

Thus, the debate about reforming the role of financial gatekeepers in Japan was driven by three factors: existing efforts to solve problems in debt and equity markets; U.S. capital market reforms following the collapse of Enron; and a series of major accounting scandals in Japan. The rest of this chapter examines the reforms of financial gatekeepers in Japan and compares them with the reforms adopted in the United States.

The Accounting System in Japan

With the end of Japan's asset boom of the late 1980s, Japanese companies were confronted with overemployment, overinvestment, and excessive debt and Japanese banks were confronted with nonperforming loans ("bad debts") and depreciating equity portfolios. In that situation, many banks and companies are known to have cooked their books—or are suspected of doing so—out of concern that accurate reporting of declining asset values would undermine their share prices or threaten their existence.

Although the initial cover-up was carried out in the belief that the decline in asset values would be temporary, unrealized losses mounted as asset values continued to decline, and from 1996 onward a series of major bankruptcies occurred as companies found themselves no longer able to disguise the facts. In almost none of those cases did auditors give investors any warning in their audit reports. As was later revealed, some accountants did not take action when they noticed manipulated financial statements and in other cases they even assisted with manipulations to satisfy corporate clients. In other words, they conducted their business for the benefit of their corporate clients, not investors.

On November 22, 1997, Yamaichi Securities, one of Japan's "Big Four" securities companies, was discovered to have ¥260 billion ($2.1 billion) of off-balance sheet debt, and the company announced that it was ceasing operations. Four days later, the *Financial Times* published an editorial criticizing the state of accounting and auditing in Japan.[1] The criticism was directed largely at the big international accounting firms that had accepted the misleading opinions of the Japanese accounting and auditing firms with which they were affiliated.

It is probably fair to say that in order to reduce the threat to the financial system, Japan's regulators initially responded by trying to make financial statements not more but less transparent. First, on December 24, 1997, as part of a package of emergency measures, the Banking Bureau of the Ministry of Finance (MOF) announced that banks could opt to value their equity portfolios at cost, rather than at the lower of cost and market value. MOF was concerned that banks' capital adequacy ratios would be significantly reduced if they reported the extent of unrealized losses on their cross-shareholdings (the shares they held in corporate clients in order to cement business ties and prevent hostile takeover bids). By arbitrarily changing the valuation method, the ministry hoped to prevent banks' capital adequacy ratios from dropping below the international requirement. If that had happened, MOF would have been forced to take prompt corrective action, which would have revealed the extent of the problem facing Japan's major banks and exacerbated the threat to the financial system—or the banks would have been forced to call in loans to bolster their capital, which would have triggered a series of corporate bankruptcies.

---

1. "Wonderland Accounting," *Financial Times*, London ed., November 26, 1997, p. 23. The description in this section of accounting reforms in Japan relies heavily on Isoyama (2002).

Next, in March 1998, the government passed the Land Revaluation Law, which allowed companies and financial institutions to value business assets such as head and branch offices and factories at market value. The sharp drop in real estate prices was putting severe pressure on the profits of banks and financial institutions that had purchased property for speculative purposes during the asset boom of the late 1980s. By allowing companies and financial institutions to revalue business assets, most of which they had acquired before the bubble at low cost, the authorities hoped to give profits a boost that would help offset the stock market decline.

The unmistakable impression from these official responses is that in Japan the problem was not confined to auditing firms but included government intervention to change accounting standards in an effort to disguise the facts.

Initial Efforts to Reform the Accounting System

At the end of 1998, the Big Five international accounting firms responded to the situation by demanding that the major Japanese accounting firms with which they had cooperation agreements include a warning in the auditor's statement accompanying the English-language version of the financial statements of their Japanese clients. The warning, which was to appear with annual reports starting with the fiscal year ending March 1999, would say that the financial statements were intended for users familiar with Japanese accounting principles and auditing standards. While the Japanese companies and auditing firms had no alternative but to agree, they were shocked to receive the same treatment as that received by their counterparts in countries such as South Korea and Indonesia, which had been under International Monetary Fund (IMF) administration following the Asian currency crisis.

In April 1999, the Certified Public Accountant Examination and Investigation Board (CPAEIB), an administrative agency under MOF, set up a working group to consider ways of making external auditors more independent and the system of supervising them more effective. The group published its findings in June 2000. Its main proposals were as follows:

—Further consideration was needed of ways to make external auditors more independent. The Japanese Institute of Certified Public Accountants (JICPA) should be responsible for supervising the independence of external auditors.

—JICPA should establish self-regulating rotation rules to govern the staff of auditing firms involved in audits.

—Audits of companies above a certain size should be carried out jointly by more than one audit firm or by a team of auditors of a suitable size from an auditing firm rather than by individual accountants.

—JICPA should improve its quality control reviews of auditing firms' internal controls and inspection systems.² Consideration should be given to a peer review system.

—The Ministry of Finance should remain responsible for the Certified Public Accountants Law, which regulates accountants and auditing firms, but it should assign more staff to the department that oversees enforcement of the law.

—The Provisions of Standard Remuneration for External Audits should be reviewed. Consideration should be given to requiring companies to disclose the number of days it takes for an audit and the fee charged.

—JICPA's powers as a self-regulating organization should be increased.

—Consideration should be given to adopting a system of limited liability for auditing firms.

—A study should be done of the consultancy work carried out by auditing firms. Firewalls need to be erected between the firms' auditing and non-auditing departments.

Of these proposals, JICPA has adopted as a self-regulating rule the one calling for a rotation system for staff involved in audits. As we shall see, however, radical reform in Japan had to await the collapse of Enron.

More Serious Reform Efforts after the Collapse of Enron

As mentioned, the Koizumi administration first proposed policies to encourage greater use of the securities markets as an alternative to the banking system in June 2001. In order to facilitate the change, the government announced programs for reforming the securities markets in August 2001 and August 2002. The second of the programs contained proposals for reforming the work of auditing firms.

Although Japan obviously needed such reforms in order to establish a securities market that investors could trust, the timing of the reform proposals was influenced by the Enron scandal. The program announced in August 2002 stated that one lesson for Japan from the U.S. scandal was the need to improve regulation of auditing firms, and it called for reviewing the certified public accountant system in Japan with a view to overhauling it as soon as possible (for example, by increasing the number and improving the quality of accountants).

In response to the problems that led to the collapse of Enron, the U.S. Congress incorporated in the Sarbanes-Oxley Act (SOX) measures to give external

---

2. Quality control reviews are conducted by JICPA staff. If any problems arise, the auditing firm is instructed to put its house in order.

auditors greater independence and to improve public supervision and regulation of their activities. Besides the U.S. Congress, the International Organization of Securities Organizations (IOSCO) examined the problem of accounting fraud. Two IOSCO reports published in October 2002 also fostered accounting reform in Japan.[3]

2003 Amendments to the Certified Public Accountants Law

Japan's efforts to reform its system of external auditing were the combined result of the drive to enhance the role of the country's securities market; the collapse of Enron; and international calls for reform (initiated by IOSCO). In December 2002 the Financial System Council's Subcommittee on the Certified Public Accountant System published a report on how to improve Japan's system of accounting and auditing.[4] After studying the report, the Liberal Democratic Party drafted amendments to the Certified Public Accountants Law. These were passed on May 30, 2003. The following were the main effects of the amendments on the gatekeeper issue:

—Self-regulating JICPA rules restricting the length of time that the same staff members of an audit firm could continue to audit a company's accounts were given legal force. It was limited to seven years. The government also adopted an ordinance prohibiting auditing firms from resuming work for a corporate client for at least two years after reaching the limit.

—Auditing firms were prohibited from soliciting non-auditing business (for example, consultancy work) from their corporate clients so long as they continued to audit their accounts.

—A new body, the Certified Public Accountants and Auditing Oversight Board (CPAAOB), was set up to oversee JICPA's quality control reviews of the internal controls and inspection systems of auditing firms.

According to a *Nihon Keizai Shimbun* survey of 200 leading listed companies in the first six months of 2005, seventy had been using the same auditing staff continuously for at least ten years and fourteen for at least twenty years.[5] The revised law stipulated that the period prior to the amendment would not count in the seven-year limitation on an auditing firm's term.

The CPAAOB was set up partly because the self-regulating status of the quality control reviews that JICPA began in 1999 limited their effectiveness and partly

---

3. "Principles of Auditor Independence and the Role of Corporate Governance in Monitoring an Auditor's Independence" and "Principles for Auditor Oversight" (IOSCO, October 2002).

4. "Reinforcement of the System of Certified Public Accountant Audits" (Japan: Subcommittee on the Certified Public Accountant System, Financial System Council, December 17, 2002).

5. *Nihon Keizai Shimbun*, July 21, 2005.

because there was felt to be a need for external monitoring on the lines of the recently established Public Company Accounting Oversight Board (PCAOB) in the United States. There were a number of alternative proposals for the CPAAOB. One was that the Financial Services Agency should do the job itself; another was that a Japanese equivalent of the U.S. Securities and Exchange Commission should be established to do the job; yet another was that an independent private sector body should be established. In the end, it was decided to reform the CPAEIB, which was a deliberative administrative body of independent experts on accounting and auditing responsible for investigating suspected regulatory violations by certified public accountants and auditing firms as well as for conducting CPA examinations.

Accordingly, the CPAAOB was established in April 2004 as a revamped and enlarged CPAEIB with the following features:

—It would have its own, permanent secretariat.

—Its chairperson and members would be appointed by the FSA, subject to the agreement of the Diet, and would perform their duties independently.

—In addition to assuming the CPAEIB's responsibilities for investigating suspected violations and conducting CPA examinations, CPAAOB is responsible for monitoring JICPA's quality control reviews.

—In monitoring JICPA's quality control reviews, CPAAOB also is responsible for checking the quality control policies and procedures as well as the independence of auditing firms. It also checks the audit certification of companies that are audited. In addition, it has the power to carry out onsite inspections when necessary.

—If a CPAAOB investigation finds that an auditing firm has failed to comply with the law or with quality control standards, it will advise the commissioner of the FSA to instruct the auditing firm to put its house in order or, if necessary, to impose sanctions. Also, if it finds that JICPA has not carried out its quality control reviews properly, it will recommend that the commissioner require JICPA to put its house in order.

Recent Problems and Further Reforms

The amendments to the Certified Public Accountants Law and the establishment of the CPAAOB have greatly improved Japan's certified public accountant system in recent years. In spite of that, the number of cases of accounting problems has increased, probably in part because the improved review process makes it more likely that problems will come to light. Nevertheless, the increase brought home the point that the changes did not solve all of Japan's accounting problems, and it forced the authorities to consider further measures.

In October 2004, Seibu Railway was found to have falsified its financial statements for many years, and several other companies have since been discovered to have committed similar offenses. In response, in November 2004, the FSA published a policy document in which it indicated that the FSA would review the system for checking companies' annual securities filings and consider requiring firms to disclose their internal audit system and the number of years that they have acted as auditors for a company.[6] Meanwhile, the CPAAOB would monitor the quality of audits by individual accountants as well as the independence and quality of auditing firms that have audited a company continuously for many years; review the audited company's assessment of the effectiveness of its internal controls on financial reporting and the auditing of the assessment by certified public accountants; and consider ways of improving disclosure of corporate governance.

Furthermore, in a second report published in December 2004, the FSA indicated, among other things, that a unit would be established either within the FSA itself or in the Securities and Exchange Surveillance Commission (SESC) to improve the system for checking companies' annual securities filings; that companies would be required to improve their corporate governance disclosure from the year ending March 2005; that the Business Accounting Council and JICPA would consider how auditing firms could tighten internal controls (for example, on inspections and operations) and improve quality control; and that the CPAAOB would monitor auditing firms (especially their internal controls) and carry out onsite inspections.[7] In particular, in order to improve corporate governance disclosure, companies were required to disclose the following information from the year ending March 2005:

—the organization, staff, and procedures for carrying out internal audits or audits by statutory auditors (audit committees) as well as the relationship between internal audits or audits by statutory auditors and external auditors

—any material interests (for example, personal, financial, or business relationships) of independent directors or independent statutory auditors in a company

—the names, positions, and number of years of continuous involvement of the certified public accountants involved in an audit; the composition of the rest of the audit team; and the arrangements for inspections when audits are certified by individual accountants.

The Business Accounting Council, an advisory panel to the FSA, conducted a review of how management assesses the effectiveness of a company's internal con-

---

6. "Measures for Ensuring Confidence in the Disclosure System" (Tokyo: Financial Services Agency, November 16, 2004).

7. "Further Measures for Ensuring Confidence in the Disclosure System" (Tokyo: Financial Services Agency, December 24, 2004).

trols for financial reporting and of how certified public accountants carry out their audits. On July 13, 2005, it issued a draft proposal that would require companies to produce an "internal control report" and accountants to produce an "internal control audit report." Once the document is amended following public comments, it is due to be incorporated in the 2006 amendments to the Securities and Exchange Law and to become obligatory for all listed companies from the year ending March 2008.

Besides the 2004 case of Seibu Railway, another case—this time of window dressing—came to light in April 2005. Kanebo, under reconstruction with the support of the Industrial Revitalization Corporation following financial difficulties, was discovered to have inflated its results by more than ¥200 billion (or $1.8 billion) in the previous five years alone. The company lost its listing on the First Section of the Tokyo Stock Exchange, and a former president and two senior managers were arrested by the Tokyo District public prosecutor's office. Furthermore, the public prosecutor's office and the SESC searched the premises of Kanebo's auditors, ChuoAoyama PricewaterhouseCoopers, and questioned the four accountants in charge of auditing the company, who were subsequently arrested on September 13, 2005. In addition, the audit firm is under investigation by the FSA.

In view of problems such as these, reform of Japan's certified public accountant system is likely to continue. It has even been suggested that auditors should be required to report to the authorities anything suspicious that they find when conducting an audit.

Comparison of Japanese and U.S. Reforms

As discussed, reform of Japan's certified public accountant system has taken place as part of the government's effort to create a financial system that relies less on banking and more on the securities markets. At the same time, international efforts have been made to boost confidence in international accounting following the collapse of Enron and Japan itself has striven to prevent a recurrence of accounting abuses. Let us compare the reforms in the United States and Japan.

STRUCTURE OF THE RULES GOVERNING CERTIFIED PUBLIC ACCOUNTANTS. In the United States, individual states award the certified public accountant (CPA) designation, and they are directly responsible for supervising accountants' work. At the federal level, the SEC is empowered under the Securities Act of 1933 to regulate certified public accountants conducting audits of public companies subject to federal disclosure requirements. Apparently, however, there have not been many cases in which the SEC has exercised that power. In September 1977, Congress considered the issue of how audits should be conducted, choosing self-regulation by the American Institute of Certified Public Accountants (AICPA) rather than regulation by the SEC. Only with the creation of the PCAOB following the collapse of Enron did the first real federal rules governing auditing come into existence.

In Japan, the Certified Public Accountants Law was passed in 1948. The CPA designation is awarded by the national government, which is also responsible for supervising the work of both individual accountants and auditing firms. JICPA was established as a self-regulating organization under the Certified Public Accountants Law and is regulated by the state. Until the Financial Accounting Standards Foundation (FASF) and its standing committee, the Accounting Standards Board of Japan (ASBJ), were established in July 2001, responsibility for setting accounting standards lay with the Business Accounting Council, an advisory panel to the Ministry of Finance.[8] Given that regulation of CPAs was vested in the national government in Japan and in individual states in the United States, it should have been easier for Japanese than U.S. authorities to take direct action to deal with serious shortcomings in the way that audits were conducted.

Even in Japan, however, the self-regulating organization was largely left to its own devices—partly because of the highly specialized nature of corporate accounting. Moreover, the Japanese state was perhaps not the ideal organization to monitor companies and gatekeepers, because, as mentioned, its behavior was motivated less by the desire to ensure the accuracy of the information that companies disclosed to investors than by other considerations, so casting doubt on the transparency of disclosure.

The recent accounting reforms are significant not only because they regulate how companies disclose information and how they are audited but also because they recognize the importance of transparency of disclosure and the role of the state in ensuring it. Let us now look at some of the differences between the accounting reforms in the United States and Japan.

CONTINUITY OF ENGAGEMENT. In the United States, the maximum period during which an auditor can continue to audit a company's accounts ("continuity of engagement" period) is five years and auditors are banned from reoffering their services for five years thereafter. In Japan, the continuity of engagement period is two years longer and the subsequent ban on reoffering services is three years shorter. When these limits were debated in the Diet, the opposition called for adopting the same rules as in the United States, but the motion was defeated.

Faced with increased criticism after the Kanebo case, JICPA decided on October 25, 2005, to shorten the allowable continuity of engagement period to five

---

8. See the FASF's website (www.asb.or.jp/e_asbj/).

years. But that decision is just a self-imposed regulation, not a law, and it applies only to the chief auditors of the Big Four firms.

THE PCAOB AND THE CPAAOB. The following are some of the major differences between the boards overseeing public accountants and accounting practices in the United States and Japan:

—The PCAOB is a nonprofit organization regulated by the SEC whereas the CPAAOB is an arm of the Japanese government, within the FSA.

—The PCAOB is funded from fees paid by members (auditing firms) and quasi-members (public companies). Some of the fees go also to fund the Financial Accounting Standards Board (FASB). The CPAAOB is funded by Japanese taxpayers, while the Financial Accounting Standards Foundation, which is responsible for accounting standards in Japan, depends on publication revenue and membership fees. Because FASF's membership has failed to increase, FASF faces financial difficulties, and there have been calls to make membership compulsory. While 86 percent of companies listed on the Tokyo Stock Exchange were members of FASF at the end of June 2005, a much lower proportion of companies listed on provincial stock exchanges belonged.[9]

—Although the PCAOB cooperates with the American Institute of Certified Public Accountants, its reviews cover individual auditing firms. The CPAAOB is responsible for monitoring quality control reviews by the JICPA, and it monitors individual auditing firms only if inspections suggest that it is necessary.

LIABILITY. Discussion about financial gatekeepers in the United States often focuses on the role of liability, sometimes as a deterrent to wrongdoing by gatekeepers and other times as a threat to their existence. The threat aspect applies to accountants since the greater number of legal suits and larger settlement amounts could jeopardize the sustainability of the Big Four regime, as Zoe-Vonna Palmrose emphasizes in chapter 4 of this book.

Lawsuits against gatekeepers are not as frequent in Japan as in the United States, even though Japan introduced similar reforms and even though the number of suits rose as a result of more major firm failures since the mid-1990s. The relative rarity of lawsuits against accountants in Japan does not mean that Japanese audit firms are less susceptible to legal risks than American ones because the existing Commercial Code in Japan permits administrative action to close down audit firms. Before amendment of the Certified Public Accountants Law, the sanctions available to the FSA were, in order of severity, "reprimand," "suspension of business," and "order to dissolve." According to the Commercial Code, if the FSA ordered an audit firm to suspend any part of its business or ordered any of

9. *Nihon Keizai Shimbun*, August 16, 2005.

the firm's auditors to suspend business, the whole firm would lose all its clients. In 2002, Mizuho, a medium-sized audit firm, was closed following such an order. The 2003 amendment of the Certified Public Accountants Law added a new sanction, "order to improve business conduct," which ranks below "suspension of business" in severity.

In April 2006, the Commercial Code will be changed to allow punishment of individual accountants involved in wrongdoing while not necessarily punishing the audit firm itself. The fate of ChuoAoyama now is uncertain because the arrest of the large firm's accountants in connection with the Kanebo incident occurred before the revision of the Certified Public Accountants Law and the Commercial Code. Even though these legal changes would reduce the threat to audit firms, there is a growing understanding in Japan that lawsuits are effective in deterring fraud and in compensating civil losses. As a result, it is highly likely that audit firms in Japan will face more legal liability in the future.

Remaining Issues in Japan

As we have seen, the 2003 amendment of Japan's Public Certified Accountants Law increased the independence of accountants but subjected them to stricter inspections. Since then—and following a number of accounting scandals—accounting reforms in Japan have followed a course similar to that of those in the United States in the wake of Enron's collapse (for example, with calls for reports by the company's management and auditor on internal controls). However, there are a number of fundamental problems that do not lend themselves to an easy solution.

THE SHORTAGE OF ACCOUNTANTS. Because there is shortage of accountants in Japan, it is difficult to be sure that all public companies have been audited to the standard that investors would like, even if accountants carry out their audits independently and to a high standard. At the end of March 2005, Japan had only 15,000 certified public accountants, whereas in the United States in 2003, AICPA had some 335,000 members. Moreover, AICPA is thought to represent only about 75 percent of the total number of accountants in the United States because many accountants belong only to state CPA associations. The small number of CPAs in Japan is clearly insufficient given that Japan has 80 percent as many listed firms as the United States. The number of CPAs per listed firm in Japan is a small fraction of that in other countries (table 2-1). Moreover, CPAs are needed not only as external auditors but also as staff employed to prepare companies' financial statements. Since these activities are essential to proper disclosure, the dearth of CPAs means that the basic infrastructure of Japan's accounting market is woefully inadequate.

Table 2-1. *Accountants and Listed Firms in Major Countries*[a]

Country	Number of accountants (A)	Number of listed domestic firms (B)	Accountants/ listed firm (A/B)
Japan	15,469	4,245	3.64
United States	335,111	5,295	63.29
United Kingdom	140,808	2,311	60.92
Germany	19,000	660	28.78
France	18,470	1,046	17.65
European Union	500,000	7,000	71.42
China	135,652	1,285	105.56

Source: See www.hi-ho.ne.jp/yokoyama-a/internationalaccounting.htm [April 2006].

a. The number of accountants is the latest data available from ICPA of each country. The number of firms is for 2003 and is taken from the World Federation of Exchanges. The figure for France refers to Eurex-listed firms.

The FSA, which is ultimately responsible for organizing CPA examinations, is aware of the need to produce more accountants. The report by the Financial System Council's Subcommittee on the Certified Public Accountant System mentioned earlier ("Reinforcement of the System of Certified Public Accountant Audits") set a target of 50,000 certified public accountants in Japan by 2018. While this is a welcome goal, it can also be seen as an admission that the shortage of accountants is unlikely to be solved in the next ten years. The shortage is related to the fact that the Japanese financial system is dominated by banks. As creditors, they can access a company's inside information without going to publicly available disclosure materials, which companies tend to treat lightly. Companies do not pay much money to auditors, and the time spent on auditing is much shorter than it is in the United States. In short, in Japan there is less demand for accountants.

INSUFFICIENT TIME FOR AUDITS. Another problem in Japan is that auditors are not given enough time to do their job properly. In October 2003, JICPA set up a project team to compare the time spent on audits in different countries. The results, published on September 16, 2004, showed that auditors in the United States, the United Kingdom, Germany, France, and Canada spent from 20 percent to 180 percent more time than auditors in Japan auditing companies of a similar size in similar sectors.[10]

---

10. "Proposal for Increasing Auditing Hours Based on International Comparison," JICPA, September 16, 2004.

JICPA recognizes that auditors must be given more time to do their job if audits in Japan are to be more reliable. In an effort to achieve that goal, it has conducted a public relations campaign among both accountants and companies that use their services. In addition, it has included "sufficient time" among the criteria in its quality control reviews. At the same time, however, it faces calls from companies seeking to cut their costs by reducing the amount of time spent on audits.

LOW AUDITORS' FEES. As with the number of accountants, Japan does not stack up well against other countries in the level of auditors' fees. For example, the range of auditors' fees in Japan is much lower than in the United States. As shown in figure 2-1, fees tend to increase with the asset size of the audited firm. According to Inoue, in both the United States and Japan asset size of the client is the single most important determinant of an auditor's fee.[11] Table 2-2 summarizes average auditing fees by asset size, showing that fees in Japan are extremely low compared with those in the United States. Non-audit fees also are far lower in Japan.

JICPA itself used to determine the standard fee table for auditors in Japan, as mandated by the Certified Public Accountants Law. The table set out the minimum basic fee for each asset class. For example, the minimum basic fee for auditing a firm with assets between ¥100 million and ¥300 million was set at ¥4.6 million per year, while the minimum for a firm with assets between ¥10 billion and ¥30 billion was set at ¥12.35 million. That is, fees for auditing a firm 100 times larger than another could be just three times more. The minimum basic fee for all firms with assets of ¥50 billion or more was set at ¥20.9 million. The extremely inelastic relationship that JICPA established between audit fees and firm size for small and medium-sized listed firms may explain why in figure 2-1 the plot for Japan differs from that for the United States. In addition to the basic fee, JICPA also set the minimum level of fees per day for each level of accountants involved in an audit.

The justification for setting minimum standardized fees was to avoid excessive competition among audit firms. In fact, competition among auditing firms has tended to depress fees since the amended Certified Public Accountants Law, which ended JICPA's role in determining fees, went into effect on April 1, 2004.

Of the ninety-eight companies responding to a *Nihon Keizai Shimbun* survey of the companies constituting the Nikkei 225 Index, 84 percent indicated that they objected to any increase in the fees paid to auditors. While 35 percent

---

11. Other factors that have been confirmed as determinants of audit fees in both the United States and Japan are complexity of the client, risk of the client, and Big Four premium. A seasonal premium was confirmed in the United States but not in Japan. See Inoue (2006).

objected because they wanted to reduce costs from non–core mission activities, 46 percent objected because they did not expect the standard of the audits to improve. Only 3 percent of responding companies accepted the need to increase auditors' fees in order to improve the quality of the information provided.[12]

Reliable auditing is crucial to making Japan's financial system more market oriented. Auditors have come under more careful monitoring and their work has been made more onerous as a result of scandals in both the United States and Japan, but a shortage of certified public accountants, inadequate time spent on audits, and low auditors' fees are major constraints on achieving the goal of improving the quality of auditing. In the short term, it is difficult to increase the number of certified public accountants significantly without sacrificing standards, and auditing fees and the amount of time spent on an audit are basically determined by private parties and not subject to intervention by the authorities. So, although the rules and regulations governing accountants in Japan are now similar to those in the United States, there are still big differences in how they are put into practice.

Credit Rating Agencies in Japan

In the United States, the value of credit rating information was highly proclaimed when there was a series of corporate bond defaults in the 1920s. A similar series of bond defaults in Japan at about the same time, rather than acting as a catalyst for the formation of credit rating agencies, led to measures to restrict corporate bond issuance in order to stabilize the financial system. To give companies access to long-term funds, the government allowed long-term credit banks and other government-controlled financial institutions to issue bank debentures.

This situation continued during the period of high economic growth from the 1950s to the 1970s, when only a handful of companies that met stringent standards were allowed to issue bonds. Those companies were considered highly unlikely to default, but, when they occasionally did, the trustee bank usually bought the bonds back at face value to avert any losses to investors. Such an environment clearly was not likely to foster the growth of credit rating agencies.

The situation began to change in the 1980s, partly as a result of the growing popularity of convertible bonds. At the same time, Japanese companies began to issue more bonds overseas, while U.S. pressure on Japan to encourage wider international use of the yen and to open up the country's financial markets led to a debate on whether the country's corporate bond market should also be deregulated.

---

12. *Nihon Keizai Shimbun*, April 21, 2004.

Figure 2-1. *Audit Fees and Asset Size, United States and Japan*[a]

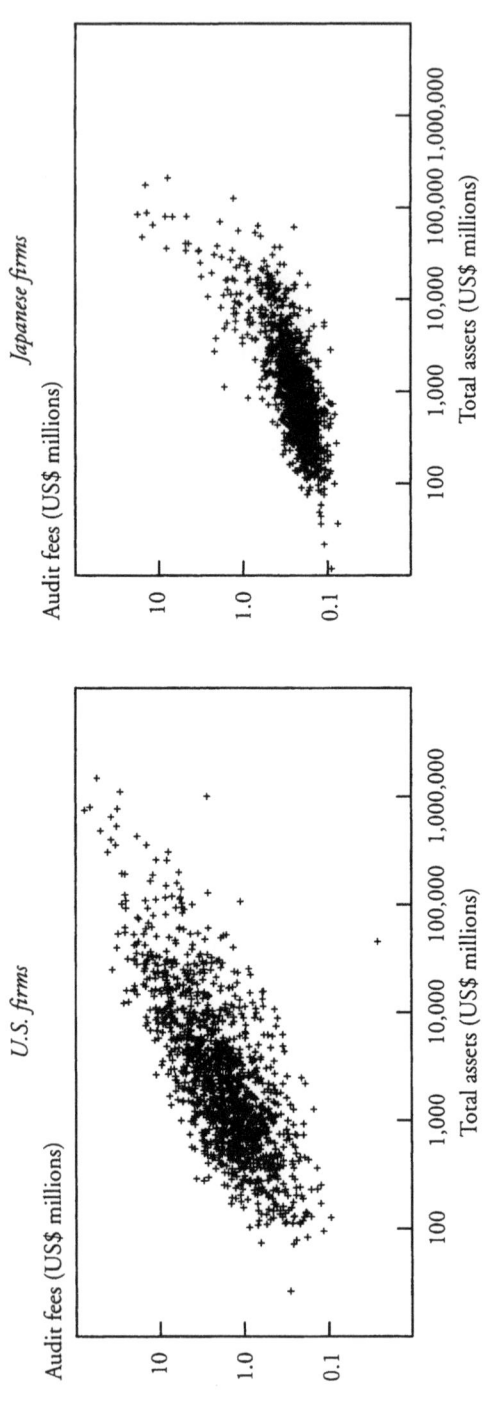

Source: Inoue (2006).
a. There are 1,344 Japanese firms, listed in the first section of the Tokyo Stock Exchange, and 1,327 U.S. firms, listed in the New York Stock Exchange. In both cases the sample consists of those firms whose latest audit fee data were available as of August 2005.

Table 2-2. *Audit Fees and Asset Size, United States and Japan*[a]
US$ million, unless otherwise noted

Firms with assets of	Number of firms	Average assets	Audit fees	Other fees
US$0.1–1 billion				
Japan	739	490.93	0.1995	0.0108
United States	419	519.81	1.0568	0.3018
US$1–10 billion				
Japan	482	2,873.47	0.3495	0.0408
United States	640	3,381.99	2.6250	0.8679
US$10–100 billion				
Japan	103	24,971.65	1.7442	0.5706
United States	224	27,028.52	7.8038	2.7660

Source: Inoue (2006).

a. See also figure 2-1. Note that 17 Japanese firms and 6 U.S. firms are excluded because their assets are below US$0.1 billion. Similarly, 3 Japanese firms and 38 U.S. firms are excluded because their assets are US$100 billion or greater.

That discussion, in turn, led to a serious debate about the need for credit rating agencies.

In its May 1984 report, the MOF's Japan-U.S. Yen-Dollar Committee recommended that Japan introduce a credit rating system.[13] According to the report, Japanese companies wanting to issue euroyen bonds would find it difficult to persuade overseas investors to accept the Ministry of Finance's issue standards and would have no alternative but to obtain a credit rating in order to free themselves of that constraint. The report also expressed the view that Japanese companies would need to obtain credit ratings from more than one agency; that credit rating agencies would need to maintain their independence; and that issuers should be prepared to bear the fees for obtaining credit ratings as investors were unlikely to be willing to do so when, at the time, all corporate bonds were secured and the risk of default was low.

The Japan Bond Research Institute (JBRI) (now Rating and Investment Information, Inc., or R&I) began bond rating activities in 1979 as an in-house unit of Nihon Keizai Shimbun, Inc. It was incorporated as a joint stock company in 1985, one year after the Japan-U.S. Yen-Dollar Committee published its report. In the same year, Japan Credit Rating Agency, Ltd. (JCR) and Nippon Investors

---

13. "Current Status and Prospects for Financial Liberalization and the Internationalization of the Yen" (Tokyo: Japan-U.S. Yen-Dollar Committee, Ministry of Finance, May 1984).

Service, Inc. (NIS) were formed and Moody's Investors Service and Standard and Poor's (S&P) opened offices in Tokyo.

The practice of credit rating in Japan grew less out of investor demand than out of the introduction of a new system of corporate finance. Japanese companies issuing bonds overseas (see above) stimulated debate about deregulating the domestic bond market, and the Ministry of Finance gradually relaxed its issue standards. Deregulation took place one step at a time to avoid disrupting the market with issues by problem companies. One interim measure adopted in 1992 required companies intending to issue a bond to obtain a minimum credit rating instead of meeting certain quantitative standards. At the same time, the authorities introduced a system of designated rating agencies, and they required companies wishing to issue a bond to use one of those agencies. Thus credit rating was introduced in Japan as a requirement for issuing corporate bonds, while in the United States credit rating began as a business.

Regulatory Use of Credit Ratings

Although the Ministry of Finance's bond issue standards were abolished in 1996, credit ratings from designated rating agencies are still required by a wide range of rules. The most important are the capital adequacy requirements for securities companies; the requirements for special-purpose companies issuing commercial paper; the eligibility criteria for shelf registration; the requirements for referenced disclosure where it is permitted; the eligibility criteria for securities held in a bond investment trust; entries in securities registration statements and prospectuses; and the eligibility criteria for purchases by the Banks' Shareholdings Purchase Corporation.

Securities registration statements and prospectuses include a column in which issuers have to enter their credit rating from a designated rating agency. (If they have obtained ratings from more than one designated rating agency, they have to enter each rating.) If they have not obtained a rating, they have to indicate that fact on the form. That means that, for all intents and purposes, a company will be unable to issue bonds unless it has a rating from one of these agencies.

Thus, as does the United States, Japan has a system for publicly approving credit rating agencies, although the reasons for introducing it were different. Furthermore, as we shall see, Japan also has many of the problems associated with credit rating agencies in the United States.

Oligopolization

The first problem is the small number of designated rating agencies. Japan currently has five such agencies. Three, Moody's, S&P, and Fitch, are non-Japanese and two, R&I and JCR, are Japanese firms. R&I was formed from the merger of JBRI and NIS in 1998. Japan has another agency, Mikuni & Co., that, although it is not a designated rating agency, is fairly widely used. As in the United States, the number of agencies with public approval is small and dwindling. But competition in Japan is relatively strong compared with that in the United States, where a duopoly pertains. With these powerful players already in the Japanese market, no other firms appear to be trying to enter and apply to become a designated rating agency.

At the same time, it should be emphasized that it is not as easy for a new firm to become a designated agency in Japan as it is to become an NRSRO (Nationally Recognized Statistical Rating Organization) in the United States. In order to become a designated rating agency, a firm must satisfy the commissioner of the FSA that it has the necessary experience, staff, structure, expertise, and independence (for example, capital structure).[14] The most important of these criteria is apparently experience—the extent to which the agency's ratings are actually used—which makes it difficult for new entrants to qualify for designation.

Ratings Lag

Two months before the collapse of Enron, a similar case involving a discrepancy between a company's credit rating and reality occurred in Japan. Mycal, Japan's fourth-largest supermarket, filed for bankruptcy protection on September 14, 2001, and defaulted on ¥350 billion ($2.9 billion) in corporate bonds. The case was of major public concern because ¥90 billion ($75 million) of those bonds, with a face value of ¥1 million ($8,333), mainly were sold to retail investors, 38,000 of whom lost money.

Mycal had issued ¥40 billion in four-year bonds on January 28, 2000, with an A rating from JCR. The company issued ¥50 billion more in four-year bonds on October 12 of the same year, even though JCR had lowered its rating to BBB on September 6. JCR lowered its rating on both bonds to speculative status on August 17, 2001, a month before the default. Although JCR was the only rating agency from which Mycal had requested a rating, other agencies had published revised ratings on the company of their own accord. For example, R&I lowered its rating on the company from BBB+ to BBB– on August 30, 2000, and to B+ on June 4, 2001. Similarly, S&P lowered its rating on the company from BB to B on March 1, 2000, while Moody's lowered its rating from Ba3 to B on July 31, 2001. Mycal's was the first default on a publicly offered bond in Japanese history,

---

14. Cabinet Office, Government of Japan, "Cabinet Order on Disclosure of Corporate Information," Article 1(13-2).

and there was considerable criticism of JCR for having maintained its investment grade rating until just a month before.

However, even if JCR had lowered its rating on Mycal's bonds sooner, that might not have been much help to the retail investors who bought them because Japan had no proper secondary market in small-denomination bonds of that kind. Some investors were able to sell them to securities companies at a discount that reflected the downgrade, but in the absence of a proper secondary market, they had to accept a large discount. Many retail investors could not imagine that a Japanese company might default and therefore decided to hold the bonds until redemption rather than take a large loss right away.

At the same time, some quarters blamed a non-Japanese firm, S&P, for setting in train the events that led to the default with its early 2001 downgrade, which coincided with a sharp decline in the price of the company's shares. This criticism is reminiscent of that levied at non-Japanese rating agencies for precipitating the end of Yamaichi Securities by downgrading the company's debt.

Ratings Bias

The case of Mycal also raised the question of agency bias toward issuers. The rating by the agency that Mycal chose as its designated rating agency was more generous than the ratings of other agencies. There is speculation that JCR tried to give a favorable rating in order to boost its fee income and that Mycal tried to choose an agency that might be inclined to be generous in its rating.

Japan's third major domestic credit rating agency, after R&I and JCR, is unique with respect to bias and in other respects. Mikuni & Co., Ltd. receives no fee income from issuers and depends entirely on income from selling its reports. It therefore has never applied to become a designated rating agency. Mikuni began marketing its credit ratings to investors and credit controllers in 1983. At first, because Japanese investors saw little risk that a Japanese company would default on its bonds, Mikuni had few Japanese clients and published all its reports in English for the benefit of non-Japanese investors. In 1995, when Japanese companies were going out of business with more frequency, Mikuni began to publish information in Japanese. As the company strongly believes that credit ratings are simply an opinion, it bases its ratings entirely on publicly available information. Mikuni has a reputation for being even more critical than Moody's. For example, it lowered its rating on Mycal from BB to B as early as August 1999 and to CCC in February 2001.

Ratings Gap and Changes since 2004

The general view, however, is that Japanese rating agencies are more generous than non-Japanese agencies, with ratings by non-Japanese agencies usually run-

Table 2-3. *Changes in Ratings of Japanese Corporations and Corporate Bonds by Four Major Rating Firms*[a]

Year	Upgrades				Downgrades			
	JCR	R&I	S&P	Moody's	JCR	R&I	S&P	Moody's
2003, 2nd half	16	5	28	12	13	20	7	5
2004, 1st half	20	20	29	19	24	17	11	0
2004, 2nd half	59	41	79	128	8	18	22	0
2005, 1st half	49	78	131	60	22	8	7	1

Source: NICMR.
a. Upgrades and downgrades include changes in both corporate ratings and bond ratings. They do not count changes in outlook.

ning two or three ranks lower than those by Japanese firms. Certainly, Japanese issuers tend to choose Japanese rating agencies. The fact that both of Japan's domestic designated rating agencies (R&I and JCR) depend almost entirely on fees from issuers does not account for their perceived generosity, since the U.S. rating agencies also depend largely on fees from issuers. The narrowing of the ratings gap since 2004, however, suggests that non-Japanese rating agencies had previously been somewhat ungenerous toward Japanese companies.

Moody's and S&P caused a stir by raising their ratings on a large number of Japanese companies in a short space of time in the second half of 2004, as shown in table 2-3. As both agencies issued more upgrades than their Japanese rivals, the ratings gap between the two groups narrowed considerably. Japanese companies and investors criticized the rush by Moody's and S&P to raise their credit ratings on Japanese companies as "playing catch-up with reality." In part, the upgrades by non-Japanese rating agencies reflected improvements in the balance sheets and income statements of Japanese companies, but they may also have reflected the agencies' belated recognition of the fact that very few Japanese companies ever actually default. S&P acknowledged that the rarity of default was the basis for reviewing its ratings.

A completely different explanation for the upgrades by the two non-Japanese rating agencies is based on the prospect of Basel II. Under Basel II most Japanese financial institutions are expected to choose the standardized approach to deciding risk weights for loans, which involves using credit ratings, and the FSA is expected to prohibit them from using unsolicited ratings for that purpose. According to this view, the non-Japanese rating agencies, concerned that they might lose out because they have tended to issue unsolicited ratings, decided to raise their ratings across the board in the hope of appearing more acceptable to potential customers.

Regulation of Credit Rating Agencies

In April 2005, the U.S. Securities and Exchange Commission proposed a rule requiring an NRSRO to establish a system to stem conflicts of interest as well as a procedure to prevent abuse of nonpublic information. Also, it introduced an effective period of the status as NRSRO and instituted periodic checks when rating agencies try to renew their NRSRO status. The Credit Rating Agency Duopoly Relief Act of 2005 submitted to Congress in June will change the definition of "NRSRO" from Nationally Recognized Statistical Rating Organization to Nationally Registered Statistical Rating Organization. That is, rating agencies will be registered and formally regulated by the SEC. Meanwhile, the SEC is working together with NRSROs to establish a framework to enhance supervision of NRSROs to the extent possible under current laws. In any event, the regulatory environment for NRSROs in the United States will be improved.

The IOSCO also is taking steps to improve regulation. Although two recent reports regarding the activities of credit rating agencies and a professional code of conduct do not have the force of official regulations, they demand that rating agencies take measures to maintain their independence, avoid conflicts of interest, control nonpublic information, and the like.[15]

In Japan, the FSA has not yet issued concrete measures to reflect changes in the United States and by the IOSCO. But since Japan has the same types of problems concerning rating agencies as the United States has, it is time for Japan to reconsider its current system of designated rating agencies.

Analysts in Japan

In Japan, as in other countries, there are sell-side analysts, buy-side analysts, and a handful of independent analysts. After a series of reforms by the Japanese Securities Dealers Association, sell-side analysts are now governed by regulations that are quite similar to those in the United States—a rather peculiar development, considering the differences between Japanese and U.S. analysts.

Differences between Japanese and U.S. Analysts

One major issue with analysts in the United States, especially after the dotcom bubble burst, was biased reporting that led to losses for many retail investors. Because analysts' remuneration had come to depend on the performance of their

---

15. "Principles Regarding the Activities of Credit Rating Agencies" (IOSCO, September 2003), and "Code of Conduct Fundamentals for Credit Rating Agencies" (IOSCO, December 2004).

employers' investment banking business, there was a tendency for them to write reports that boosted that business. A second issue is that close contact between analysts and the management of the companies that they write about gives them access to information unavailable to ordinary investors and makes them vulnerable to pressure from those companies. That contact stems from the traditional practice whereby investor relations officers and senior managers of U.S. companies offer their comments to analysts on their earnings forecasts and analyses before they are published. A third problem acknowledged by many U.S. securities companies is that their analysts own shares in some of the companies that they cover—a practice that could compromise the objectivity of their reports.

In response to these concerns, the New York Stock Exchange and the National Association of Securities Dealers adopted a series of rules designed to ensure the neutrality of analysts, while the SEC adopted Regulation AC (Analyst Certification). Those measures helped to reduce the risk that analysts would become involved in conflicts of interest; however, the so-called Global Settlement between U.S. regulators and the top ten U.S. securities firms, which was reached on April 28, 2003, had a much greater impact. Among other things, the settlement obliged securities firms to provide investors with independent, third-party research; prohibited analysts from taking part in the sales activities of their investment banking divisions or in issuers' roadshows; and required securities firms to publish data on their analysts' performance.

The position of analysts in Japan is different from that of their counterparts in the United States, in at least five respects:

— First, if analysts in Japan were found to write misleading reports, it would not be likely to cause an outcry of the same scale as the one that occurred in the United States after the Internet bubble burst, when many investors lost money because of such reports. That is because the number of retail equity investors in Japan is small. Individual Japanese have traditionally invested only a small proportion of their personal financial assets in equities and equity investment trusts. Moreover, although a growing number of people have taken to buying and selling equities as brokerage commissions decline and Internet access increases, many of them are day-traders, who tend not to be interested in fundamental research.

—Second, analysts in Japan do not have the charisma or the popular influence that U.S. analysts wield, partly because of the small number of retail equity investors in Japan and the rise of day-trading. Without that kind of influence, analysts in Japan do not contribute to winning investment banking business for their employers to the same extent that their U.S. counterparts do.

—Third, analysts in Japan do not get early word from companies about their earnings. Companies themselves release their own earnings forecasts regularly and are expected to revise them if necessary. The practice among U.S. companies of giving analysts hints about earnings is intended to avoid the confusion that might result if the market consensus was wide of the mark.

—Fourth, securities companies in Japan normally have a long-standing rule forbidding or severely restricting their analysts from investing in their own accounts, unlike in the United States, where the practice is common.

—Fifth, analysts in Japan have not been as involved in investment banking as those in the United States and their remuneration is not normally linked directly to the performance of the investment banking division of their firm.

Japan also has recently tightened rules on equities analysts, but Japanese securities companies have not been forced to accept the same degree of regulation as U.S. securities houses under the Global Settlement. That seems to be justified in light of the different position of analysts in Japan.

Rules Governing Japanese Analysts

Tighter regulation in the United States, discussions by the IOSCO, and various domestic problems led the Japan Securities Dealers Association (JSDA) to amend its resolution regarding the handling of research reports and led individual securities companies to revise their internal rules. The JSDA has dual roles as a self-regulating organization and as an industry association. Part of the impetus for amending the JSDA resolution (the board adopted the new version in January 2002) came from several events that transpired in the United States. First, in June 2001 the Securities Industry Association (SIA, an organization representing 600 U.S. securities dealers) issued a set of best practices for operating securities firms and compiling analysts' reports.[16] In addition, the U.S. Congress began hearings on analyst conflicts of interest in June 2001. Finally, the collapse of Enron, which occurred while the hearings were taking place, focused attention on the issue.

The direct trigger for the JSDA's revised resolution, however, was an analyst's report published in Japan. ING Baring Securities Japan Ltd., Tokyo Branch (ING) published a report on Daiwa Bank on May 25, 2001, that mistakenly gave Daiwa Bank's (Tier 1) capital adequacy ratio for the year ended March 2001 as 4.79 percent instead of 7.49 percent. The report claimed that the bank had suffered a sharp decline in deposits, causing depositors to question its future when in fact the bank's deposits had actually increased. In addition, the report gave ¥50 ($0.4) as the fair value for the bank's shares, which had been trading at more than ¥150 ($1.25) before the report was published, and gave them a "sell" rating.

16. "Best Practices for Research" (Tokyo: Securities Industry Association, June 2001).

As a result, Daiwa's share price dropped to just over ¥130 ($1.08), and institutional investors who had shorted the bank's shares on the basis of the ING report made a profit. Moreover, before the report was published its contents had been leaked to ING's proprietary trading desk, which also made a profit by shorting Daiwa Bank's shares, although the person responsible for the short sales was apparently unaware of the report's existence.

Daiwa Bank lodged a complaint against ING for the claim that the fair value of its shares was ¥50 ($0.40) on the grounds that the reasons given were unclear. In response, in June 2001, ING published amendments and an apology in the national press. The matter was also investigated by the FSA, which published its findings and issued a business improvement order on August 20, 2001. The FSA found that the ING report contained erroneous figures that could mislead investors in a number of important respects and that ING had solicited business on the basis of the report—conduct incompatible with Article 4(i) of the Cabinet Order on the Rules of Conduct for Securities Companies. This cabinet order details the activities in which securities companies and their officers and employees are prohibited from engaging under Article 42 of the Securities and Exchange Law and prohibits securities companies from publishing erroneous and misleading information. The FSA found that ING had not employed anyone to check its analyst's reports. In addition, it found that the research section in which the analyst concerned worked was housed in the same department as the equity trading section and that there were no firewalls to prevent leaks between the two sections.

The FSA then took action against ING. First, it required ING to draw up and implement measures to prevent a recurrence by establishing rules and a system for checking analysts' reports objectively and thoroughly; proper firewalls between the equity research and trading/investment departments; and specific procedures for informing proprietary trading departments of any changes in recommendations and coverage in order to prevent them from trading in the securities of a company before a report on that company is published. Second, the FSA required ING to clarify who was responsible for the problems. The FSA also asked the JSDA to consider drawing up rules to ensure that its members established firewalls between their equity research and trading/investment departments in order to prevent analysts from front running.

RULES INTRODUCED IN 2002. In response, in January 2002, the JSDA board adopted a resolution calling on members to

—establish a system of internal supervision to ensure that reports are both appropriate and reasonable in content

—ensure the security of material information when analysts are either working for other departments or passing on material information to other departments

—ensure that analysts are free from interference or intervention by other departments when writing their reports and guarantee their independence of opinion by ensuring that directors of underwriting and investment banking departments do not make clients or prospective clients any promises about the contents of such reports

—set up a committee to check and assess the content of analysts' reports and try to improve their quality

—forbid analysts from either dealing in or owning the securities of any of the companies that they cover unless expressly permitted and ensure that executives and employees do not deal on their own account on the basis of any material information obtained from an analyst's report or research.

In addition, the resolution required members to draw up written internal rules and procedures incorporating those requirements.

RULES INTRODUCED IN 2003. Shortly after JSDA's rule changes, the U.S. Congress passed the Sarbanes-Oxley Act. The New York Stock Exchange and the National Association of Securities Dealers also adopted self-regulating rules governing analysts, and the SEC carried out further investigations of leading Wall Street firms. Meetings of the IOSCO also featured discussion of various issues involving analysts.

In view of those developments, the FSA decided to ask the JSDA board to amend its resolution. In January 2003, the JSDA added rules that require disclosure of conflicts of interest and the establishment of a proper analyst remuneration system and that forbid securities firms from letting issuers review analysts' reports prior to distribution. The new rules on disclosing conflicts of interest required JSDA members to do the following:

—Disclose any situation that could arise between them or one of their analysts and a company that is the subject of an analyst's report if there is a high likelihood that it might compromise the analyst's independence.

—Disclose the fact that a company that is the subject of an analyst's report was the lead manager of an initial or secondary offering of securities when not more than twelve months have passed since the day that the registration statement of the offering was submitted.

—Refrain from publishing in an analyst's report any investment ratings or target prices for shares when the member has been the lead manager of an initial or secondary offering of shares as part of a listing on a stock exchange or registration with the Japan Securities Dealers Association until ten business days have passed since the listing or registration ("quiet period").

Tighter Regulation of Analysts since 2003

Following the amendments to the JSDA resolution in 2002 and early 2003 tightening the regulation of analysts, further measures were implemented, triggered by events in the United States as well as Japan. In the United States, the Global Settlement was announced in April 2003 and Regulation AC came into force around the same time. In Japan, two events cast doubt on the arrangements made by securities companies for dealing with reports produced by outside analysts:

—A securities analyst who had signed an agreement to write reports for a securities firm repeatedly bought shares of the companies that he recommended before the reports were published and sold them afterward when the price had risen. When the securities company asked the analyst to transfer his trading account to them, he refused. The firm simply included in its agreement with the analyst a clause referring to the need to comply with the law. It did not mention anywhere in the analyst's reports the fact that he had a position in the securities that he was recommending.

—Another securities firm commissioned reports from an outside source that it made available to its clients free of charge on its website. The securities firm specified the companies covered in the reports and paid the outside source for its services in accordance with the agreement between them, but it did not disclose that information to its clients, who were given the impression that the authors of the reports had chosen the stocks themselves. The Securities and Exchange Surveillance Commission ruled that its omission amounted to presenting information about an important matter in a way that was likely to mislead investors, a violation of Article 4(i) of the Cabinet Ordinance Governing the Activities of Securities Companies on the Basis of Article 42(1)(ix), which is based on Article 42(1)(ix) of the Securities and Exchange Law.

Following those events, in December 2003, the SESC told the FSA that securities companies that used outside analysts' reports to recommend securities to their clients needed to make proper arrangements for dealing with such reports and the analysts who had written them. In response, on March 17, 2004, the JSDA board adopted a second set of amendments to its "Resolution on the Handling of Research Reports." Like the measures that had been taken in the United States, these new amendments consisted of restrictions on the involvement of securities analysts in underwriting and investment banking activities. Specifically, the amendments forbade them from taking part in promotional activities (for example, investor briefings) involving the two departments.

According to the amended resolution, "promotional activities" refers to any activities intended to win underwriting or investment banking deals or transactions. As examples it gives a case in which an analyst takes part in a meeting concerning his or her employer's underwriting or investment banking department attended by a member or a client of either of those departments; a case in which the analyst makes a recommendation to a company on behalf of the employer's underwriting or investment banking department; and a case in which the analyst produces written material to support the promotional activities of the employer's underwriting or investment banking department.

The amendments also include provisions for how securities firms should handle reports that they commission from outside analysts. Securities firms are now required to ensure that any material conflicts of interest between outside analysts and the companies that they cover are disclosed in analysts' reports and to inform their clients if they have paid outside analysts for reports or instructed them to write about particular companies.

Regulating Analysts and the Implications for Their Future

The rule that probably has had the biggest impact on analysts working for securities firms in Japan is one in the latest set of amendments to the JSDA resolution that restricts analysts' involvement in investment banking activities. Although in Japan the remuneration of analysts working for securities companies is rarely linked to specific investment banking deals, how securities firms can recoup the costs of their research departments is a key issue and relations between analysts and the investment banking activities of their employers cannot simply be ignored.

The European Commission's Forum Group on Financial Analysts proposed a more indirect approach to the conflict-of-interest issue than that taken in the United States and Japan.[17] The group argued that there is no need to forbid securities analysts from taking part in activities that promote their investment banking departments; financial institutions should simply ensure that none of their analysts make any investment recommendations while they are involved in investment banking activities. That approach reflects the understanding that analysts' reports and valuations are important in the price discovery of initial public offerings.

The rules in the United States and Japan take a much more direct approach to eliminating the risk of compromising an analyst's independence by forbidding analysts from involvement in promotional activities, where they are most likely to be subject to pressure from their investment banking departments. Analysts'

---

17. Recommendations from the Forum Group to the European Commission, "Financial Analysts: Best Practices in an Integrated European Financial Market," September 4, 2003.

involvement in those activities is restricted to screening potential clients and carrying out due diligence once a securities firm has been appointed as adviser or lead manager.

It has been argued that under these rules, sell-side analysts working for U.S. investment banks and Japanese securities companies face a big reduction in income (both direct and indirect) for the investment banking work that they do and that both their remuneration and the number of companies that they cover will be affected. Rules are not the only factor that can influence the future of sell-side analysts, however. Other factors include the growing use of passive management, the increase in the number of speculators, soft-dollar rules, and Regulation FD (Fair Disclosure). Although there have not been any moves to introduce soft-dollar rules in Japan, their introduction in the United States or the United Kingdom would lead to more intense discussion of their possible introduction in Japan. As for Regulation FD, some think that it is not as important in Japan as in the United States, since analysts in Japan have never performed the peculiar role that U.S. analysts play in bridging the information gap between companies and the market regarding earnings forecasts. Nevertheless, in a report issued in July 2005, the Financial System Council's Working Group on Disclosure concluded that Regulation FD will require further consideration in light of the IOSCO discussions.

Such developments raise the specter of a decline in the supply of high-quality company research reports to a level that is socially undesirable. However, it also is possible to take the view that there is dire need of change in the current state of affairs, in which stock-picking equity analysts are traditionally paid more than asset allocation advisers even though it has long been known that asset allocation is the most important factor affecting investment performance and that stock selection is relatively unimportant.

Leaving aside the issue of remuneration, there probably will always be investors who are prepared to pay (either directly or indirectly) for high-quality research. What is not so clear, however, is whether sell-side analysts will continue to be the main producers of such reports. Institutional investors may feel that they are served well enough by buy-side analysts or independent analysts, and retail investors may feel that information that is free or available at low cost on the Internet is adequate, even though such information may generally be inferior to the research traditionally provided by sell-side analysts.

In the United States, large securities brokers are obliged by the Global Settlement to distribute reports by independent research firms, a policy that can be regarded as intent to alter the structure of the investment research industry by subsidizing and facilitating the development of independent analysts and penalizing sell-side analysts. Introduction of such a policy in Japan has not been proposed.

Who Should Regulate Analysts?

Any consideration of the future for analysts in Japan needs to take account of one more factor: the pressure that they face from bureaucrats and politicians. As discussed, the FSA and the JSDA have strengthened controls and regulations to prevent sell-side analysts from providing investors with biased reports. However, it is not altogether clear whether their motive for doing so has been solely to safeguard the interests of investors.

The controversial ING report was probably not the first analyst's report to contain erroneous information. Nor was it the first time that the issue of firewalls between research and proprietary trading departments had been raised. The reason that the FSA paid unprecedented attention to the errors in the ING report was partly the scale of the errors, but also partly the fact that Japan's bad debt problem was the focus of international attention at that time. If the FSA had not been so concerned about the decline in banks' share prices and the threat to the financial system, it probably would not have paid so much attention to a "sell" recommendation (albeit an extremely negative one) by a foreign securities company.

Japanese politicians and bureaucrats were critical of foreign securities companies and investors for making money by driving down the share prices of Japanese companies and banks, and they accused foreign market participants, who they felt did not know what was going on in Japan, of undervaluing Japanese equities. That was particularly true since the beginning of 2001, when Japanese politicians and bureaucrats did their best to prevent increased speculation about Japan's financial system after the G7 raised the subject of bad debt.

As well as taking action against ING, the FSA criticized the IMF for quoting market analysts' views on the scale of Japan's bad debt problem and the authorities' response in its Article IV consultation report on Japan. In the FSA's view, it was irresponsible of a prestigious supranational agency such as the IMF to quote the views of a market analyst without confirming their accuracy.

That was not the first time that the Japanese government had taken a securities company to task for the content of one of its research reports. Reportedly, the authorities previously protested informally to the senior managers of a securities company about bearish stock market forecasts by strategists who worked for them. In other words, politicians and bureaucrats have sometimes objected to analysts' opinions for reasons other than their desire to safeguard investor interests. Since securities companies are regulated by the FSA, analysts who work for securities companies may be subject to political or bureaucratic pressure, while independent analysts are not. If independent analysts became more influential, the authorities might be more tempted to take action against them for political reasons.

Be that as it may, the authorities should beware that such action would be an abuse of their power. If analysts need to be regulated, it should be to ensure that they fulfill their duty as gatekeepers, and any rules should be enforced solely for that purpose and not to achieve some other public objective.

Lessons about Financial Gatekeeping from Japan's Experience

As the preceding discussion shows, the regulatory environment for financial gatekeepers in Japan has been strongly affected by developments in the United States. As a result, gatekeepers in Japan now face regulations very similar to those in the United States. There are, however, important differences in the regulations of the two countries. For example, by and large, financial gatekeepers are less heavily regulated in Japan than in the United States. Are such differences justifiable? How should gatekeepers should be regulated and who should regulate them?

Why Should Financial Gatekeepers Be Regulated?

Securities regulations traditionally focused on securities transactions per se—on issuers and intermediaries like brokers, on mutual funds, and on stock exchanges. But now, regulators in Japan as well as in the United States are focusing on financial gatekeepers. In considering the need to regulate financial gatekeepers, it is important to notice that not all financial gatekeepers are treated equally. Different regulatory environments are being introduced or discussed for different types of gatekeepers.

In comparing the current regulatory environments in the United States and Japan, one can see that accountants are the most highly regulated of the three types of financial gatekeepers. A specialized monitoring agency is dedicated solely to accountants, and laws and rules are promulgated to ensure their independence and to avoid conflicts of interest. With the exception of the not-so-clear qualifications for NRSRO status, rating agencies are relatively unregulated at present. Sell-side analysts are subject to greater oversight than rating agencies, but there is no specialized monitoring agency for them as there is for accountants. Actually, it is not analysts per se who are regulated, but the treatment of analysts' functions by securities brokers and dealers. Meanwhile, regulation of buy-side analysts and independent analysts has not come up in the current discussion.

Two variables explain the different regulatory environments for different financial gatekeepers. One is how much influence the information that they provide has on securities trades and the other is how uncertain or subjective their information is. Those two variables also represent two fundamental considerations in the need to regulate financial gatekeepers—the importance of protecting investors and the importance of protecting freedom of information.

Those who advocate greater regulation of financial gatekeepers would say that to fully protect investors it is not enough to regulate securities transactions; it is necessary to regulate the way that information is provided to investors—that is, the conduct of financial gatekeepers. On the other hand, those who favor laxer regulation would point to the importance of the freedom to provide information to investors and of the freedom of investors to receive it, because increasing the amount of information that market participants have increases market efficiency. Free provision of information is therefore as important for markets as freedom of speech is for democracy. Moreover, they note that it is impossible or unrealistic to regulate the provision of all information for investment decisionmaking, since information comes in so many forms, is so prevalent, and is a common part of economic activity.

Given the close link between information and securities trading and the fact that the current regime regulating securities transactions is based on the need to protect investors, regulating the provision of information is necessary to achieve that goal. There is less risk that introducing additional regulation will constrain the provision of information when information is for the most part certain and objective or when individual information providers with some professional expertise are likely to reach similar conclusions. The variation in information is small and less valuable when information is objective by nature. If accountants and sell-side analysts are compared on the basis of the two variables mentioned—their influence on securities trades and the uncertainty and subjectivity of the information that they provide—it is easy to understand why accountants are more regulated than sell-side analysts.

—*Influence on trades.* The core of securities regulation in both the United States and Japan is disclosure, and the quality of disclosure is endorsed by accountants. Thus these gatekeepers are clearly important providers of information for securities transactions. In fact, securities laws in both countries already formally require the regulation of accountants, so recent enhanced regulations just reinforce what the system was designed to do from the start.

Regulations on the conduct of securities brokers and dealers already regulate conduct of analysts employed or used by securities brokers and dealers. Certainly, sell-side analysts have great influence over trading, since the information that they provide is intended from the outset to induce transactions. On that basis, one can say that sell-side analysts need to be regulated. At the same time, not regulating

Figure 2-2. *Need to Regulate Financial Gatekeepers Explained by Two Variables*

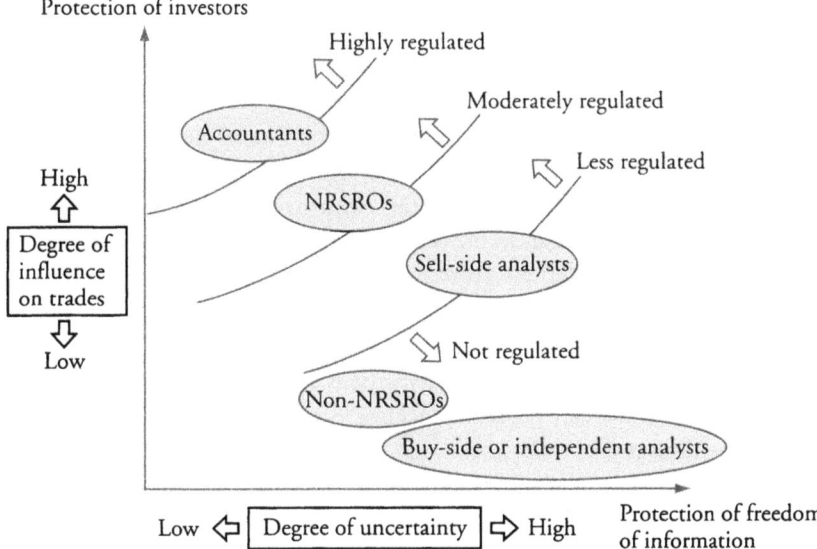

Source: Nomura Institute of Capital Markets Research.

them as tightly as accountants is reasonable. Sell-side analysts do not wield as much influence over trades as accountants because there are many analysts' reports and other forms of information from which investors can choose.

—*Uncertainty and subjectivity.* Since the information provided by accountants is prepared in accordance with generally accepted accounting principles (GAAP), the information can be considered relatively objective; it does not depend on the individual accountant who does the work. In that respect, regulation is not necessary to protect the provision of information, but because the information is central to investors' trading decisions, it is necessary to assure investors that accountants have followed those principles. In contrast, the information provided by analysts is subjective and uncertain, and it is valuable for investors to have access to as wide a variety of information as possible. For that reason, there is less need to regulate analysts than accountants.

Figure 2-2 depicts how the two variables—influence of information on securities trades and uncertainty and subjectivity of information—affect the need to regulate different financial gatekeepers. It is easy to understand why buy-side and independent analysts are not as regulated as sell-side analysts. In terms of the subjectivity of the information that they provide, all analysts are basically the same. But in terms of their influence on trades, other types of analysts have much less influence than those employed or used by securities brokers and dealers.

The location of rating agencies in figure 2-2 needs explanation. Because various securities regulations refer specifically to the ratings of NRSROs, these rating agencies are closely involved in securities transactions and need to be regulated. Also, since investors do not have many alternatives to the ratings of NRSROs in evaluating fixed-income securities, those ratings seem to have greater influence over transactions than the information provided by sell-side analysts. For that reason, it seems that NRSROs should be regulated more heavily than sell-side analysts, and since non-NRSROs do not have the same degree of influence in transactions, they should be treated like independent analysts, who are not regulated.

In terms of uncertainty or subjectivity, credit rating information ranks higher than information provided by accountants but lower than that provided by equity analysts since ratings deal only with credit risk and often focus only on whether an issue is investment grade. In that respect also, NRSROs in the United States and designated rating agencies in Japan should be subject to more regulation than sell-side analysts.

The reality is that whether rating agencies are NRSROs or not, they are not regulated to the same extent as sell-side analysts. To explain this situation, one might consider the nature of the problems with financial gatekeepers that have occurred so far. Among the recent corporate scandals, in many instances accountants and sell-side analysts actually colluded with the firms that they audited or researched to distort information disseminated to investors. But no such striking misdeeds by rating agencies have been reported. Moreover, since both accountants and securities brokers and dealers already are regulated, all that the authorities had to do in response to the scandals was to amend the existing regulatory framework. But since rating agencies are not regulated, regulators would have to start by confirming the need to regulate them.

Lack of evidence of serious problems does not preclude the need for formal regulation of NRSROs because the information that they provide is so influential in securities transactions. On the other hand, if NRSRO ratings were not required by various securities regulations and if the system designating certain rating agencies as NRSROs did not exist, then rating agencies would have much less influence and there would be less need to regulate them. The actual trend is moving in the opposite direction, however, toward using rating information in more regulations, such as Basel II.

As in the case of rating agencies, the location in figure 2-2 of each type of financial gatekeeper can shift depending on changes in its nature or in public policies. For example, today accounting information is becoming more and more subjective because fair-value accounting requires judgment regarding future cash flows. Also, investors may become less influenced by financial information and more by nonfinancial information, such as customer satisfaction, patents, and market share. If such trends continue, there might be less need for such rigorous regulation of accountants in the future.

It is also interesting to consider the possible location of other types of information providers in the figure. For example, investment advisers in the United States already are subject to formal regulation through the Investment Advisers Act of 1940—and understandably so, because their advice, even though it is rather subjective, is so influential in securities trading. At the same time, if financial planners do not refer to securities investments, it is reasonable not to require them to register as investment advisers. Also, there should be a wide variety of creative financial advice available to suit the needs of various individuals.

The difference between the regulatory environment for financial gatekeepers in the United States and Japan also can be explained in terms of the two variables discussed. For example, the fact that sell-side analysts in Japan are less regulated than in the United States is justified because they do not play as charismatic a role with individual investors and because they are not as involved in the investment banking business. Also, in Japan, earnings outlooks are usually disclosed by firms as part of timely disclosure requirements and analysts do not play an important role in pinpointing them, as they do in the United States.

Accountants also are less closely regulated in Japan than in the United States. Japan's Certified Public Accountants and Auditing Oversight Board only checks JICPA's reviews of audit firms whereas the U.S. Public Company Accounting Oversight Board itself performs checks of audit firms. Also, the rotation period for audit staff is seven years in Japan instead of five years as in the United States. Japan's more lenient treatment of accountants is hard to explain by the logic of the analysis presented in this chapter, since accounting information is as influential to securities trading in Japan as it is in the United States. In the wake of recent accounting scandals in Japan, the regulatory environment of accountants in Japan may well be tightened.

How Should Financial Gatekeepers Be Regulated?

The previous section discussed the necessity for regulating certain financial gatekeepers. The next point to consider is how financial gatekeepers should be regulated if regulation is justified. Two issues seem to be important when considering optimal regulation of financial gatekeepers: one is competition and availability, and the other is conflicts of interest.

COMPETITION AND AVAILABILITY. In general, the optimal number of service providers is determined by market forces if there is a free and efficient market for the service. But with some types of financial gatekeepers, regulation to protect investors may, for example, restrict new entries. Therefore market forces alone cannot decide the number of each type of financial gatekeeper and the actual number might be less than optimal.

Limited competition and availability among a certain type of gatekeeper will tend to increase that group's influence on trades. Also, the fewer the number of gatekeepers in one area, the greater the potential for problems with one gatekeeper. These observations suggest that there is greater need for regulation if competition among and availability of financial gatekeepers is limited. But stricter regulation could result in restricting the supply of financial gatekeeper services and thereby aggravating the problems.

On the other hand, sufficient numbers of financial gatekeepers and competition among them could help keep potential problems in check because the market would discipline their behavior. In that case, there would be less need for regulation. Therefore, even if a certain type of financial gatekeeper should be regulated, it would be necessary to design the regulation so that at least it would not reduce the availability of and competition among these gatekeepers. A better policy might be to actively promote the availability of gatekeepers and the competition among them.

One of the Japanese government's policy objectives is to foster the development of a financial system that depends less on the banking industry and more on financial markets. At the moment, however, there is a (relative) shortage of accountants in Japan, so one of the government's aims is to increase their number. In Japan the title of CPA is awarded by the government, which traditionally has controlled the number of accountants entering the profession by controlling the number of candidates who pass the state examination. But attempting to relieve the shortage of accountants by increasing the number of successful candidates in a short space of time could lead to a drop in quality. Moreover, those who have already qualified as CPAs have a vested interest in opposing a sharp increase in the number of new entrants.

Although reform of the accounting profession in Japan has included attempts to increase the number of new entrants, the increased regulatory burden placed on accountants makes the profession less attractive and makes it difficult to solve the problem of availability. For example, the rules on auditors' non-auditing activities have been tightened at the same time that their auditing responsibilities have been increased. That has made it increasingly difficult for auditing firms to turn a profit. Japan's leading auditing firms have already formed alliances with their counterparts in the United States, and the auditing business is increasingly becoming an oligopoly just as it is in the United States. Unless companies appreciate the value of well-conducted audits and are prepared to pay what they are worth, there is a risk of a shortage of auditors. Therefore, a careful eye must be kept on how the recent changes in the rules governing auditors in both Japan and the United States affect the availability of auditing services.[18]

When some providers among one type of gatekeeper are regulated (for example, NRSROs and sell-side analysts) and others are not, the market should determine the demand for and supply of those that are not regulated—just as for any other normal good or service. And whether regulation hampers the availability of and competition among the providers that are regulated should be examined. In the case of rating agencies, the system of designated rating agencies in Japan hampers achievement of the optimal supply of players. Abandoning the system might reduce the need to regulate rating agencies since their influence on trades will decline and competition and market discipline will increase.

The recently adopted policy mix in the United States—penalizing sell-side analysts with relatively harsh regulations and subsidizing independent analysts—implies that sell-side analysts were judged to be oversupplied and independent analysts undersupplied under market forces, making policy intervention necessary.

If it is necessary for the authorities to intervene to foster independent research in the United States, the world's largest capital market, then it would appear that they would need to do even more in smaller and less developed markets, such as Japan, if the dominance of sell-side analysts is to be reduced. A decline in market demand for and the market value of sell-side analysts is unlikely to be enough in itself to boost demand for independent research. This raises the question of whether governments in countries other than the United States should actively pursue policies to foster the development of independent research.

Generally speaking, if market forces alone cannot achieve the optimal supply of financial gatekeepers, there are several policy alternatives. The government might fully control the number of new entrants, give subsidies to encourage new entrants, or even control fees for certain financial gatekeepers to keep the industry profitable. Another less interventional approach would be to give financial gatekeepers as much freedom as possible so that they could stay in business more easily and new entrants would have more room. For example, the government

---

18. There is another aspect to the availability problem for auditors. As discussed, the increasing legal liability and financial settlements facing auditors could jeopardize the Big Four American accounting firms, and such a threat may become real in Japan in the future.

could allow financial gatekeepers to adopt a wide range of business models and keep enough revenues from the nonfinancial business that they generate through their capacity as financial gatekeepers to maintain their gatekeeping business. Such an approach seems difficult to follow because is raises concern over conflicts of interest.

CONFLICTS OF INTEREST. One pillar of regulation of financial gatekeepers is to avoid conflicts of interest. Conflicts of interest are inherent in most financial gatekeeping relationships because gatekeepers find it difficult to collect fees from the users of their information and so must find other sources of revenue. That is, accountants depend on fees from the companies that they audit, rating agencies depend on fees from the bond issuers that they rate, and sell-side analysts depend on fees from the securities businesses for which they work.

In both the United States and Japan, accountants are prohibited from providing both audit and non-audit services to the same client; sell-side analysts are barred from involvement in investment banking business; and rating agencies are criticized for depending on fees from issuers that they rate.

There might be various ways to protect investors from the damage caused by conflicts of interest. What is important is to control the damage but not necessarily limit the freedom of gatekeepers to adopt various business models or organizational structures because they could possibly induce conflicts of interest. If financial regulation is viewed as a whole, two reform trends can be observed heading in opposite directions when it comes to conflict of interest. The first is in the area of banking regulation, where the barriers separating banking and securities businesses that had been established to avoid conflicts of interest have been lowered. The second can be seen in the many provisions of the Sarbanes-Oxley Act that emphasize the importance of having independent agents in various areas to avoid corporate fraud and conflicts of interest.

Benston and others criticize the U.S. decision to prohibit accountants from providing both audit and non-audit services to the same company.[19] One might also question whether it was necessary to completely ban analysts' involvement in the investment banking business. Instead of imposing the strict separation of businesses, especially where availability and competition are limited, authorities could allow financial gatekeepers more freedom in composing their business portfolios and choosing their organizational structures and enhance the system to monitor potential abuses. That is exactly the model that regulators are following in dealing with conflicts of interest in banks' securities business.

19. Benston and others (2003).

Who Should Regulate Financial Gatekeepers?

So far, it seemingly has been taken for granted that a government organization should regulate financial gatekeepers. But, as the Japanese experience in particular suggests, governments sometimes fail to regulate financial gatekeepers to protect investors' interests, because governments and government authorities have their own interests. For example, governments may issue bonds and become shareholders in companies that are being privatized. Also, a banking regulator's interest in avoiding financial panic may put it at odds with a financial gatekeeper if the gatekeeper's report reveals weaknesses in the banking system. Besides, political pressure may distort regulators' decisions, as happened with the U.S. regulators' decision on the accounting treatment of stock options.

The ideal might be an organization solely devoted to protecting investors, one that was politically independent and whose policy objectives were separate from other government policy objectives. Such an organization would be comparable to a central bank; central banks are narrowly focused on monetary policy and their political independence is legally guaranteed. Such an organization should also be financially independent.

Litan argues that the United States should have given the Securities and Exchange Commission the job of dealing with the problem of conflict of interest among accountants rather than establish the Public Company Accounting Oversight Board.[20] Financial independence of regulators is certainly an issue in Japan. Because the Certified Public Accountants and Auditing Oversight Board is under the authority of the Financial Services Agency and is financed by taxes, it could be influenced by other policy objectives of the FSA or of politicians.[21] Moreover, the Accounting Standards Board of Japan is barely financed by corporate membership fees and publications, unlike its U.S. counterpart, the Financial Accounting Standards Board, which is now financially supported by PCAOB.

In Japan, some argue for introducing a commission like the U.S. SEC, but others question the logic of having separate regulators for securities markets, the banking system, and insurance companies in this day of financial conglomerates.[22] Japan is also actively debating the role of various self-regulated organizations (SROs). The issue of who should regulate financial gatekeepers, then, is

---

20. Benston and others (2003, pp. 12–13, 67–68).
21. Japan's FSA is not only a regulator for investor protection but also a banking and insurance supervisor.
22. Some Americans do not seem to be satisfied with the current regulatory structure, as seen in the Government Accountability Office report *Financial Regulation: Industry Changes Prompt Need to Reconsider U.S. Regulatory Structure*, GAO-05-61 (October 2004).

bound up with the structure of the regulatory system, a topic that is beyond the scope of this chapter.

References

Benston, George, and others. 2003. *Following the Money: The Enron Failure and the State of Corporate Disclosure.* Washington: AEI-Brookings Joint Center for Regulatory Studies.

Inoue, Tomoo. 2006. "Determinants of Audit Fees for Listed Japanese Companies." Mimeo. Seikei University.

Isoyama, Tomoyuki. 2002. *World Competes in Setting International Accounting Standards* [in Japanese]. Tokyo: Nikkei BP.

COMMENT BY
Paul Stevens

YASUYUKI FUCHITA has produced a very thorough and useful chapter. It is always valuable to look to the experiences of other markets when trying to make sense of what is going on at home. While the context may be different, the United States and Japan are grappling with many of the same problems.

In the United States, the term "financial gatekeeper" applies to a range of entities that facilitate, grant, or condition access to the public capital markets by issuers of publicly traded securities by providing oversight and analysis of firms and transactions. After Enron and other recent scandals, the focus has been on accountants, obviously; on investment banks and analysts; on lawyers, a group not mentioned by Fuchita; and, to a somewhat lesser extent, on the ratings agencies. It is important to note that attention to gatekeepers is not entirely new. In the 1970s, the Enforcement Division of the Securities and Exchange Commission (SEC) administered its responsibilities on the basis of what was then called "the access theory," which held that major corporate fraud was not possible without the complicity, connivance, or indifference of the gatekeepers involved. Over time, of course, as Coffee could relate in exquisite detail, the liabilities of gatekeepers have grown enormously, under both U.S. public law—SEC statutes and criminal laws—and civil law.

The core concern emphasized in this chapter is, I think, exactly the right one: typically accountants and other gatekeepers are paid by the issuers of securities who are seeking to get through the gate that controls access to public capital.

This setup can result in substantial conflicts of interest, since the gatekeepers can be torn between serving the private, profit-driven interests of the companies that hire them and the public interest in maintaining transparent, efficient markets.

It is interesting, given the size of Japan's financial markets, that gatekeepers have a relatively minor role in that economy. Perhaps the situation will change over time. Fuchita aptly connects the lack of demand for gatekeepers in Japan with the dominance of banks, which do not rely on them as much as other types of financial firms do. The chapter also notes correctly that in Japan individual investors hold a far smaller portion of equity securities than those in the United States do. A survey that the Investment Company Institute and the Securities Industry Association have conducted jointly over a number of years shows that equity ownership by U.S. households has increased threefold since the early 1980s.[1] Today, more than half of U.S. households own equities directly or through mutual funds. Ninety percent of equity-owning households invest in stock mutual funds, which increasingly are how individual U.S. investors are accessing the equity marketplace. More widespread participation in equities markets by firms and individuals in the United States may help explain why gatekeepers are more prominent and influential here. Another lesson that I draw from the chapter is that the strength and independence of a gatekeeper depends in part on the prestige associated with that profession in a particular society, and professional prestige is another aspect in which Japan's gatekeepers lag somewhat behind those in the United States.

I want to highlight a few issues surrounding the major forms of gatekeepers in the United States, starting with the ratings agencies. The United States is hopelessly muddled about how to think about ratings agencies. On the one hand, they are thought to enjoy a form of protected speech and to exercise First Amendment rights, as commentators or journalists might; on the other hand, they are thought of as gatekeepers who perform some quasi-governmental function, sometimes one written into the fabric of our securities regulations. The tension between these two roles makes it more difficult for the agencies themselves to do their job, as well as for others to assess their performance or design ways to improve it. Fuchita correctly notes that in the United States ratings agencies began as a business to fulfill a need in the private marketplace but have since become convenient mechanisms for government to build regulations around; he describes a similarly convoluted public-private relationship that hampers ratings agencies in Japan.

---

1. Investment Company Institute and Securities Industry Association, *Equity Ownership in America* (Washington: 2005). See www.ici.org/stats/res/index.html#Equity%20Owners.

On the issue of securities analysts, I personally think that sell-side analysts—at least those associated with securities dealers and investment banks—are hopelessly, irreconcilably conflicted. I am skeptical about the efficacy of various disclosure or other provisions designed to separate one portion of such a firm's business from another or otherwise bolster the analyst's integrity and objectivity. These types of provisions are well intended, but they probably will suffice to prevent only the most egregious forms of fraud. One problem that sell-side analysts will face, if they cannot be paid directly by issuers, is how to recoup the costs of their research. But the market should take care of that, and, in order to generate sufficient demand for their services, analysts will have to produce better quality analysis. Clearly, there also will be some shift to independent and buy-side analysis, which has recently become more robust.

Fuchita rightly points out that indexing strategies will make the analyst conflict-of-interest concern less significant. The rise of mutual funds as a way of investing in U.S. equity markets is important also because the fund's investment adviser has every incentive to filter out analysis that is not worthwhile or clearly value added. I also think that the importance of robust third-party independent research has been reaffirmed. In the United States the idea of prohibiting the use of soft dollars to access that kind of research has been discussed and resoundingly rejected, indicating that the role and contribution of independent research is now more highly valued.

Finally, I want to comment on the author's suggestion about the variables that ought to guide regulation, that is, the influence that gatekeepers have on information in the market and how uncertain or subjective that information is. Based on these variables, the author makes a convincing case that accountants ought to be the most highly regulated gatekeepers of all. I do worry, however, about a broader issue, which is the effect of regulation on competition and access.

There are many who are concerned that the government is regulating gatekeepers into extinction. As a lawyer in private practice, I have been involved, on behalf of various mutual fund boards, in their search for new public accounting firms for these funds. Surprisingly, when all is said and done, when technical independence requirements and business realities are taken into full account in such a process, there may be only one option available to a board. It is an odd situation: regulations encourage boards to exercise the highest prudence and circumspection in choosing their auditors, but they also severely restrict the pool of eligible candidates. It is reminiscent of the early days of the automobile: you can have your choice of any color, said Mr. Ford, so long as it is black!

In the United States, it is clear that there will be two tiers of audit firms, largely because of liability concerns—a very small, elite group, which is going to venture into the realm of public company auditing, and many others, which are fine firms but will restrict themselves to the private marketplace. Analysts, I believe, will always be in abundant supply, and eventually we will resolve the question about rating agencies in a way that allows many more to come to the market and to function in a transparent manner so that people can see what value they add and then make their own decisions. But the competition issue and the availability of services with respect to accountants is and likely will remain a very important public policy concern for the foreseeable future. The trajectory of our regulation of this particular gatekeeper should reflect these concerns.

Again, I commend Fuchita for a thorough and insightful treatment of these topics.

FRANK PARTNOY

3

How and Why Credit Rating Agencies Are Not Like Other Gatekeepers

IN SEPTEMBER 2005, the Brookings–Tokyo Club Seminar addressed perhaps the most important policy question related to the recent wave of corporate scandals in the United States and Japan: What should be the role of private financial market gatekeepers?[1] In this chapter I assess potential answers to this question with respect to the least-understood gatekeeper: the credit rating agency.

Credit rating agencies clearly belong within the broad classification of financial market gatekeepers.[2] They play a verification function in the fixed-income markets by designating alphabetical ratings of debt. They have a substantial stock of resources to pledge as reputational capital in the event that they are found to

---

I am grateful to Laura Adams, David DeVito, Kristen Jaconi, Shaun Martin, Justin Pettit, and Lawrence White for comments on a draft of this chapter as well as to Barry Bosworth, Robert Litan, and the participants in the Brookings–Tokyo Club Seminar.

1. The pre-2002 literature on gatekeepers was extensive. See, for example, Partnoy (2001), assessing a proposal that gatekeepers be subject to a modified strict liability regime, and Coffee (1997), discussing the role of underwriters, accountants, lawyers, and directors as "gatekeepers" and "reputational intermediaries." See also Choi (1998); Kraakman (1986); Gilson and Kraakman (1984), discussing the role of investment bankers as gatekeepers; Kraakman (1984); and Dooley (1972). The literature on gatekeepers has experienced something of a renaissance in response to the collapse of Enron and WorldCom. For a more recent discussion, see Coffee (2004a), Partnoy (2004), and Coffee (2004b). See also Oh (2004) and Cunningham (2004). There also is an extensive literature on lawyers as gatekeepers. See Coffee (2003) and Zacharias (2004).

2. See Coffee (2004a, p. 308).

have performed poorly.³ They act as agents, not principals, and are paid only a fraction of the proceeds of debt issues.⁴

However, credit rating agencies differ from other gatekeepers in several important ways. Although they have performed at least as poorly as other gatekeepers during the past five years, their market values have skyrocketed. Since 2002, as securities firms have restructured their approach to rating shares in response to a wave of private litigation and government prosecution (and to the general decline in the reputation of the ratings of securities analysts), the credit rating process has remained largely intact and credit ratings have become more prominent, important, and valuable.

In addition, credit rating agencies continue to face conflicts of interest that are potentially more serious than those of other gatekeepers: they continue to be paid directly by issuers, they give unsolicited ratings that at least potentially pressure issuers to pay them fees, and they market ancillary consulting services related to ratings. Credit rating agencies increasingly focus on structured finance and new complex debt products, particularly credit derivatives, which now generate a substantial share of credit rating agencies' revenues and profits. With respect to these new instruments, the agencies have become more like "gate openers" than gatekeepers; in particular, their rating methodologies for collateralized debt obligations (CDOs) have created and sustained that multi-trillion-dollar market.⁵

Why are credit rating agencies so different from other gatekeepers? Part of the reason is that the most successful credit rating agencies have benefited from an oligopoly market structure that is reinforced by regulations that depend exclusively on credit ratings issued by Nationally Recognized Statistical Rating Organizations (NRSROs).⁶ These regulatory benefits—which I call "regulatory licenses"—generate economic rents for NRSROs that persist even when they perform poorly

---

3. As noted in the later discussion of the profitability of credit rating agencies, there are serious questions about whether fluctuations in their reputation affect their stock of capital. For example, during the past five years, as the market capitalization of most financial market gatekeepers has fallen, the market capitalization of the major rating agencies has increased. Not coincidentally, over the same period, rating agencies have not been subject to civil or criminal liability for malfeasance.

4. Rating agency fees are in the range of 3 to 4 basis points of the face amount for rating a typical corporate bond issue and substantially more for complex issues. See discussion of agency profitability.

5. I discuss credit derivatives in greater detail in the section on the agencies' role in rating new structured finance issues.

6. The Securities and Exchange Commission controls the NRSRO designation process, although numerous regulations outside the securities area depend on NRSRO ratings. For an excellent description of the structure of the credit rating business, see White (2002, pp. 41–64).

and otherwise would lose reputational capital. Until recently, there were only three NRSROs: Moody's, Standard & Poor's, and Fitch.[7]

Another reason that credit rating agencies differ from other gatekeepers is that they have been largely immune to civil and criminal liability for malfeasance. Some rules specifically exempt credit rating agencies from liability. More important, several lower-court judges have accepted—wrongly, in my opinion—the rating agencies' argument that ratings are opinions protected by the First Amendment.

Various proposals have been put forth to reform credit rating agencies, particularly NRSROs. Some initiatives have been directed at increasing competition among agencies by opening the process of designating NRSROs,[8] while a few commentators have proposed eliminating the NRSRO designation entirely.[9] Recently introduced legislation would require credit rating agencies to register with the Securities and Exchange Commission (SEC), just as investment advisers and broker-dealers must; although the legislation would require reporting and record-keeping, it would not impose onerous substantive requirements.[10] Since 1999, I have advanced a proposal to substitute market-based measures—such as credit spreads—for credit ratings in the numerous regulations that depend on NRSRO ratings.[11]

Credit ratings continue to present an unusual paradox: rating changes are important, yet they possess little informational value.[12] Credit ratings do not help parties manage risk, yet parties increasingly rely on ratings. Credit rating agencies are not widely respected among sophisticated market participants, yet their franchise is increasingly valuable. The agencies argue that they are merely financial journalists publishing opinions, yet ratings are far more valuable than the opinions of even the most prominent and respected financial publishers.

In this chapter I argue that optimal policy with respect to credit rating agencies should account for the ways in which agencies differ from other gatekeepers, and I explain some of the reasons why these differences have persisted and

---

7. The SEC recently approved two additional NRSROs. Currently, Moody's, S&P, Fitch, DBRS, and A. M. Best Company are designated as NRSROs.
8. See SEC (2005).
9. See Pollock (2005).
10. See H.R. 2990, The Credit Rating Agency Duopoly Relief Act (2005), sponsored by Rep. Michael Fitzpatrick (R-Pa.), 109 Cong., June 20, 2005.
11. See Partnoy (1999, p. 619).
12. See Partnoy (2002, pp. 65–84); see also Schwarcz (2002). Although initial credit ratings provide some guidance to purchasers at the time of issuance, it is not clear that they provide any information beyond that already reflected in the "price talk" associated with a fixed-income instrument (that is, information available before the instrument is issued).

in some cases widened. I next assess various policy proposals and argue that an ideal policy should both reduce the value of regulatory licenses and increase the threat of rating agency liability. Simply put, the best proposals would help resolve the paradox of credit ratings by creating incentives for credit rating agencies to generate greater informational value while reducing the impact of ratings on markets.

How Credit Rating Agencies Differ from Other Gatekeepers

The differences between credit rating agencies and other gatekeepers are stark. Credit rating agencies are more profitable than other gatekeepers, they face different and potentially more serious conflicts of interest, and they are uniquely active in structured finance, particularly with regard to collateralized debt obligations.

Profitability

The profitability of credit rating agencies can be considered from two perspectives, one historical, the other more recent. A brief examination of the history of these agencies reveals that the business of rating bonds generally was not highly profitable. A close look at the performance of the agencies over the past five years, however, reveals an extraordinary increase in their profitability. The performance of credit rating agencies is precisely the opposite of that of other gatekeepers, which, although they were consistently profitable during the twentieth century, have experienced difficulties during the past five years.

To put the profitability of modern credit rating agencies in context, it is worth remembering that before the 1970s, the agencies' business model was radically different from what it is today. Before the 1970s, when the Securities and Exchange Commission created the NRSRO designation and various regulations began to depend on NRSRO ratings, credit rating agencies made money by charging subscription fees to investors, not ratings fees to issuers. In contrast, today roughly 90 percent of credit rating agencies' revenues are from issuer fees.[13]

The modern credit rating industry grew out of various American firms that began classifying bonds, primarily railroad bonds, during the late nineteenth century. By 1890, Poor's Publishing Company, predecessor of today's S&P, was publishing *Poor's Manual*, an analysis of bonds.[14] During the following two decades,

---

13. See Moody's Corporation Form 10-K Filing, March 8, 2005, pp. 18–22.
14. See, for example, In re Bartol, 38 A. 527 (Pa. 1897), approving of reference to *Poor's Manual* of 1890.

numerous analysts issued railroad industry reports with elaborate statistics and details about operating and financial data for individual companies.[15]

John Moody collected these details, believing that investors would pay for a service that synthesized the mass of information into an easily digestible format.[16] He published his first rating scheme for bonds in 1909, in a book entitled *Analysis of Railroad Investments*, but there was not much demand for his ratings until the market boom of the 1920s. By 1924, the market for bond ratings was more competitive than it is today: in addition to John Moody's rating company, Poor's, Standard Statistics Company, Inc., Fitch Publishing Company, and others published ratings.[17] These early agencies made money by charging investors subscription fees; they did not charge issuers.

Following the 1929 stock market crash, the credit rating industry went into a general decline.[18] Investors were no longer very interested in purchasing ratings, particularly given the agencies' poor track record in anticipating the sharp drop in bond values beginning in late 1929. One infamous case involved a default by the Chicago, Rock Island & Pacific Railroad on bonds that all of the major agencies had given their highest ratings.[19] Investors recognized that the ratings were not of especially great value and that in any event they were based largely on publicly available information.

The rating business remained stagnant for decades. According to a study of 207 corporate bond rating changes from 1950 to 1972, credit rating changes generated information of little or no value. The changes merely reflected information already incorporated into stock market prices—and indeed lagged that information by as much as eighteen months.[20] Concern about the failure of the

---

15. In 1906 and 1907, two prominent reports were published on the railroad industry, "The Earning Power of Railroads," by Floyd Mundy, and "American Railways as Investment," by Carl Snyder. John Moody relied heavily on both reports. See Partnoy (1999, note 79).

16. According to Moody, "While no one in this country had attempted such a thing as investment ratings by means of symbols, yet even in those days bonds were classified into groups according to quality and salability, especially by large investment institutions, such as insurance companies. Moreover there had existed for a considerable time, I think, a bond rating system in Vienna and also, I believe, in Berlin. These foreign systems had been developed by symbols and the Austrian Manual of Statistics, which carried these symbols, was quite well known in Europe, although not at all in this country." Harold (1938), quoting from John Moody, in a letter to Harold dated August 21, 1934.

17. Partnoy (1999, p. 639).

18. There is some evidence that regulations from the 1930s that depended on credit ratings encouraged the use of ratings and led to some resurgence in the industry. However, that resurgence was short lived, and by the end of World War II, credit rating agencies were not especially profitable.

19. See Partnoy (1999, p. 643).

20. See Pinches and Singleton (1978, pp. 29, 39).

rating agencies to generate accurate and reliable information led to public arguments for regulation of the credit rating industry.[21]

Yet the agencies were not regulated, in part because regulators perceived that they did not play a prominent role in the financial system. During the early 1970s, the SEC decided that instead of regulating the credit rating industry, it would begin relying on the ratings of a handful of major credit rating agencies in making certain regulatory determinations, beginning with the calculation of net capital requirements for broker-dealers.[22] In adopting its net capital rules, the SEC created the NRSRO concept, although it neither defined the term nor indicated which agencies qualified as NRSROs. During the following years, the SEC suggested through a series of no-action letters that the major established credit rating agencies qualified for NRSRO designation but that smaller agencies did not.

Over time, the SEC—and then other administrative agencies, as well as Congress—established additional legal rules that depended on NRSRO ratings.[23] This shift in regulatory approach corresponded to a change in the economics of the credit rating industry. In particular, credit rating agencies abandoned their historical practice of charging investors for subscriptions and instead began charging issuers for ratings on the basis of the size of the issue. As additional regulations came to depend more on NRSRO ratings, those ratings became more important and more valuable. Despite those changes, during the 1980s the business of rating bonds grew only modestly. In 1980, there had been just thirty professionals working in the S&P Industrials group; by 1986, there were only forty.[24]

The number of bonds that the major agencies rated increased dramatically during the 1990s. By 1997, Moody's was rating 20,000 public and private issuers in the United States and about 1,200 non-U.S. issuers, including both corporations and sovereign states. S&P rated slightly fewer in each category. Moody's rated $5 trillion worth of securities; S&P rated $2 trillion. Both companies' operating margins were thought to be in the range of 30 percent (Moody's had not yet gone public, and McGraw-Hill, S&P's parent, did not publish much information about S&P's profitability).[25] The agencies' power and profitability at that time

---

21. Wakeman (1981, p. 19). Wakeman found that by the 1970s, bond ratings simply mirrored the market's assessment of a bond's risk and generated little information not already reflected in the market price of the bonds. See also Hickman (1958), assessing default rates of investment grade and non–investment grade bonds through 1943.

22. SEC rule 15c3-1 set forth certain broker-dealer net capital requirements and required a different haircut for securities based on credit ratings assigned by NRSROs.

23. See Partnoy (2002, 74–78).

24. Partnoy (1999, p. 649).

25. Partnoy (1999, p. 650). Moody's was owned by the Dun & Bradstreet Corporation prior to its spin-off in September 2000.

Table 3-1. *Moody's Income Statement Data, 2000–04*
US$ million

Data	2000	2001	2002	2003	2004
Revenue	602	797	1,023	1,247	1,438
Expenses	314	398	485	584	652
Operating income	288	399	538	663	786
Net income	159	212	289	364	425

Source: Moody's Corporation Form 10-K Filings, various years.

were reflected in commentator Thomas Friedman's quip that there were only two superpowers in the world, the United States and Moody's, and that sometimes it wasn't clear which was more powerful.[26]

It is remarkable that the recent meteoric ascent of credit rating agency revenues and profits began only several years after Friedman's quote. Consider table 3-1, which depicts the increase in the revenues and net income of Moody's during its life as a public company since 2000. As of early September 2005, Moody's market capitalization was more than $15 billion, roughly the same as Bear Stearns Companies Inc., a major investment bank. Yet Bear Stearns had 11,000 employees and $7 billion of revenue, whereas Moody's had 2,500 employees and $1.6 billion of revenue. Moody's operating margins have consistently been more than 50 percent since 2000, even higher than they were during the 1990s. Moody's share price trades at a significantly higher multiple than the typical publicly traded gatekeeper, such as an investment bank. Moody's diluted earnings per share (EPS) for 2004 was just $2.79, and its stock price in 2005 was in the range of $50 to $60 per share, based on public reports of trading prices. In contrast, investment bank price-to-earnings (P/E) ratios have been closer to 10. Perhaps most remarkable is that Moody's $15 billion market capitalization is supported by assets of just $1.4 billion.

Moody's success is even more striking because of the simplicity of its business. The vast majority of the company's income is fees from ratings. For example, Moody's has not used derivatives and has not had any off–balance sheet arrangements with unconsolidated entities or financial partnerships. Nor does Moody's take on substantial interest rate or credit risk.

Although similar data are not available for S&P Ratings Services, whose stock is not publicly traded, it appears to be similarly profitable. As of September 2005,

26. Thomas L. Friedman, interview, *NewsHour with Jim Lehrer*, PBS, February 13, 1996.

S&P had credit rating opinions outstanding on approximately $30 trillion of debt, including 745,000 securities issued by roughly 42,000 obligors in more than 100 countries.[27] Moody's numbers were roughly the same.[28] And, as noted above, S&P and Moody's charge similar fees.

In financial terms, the credit rating agencies and other gatekeepers have been moving in opposite directions. While the value of Moody's shares has increased by more than 300 percent during the past five years, most banks' shares have declined in value. Accounting firm profits also have declined, at least until the Sarbanes-Oxley Act of 2002 generated new opportunities.[29] Arthur Andersen is gone, and KPMG barely survived. Most gatekeepers have experienced high volatility during the past five years. But Moody's shares steadily increased during that period, as depicted in figure 3-1.

A portion of the relative increase in the value of credit rating agencies reflects the legal settlements and future expected liability of other gatekeepers, particularly banks and accounting firms. While other gatekeepers have paid billions of dollars in legal settlements since 2002, credit rating agencies have paid virtually nothing. The primary reason for the difference is that the rating agencies have successfully defended themselves against litigation by claiming that their business is financial publishing and that their ratings therefore are "opinions" protected by the First Amendment.

Although Moody's might say that it is in the financial publishing business, market participants do not believe it. Moody's is substantially smaller than the other major financial publishers and generates less revenue than they do, but it has a much higher market capitalization. Consider the financial data in table 3-2 from Moody's, along with that of two major financial publishers, Dow Jones and Reuters.[30]

As of September 2005, Dow Jones had revenues that were slightly higher than those of Moody's and nearly three times as many employees, yet Moody's shares were worth nearly five times as much. Reuters, a much larger firm than Moody's by most measures, has a much smaller market capitalization. The reasons are obvious: Moody's has much higher operating margins. Investors will pay five times more for a dollar of Moody's revenue than for a dollar of the revenues of Dow Jones or Reuters. Each Moody's employee is associated with ten times more market value than each Dow Jones or Reuters employee. By virtually any financial

---

27. See Rita M. Bolger, testimony, Capital Markets, Insurance, and Government-Sponsored Enterprises Subcommittee of the House Financial Services Committee, June 29, 2005, exhibit A, p. 1.
28. Moody's Corporation Form 10-K Filing, 2004, p. 3.
29. Law firm profits also have increased in the aftermath of the Sarbanes-Oxley Act.
30. The comparison is similar for other publicly traded companies in the publishing industry.

Figure 3-1. *Change in Moody's Share Price versus S&P 500 versus Major Investment Banks*
Percent change

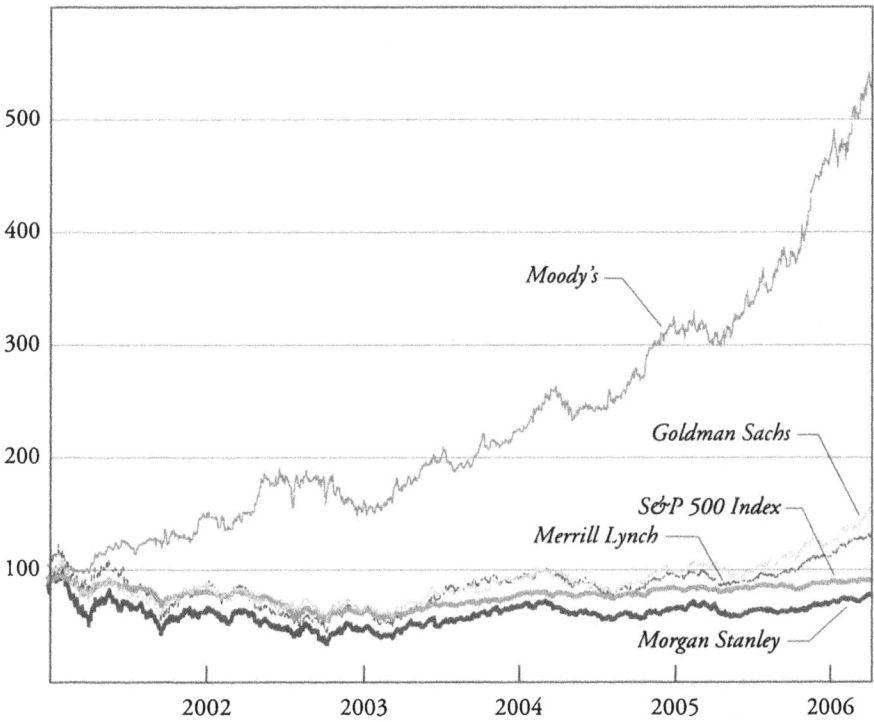

Source: http://finance.yahoo.com.

Table 3-2. *Moody's versus Major Financial Publishers*

Company	Market cap (billions)	Revenue (billions)	Employees (number)	Operating cash (millions)	Operating margin (percent)	Price/ revenue	Price/ employee
Dow Jones	$3.3	$1.7	7,143	$224	9	1.9	$461,991
Reuters	$9.3	$5.3	15,475	$413	11	1.8	$600,969
Moody's	$15.2	$1.6	2,500	$632	54	9.5	$6,080,000

Source: http://finance.yahoo.com.

measure, Moody's has a much more valuable franchise than other financial publishing firms and is much too profitable to be considered a financial publisher. If Moody's were in the same business as financial publishing firms, one would expect these ratios to be close.

In sum, credit rating agencies have been more profitable than other gatekeepers. Unlike the "opinions" of other gatekeepers, the ratings of NRSROs are increasingly important and valuable.[31] That is true notwithstanding the abysmal recent performance of credit rating agencies.[32]

Conflicts of Interest

All of the major gatekeepers have been accused of serious conflicts of interest. However, the conflicts at credit rating agencies are different from those at other gatekeepers and potentially more serious, not only because agencies are paid directly by the issuers that they rate, but also because the vast majority of rating agencies' revenues are from those fees. In addition, those credit rating agencies with market power, specifically S&P and Moody's, have been developing ancillary businesses, including consulting, that other non–credit rating agency gatekeepers are now restricted in developing.

The SEC recently conducted formal examinations of the three major NRSROs and reported serious concerns about conflicts of interest. The first and most obvious conflict arises from the fact that issuers pay NRSROs for their ratings. This conflict has existed since the 1970s, when the SEC began implementing NRSRO-dependent rules and rating agencies switched from charging investors to charging issuers for ratings. However, the SEC has pointed to an increase in potential conflicts in recent years.

---

31. Both anecdotal evidence and academic studies suggest that rating changes are increasingly important events. See Securities and Exchange Commission (2003, p. 5), noting that "the importance of these opinions to investors and other market participants, and the influence of these opinions on the securities markets, have increased significantly."

32. Although the credit rating agencies argue that their rating changes are correlated with actual defaults, virtually anyone's rating changes would be if the person simply read the newspapers. The market value and regulatory importance of ratings suggest that agencies are at least trying to do something more than merely publish ratings that are correlated after the fact with default experience. Indeed, it was the agencies' poor performance in assessing companies before the recent wave of corporate defaults that led Congress to study and then criticize the industry. For example, consider the following statement from Senator Joseph Lieberman, whose Senate committee held the first hearings on Enron: "The credit-rating agencies were dismally lax in their coverage of Enron. They didn't ask probing questions and generally accepted at face value whatever Enron's officials chose to tell them. And while they claim to rely primarily on public filings with the SEC, analysts from Standard and Poor's not only did not read Enron's proxy statement, they didn't even know what information it might contain." Senate Committee on Governmental Affairs, press release, "Financial Oversight of Enron: The SEC and Private-Sector Watchdogs" (October 8, 2002).

As noted above, approximately 90 percent of rating agency revenues come from issuers who pay for ratings.[33] Rating agency fees vary depending on the size and complexity of the issue.[34] For corporate debt, the fees are in the range of 3 to 4 basis points of the size of the issue, with minimum amounts in the range of $30,000 to $50,000 and maximum amounts in the range of $300,000.[35] For structured finance issues, fees range up to 10 basis points, and fees for complex transactions are substantially higher, up to $2.4 million.[36]

The rating agencies recognize that conflicts arise from having issuers pay for ratings, but they say that historically they have been able to manage those conflicts. For example, S&P has adopted procedures designed to ensure that no individual is able to link credit rating opinions to fees.[37] Of course, credit rating agencies and other gatekeepers face some of the same actual and potential conflicts. For example, credit rating agency board members serve in various capacities for companies that the credit rating agencies rate. For example, WorldCom shared a director with Moody's and received favorable ratings even after its bonds were trading at non–investment grade credit spreads.[38] Unlike other financial intermediaries, credit rating agencies have not been pressured to eliminate such conflicts.

To illustrate the differences between credit rating agencies and other gatekeepers with respect to conflicts, I have focused on two areas of conflict—ancillary services and unsolicited ratings—where credit rating agencies have not been

---

33. Because rating agencies rate thousands of bond issues, they do not depend on any particular issuer, so the concern about conflicts is more systemic than individualized. For example, S&P has stated that no single issuer or issuer group represents more than about 2 percent of the total annual revenue of its rating business. See SEC (2003, p. 41). In this way, credit rating agencies are unlike auditors, who might depend on one company for a more substantial share of revenue.

34. Standard & Poor's Ratings Services, "U.S. Ratings Fees Disclosure," April 20, 2005 (www.standardandpoors.com).

35. High-volume issuers and purchasers of multi-year ratings receive discounts. In addition, the agencies charge monitoring fees, cancellation fees, and initial confidential rating fees, which can be in the range of $20,000 to $50,000.

36. Buried in the copyright terms on its website, Moody's makes the following disclosure: "MOODY'S hereby discloses that most issuers of debt securities (including corporate and municipal bonds, debentures, notes and commercial paper) and preferred stock rated by MOODY'S have, prior to assignment of any rating, agreed to pay to MOODY'S for appraisal and rating services rendered by it fees ranging from $1,500 to $2,400,000" (www.moodys.com/moodys/cust/AboutMoodys/AboutMoodys.aspx?topic=copyright).

37. See Standard & Poor's Ratings Services, "Code of Practices and Procedures," September 2004. Update to Standard & Poor's Ratings Services, "Code of Conduct," October 2005 (http://www.standardandpoors.com/ratings/).

38. Clifford L. Alexander Jr., former chairman of Moody's, served on the board of WorldCom/MCI for nineteen years, as well as the board of Wyeth, another company that Moody's rated. Alec Klein, "Moody's Board Members Have Ties to Clients," *Washington Post*, November 22, 2004, p. A09.

subject to as much regulatory intervention as other gatekeepers.[39] First, with respect to ancillary services, credit rating agencies market pre-rating assessments and corporate consulting.[40] For an additional fee, issuers present hypothetical scenarios to the rating agencies to understand how a particular transaction—such as a merger, asset sale, or stock repurchase—might affect their ratings. Although the rating agencies argue that fees from ancillary services are not substantial, there is evidence that they are increasing.[41]

In addition, Moody's, S&P, and Fitch each offer risk management consulting services. According to the SEC, the products and services offered include "public and private firm credit scoring models, internal ratings systems services, and empirical data on default incidence, loss severity, default correlations, and rating transitions."[42] The SEC found that these marketing activities exacerbated the conflicts of interest at the agencies.

These ancillary services resemble consulting services offered by accounting firms. Just as an issuer might feel pressured by its auditor to use the auditor's consulting services, they might similarly feel pressure to use a credit rating agency's consulting services. Issuers might worry that if they did not purchase other services from the agency, the decision would have a negative impact on their rating. Conversely, issuers might believe that if they did purchase ancillary services, their rating would improve. In addition, with respect to rating agency assessment services, once an agency has indicated what rating it would give an issuer after a corporate transaction, the agency would be subject to pressure to give that rating. For example, if an agency were paid a fee for advice and advised an issuer that a stock repurchase would not affect its rating, it would be more difficult for the agency to change that rating after the issuer completed the repurchase.

Again, the rating agencies claim that they are able to manage these conflicts. They have implemented policies and procedures to separate their consulting and ratings functions. However, evidence gathered by the SEC suggests that those

---

39. CDOs, discussed later, also present unique conflicts of interest. For example, Fitch has alleged that S&P and Moody's have engaged in anticompetitive practices in the structured finance market by "notching": lowering their ratings on or refusing to rate structured finance securities unless a substantial portion of the assets in the pool also are rated by them. See press release, Fitch Ratings, "Survey Shows Majority of Structured Finance Executives Oppose Notching as Practiced by Moody's and S&P," March 27, 2002.

40. In September 2005, S&P announced that it was abandoning its practice of providing corporate governance ratings, an ancillary service that was in potential conflict with its practice of providing credit ratings.

41. See McGraw-Hill Companies Form 10-K Filing, 2001: "[S&P's] revenue from rating evaluation services . . . increased substantially during 2000."

42. See Securities and Exchange Commission (2003, p. 42).

policies are not effective and that rating agency analysts both perform ancillary assessments and participate in marketing consulting services.[43]

Obviously, the primary difference between credit rating agencies and other gatekeepers with respect to conflicts related to ancillary services is that regulators have not restricted credit rating agencies' consulting services. In contrast, accounting firms and corporate boards face new rules regarding conflicts of interest and research analysts at investment banks must comply with restrictions on their activities and compensation. Yet no such rules govern credit rating agencies.

A second area of conflict arises from the unsolicited ratings that the agencies give to some issuers. Unsolicited credit ratings, which are highly controversial, have been the subject of ongoing litigation and scrutiny but no new regulations. Moody's has estimated in the past that 1 percent of its ratings have been unsolicited; S&P and Fitch have not publicly stated how frequently they issue unsolicited ratings, although they admit to engaging in the practice.[44] Although it is not clear precisely how frequently credit rating agencies issue unsolicited ratings, it is clear that they do. The vast majority of ratings are solicited by issuers, but on the basis of available data and empirical evidence, it seems reasonable to assume that roughly 1 percent of corporate credit ratings are unsolicited. It is not clear what the percentage might be with respect to structured finance ratings.

During the past decade, the Department of Justice has opened investigations into the practice of giving unsolicited ratings, but it has not yet brought a prosecution. On July 29, 2005, Moody's disclosed that it had received subpoenas from Eliot Spitzer, New York's attorney general, seeking information about its issuing of unsolicited ratings. It seems likely that regulators will continue to scrutinize unsolicited ratings.

The controversy surrounding the practice of unsolicited ratings began in 1993, when the Jefferson County (Colorado) school district decided to issue new bonds to take advantage of lower interest rates.[45] Although it had hired Moody's for previous bond issues, it decided to hire S&P and Fitch instead for those particular bonds.[46] On October 20, 1993, the school district priced the bonds, and initially

---

43. Securities and Exchange Commission (2003, p. 43).
44. Alec Klein, "Credit Raters' Power Leads to Abuses, Some Borrowers Say," *Washington Post*, November 24, 2004, p. A01. The extent to which Moody's continues to issue unsolicited ratings remains unclear. See *Compuware v. Moody's Investors Services, Inc.*, 324 F. Supp.2d 860 (E.D. Mich. 2004).
45. See *Jefferson County School District No. R-1 v. Moody's Investors Services, Inc.*, 175 F.3d 848 (10th Cir. 1999).
46. See Leslie Eaton, "Judge Dismisses Lawsuit against Moody's Service," *New York Times*, May 10, 1996, p. D2.

they were selling well. However, two hours after the pricing, Moody's issued a "negative outlook" on the bonds.[47] Several buyers immediately canceled their orders, and the school district was forced to reprice the bonds and pay a higher rate. It sued Moody's, alleging that this "negative outlook" contained falsehoods and had increased the cost of issuing the bonds by $769,000. Moody's defense was that its evaluation of the school district's bonds was a constitutionally protected "opinion." The court agreed, and its dismissal of the claims was upheld on appeal.[48] For now, I want to set aside the First Amendment implications of this case (and others), which I address later, and focus on the implications of unsolicited ratings.

The decision in the Jefferson County case suggested to credit rating agencies that the courts would protect them from litigation if they issued unsolicited ratings. Anecdotal evidence suggests that the agencies have continued to issue unsolicited ratings, despite the investigation by the Department of Justice.[49] With respect to unsolicited ratings, the credit rating agencies are unique among gatekeepers. In particular, the conflicts involving securities analysts are the reverse of those associated with credit ratings: the allegation is that analysts give unduly favorable ratings to persuade issuers to pay additional fees for other services, not that they give unduly unfavorable ratings to persuade issuers to pay for the ratings. In other words, the securities analyst conflicts are "pull" conflicts in which the analyst dangles the prospect of favorable ratings to obtain future fees, whereas the rating agency conflicts are "push" conflicts in which the agency threatens the issuer with unfavorable ratings to obtain fees now.

With respect to other gatekeepers, such as auditors, the notion of unsolicited ratings makes little sense. An accounting firm would not likely give an audit

---

47. Moody's said, "The outlook on the district's general obligation debt is negative, reflecting the district's ongoing financial pressures due in part to the state's past underfunding of the school finance act as well as legal uncertainties and fiscal constraints." *Jefferson County School District No. R-1* v. *Moody's Investors Services, Inc.*, 175 F.3d 848, 850 (10th Cir. 1999).

48. Moody's was separately fined $195,000 in 2001 for obstructing justice by destroying documents in the investigation. See Alec Klein, "Credit Raters' Power Leads to Abuses, Some Borrowers Say," *Washington Post*, Nov. 24, 2004, p. A01.

49. For example, Michigan Municipal Bond Authority officials said that they received a Moody's bill for an unsolicited rating after they chose Fitch to rate some bonds that they issued in spring 1995. They returned the bill unpaid. See "Watching the Watchers: Justice Department Launches Probe of Moody's Ratings," *Tulsa World*, March 28, 1996, p. E1. In one publicized case, Moody's began publishing credit ratings of the bonds of Hannover Re, a large German reinsurer, after it told Moody's it did not see the value in a Moody's rating (it already was paying S&P and Fitch ratings fees). As Hannover Re continued to refuse to pay Moody's for a rating, Moody's continued to downgrade its debt. When Moody's finally cut Hannover Re's rating to below investment grade in 2003, the company's share value declined by $175 million. See Alec Klein, "Spitzer Examining Debt Ratings by Moody's," *Washington Post*, July 30, 2005, p. D01.

opinion to a non-client; indeed, it likely would find doing so cost prohibitive. It is interesting that credit rating agencies believe that they are capable of publishing accurate unsolicited ratings even if they have no access to management or inside information and are merely making judgments based on publicly available information.[50]

Finally, one twist to the practice of unsolicited ratings is that credit rating agencies might feel obligated to issue them to preserve their First Amendment defense. If the agencies rate bonds only when they receive payment from issuers, their ratings appear less like protected speech. But if the agencies are publishing "opinions" about issuers who are not paying fees, they appear to be acting more like journalists. As noted above, the evidence indicates that financial market participants do not believe that credit ratings are merely the opinions of journalists. If they did, Moody's shares would be worth $3 billion, not $15 billion. But if credit rating agencies never issued unsolicited ratings, they would appear to be even less like financial publishers and therefore even less likely to be protected by free speech principles.

Structured Finance

Perhaps the starkest difference between credit rating agencies and other gatekeepers in recent years has been the increasingly substantial role that the agencies play in rating new structured finance issues, particularly credit derivatives.[51] Financial institutions first began using credit derivatives during the mid-1990s as a mechanism to transfer credit risk, primarily because it enabled them to hedge the risk associated with their lending operations and to reduce balance sheet capital requirements.

The simplest form of credit derivative—the credit default swap (CDS)—facilitates the transfer of credit risk and does not directly implicate or involve credit rating agencies. In a CDS, one party agrees to pay money to another party if a specified "credit event" occurs, typically a default on a specified bond: one party is "selling" protection against default and will pay in the event of a default; the other party is "buying" protection against default and will be paid if a default

---

50. There is an argument that unsolicited ratings are a sign of market failure in the credit rating business, because they indicate that some agencies, particularly Moody's, believe that they can extract fees from issuers by threatening to publish unduly unfavorable ratings. Such a strategy would work only if issuers believed that competition was insufficient to obtain a more accurate rating.

51. Credit derivatives are private contracts in which parties agree to transfer the credit risk associated with one or more issuers. The credit derivatives market did not exist a decade ago, but it suddenly has become a multi-trillion-dollar market. See, for example, JP Morgan, "Credit Derivatives: A Primer," JPMorgan Credit Derivatives and Quantitative Research, January 2005, p. 1, citing an estimate that at the end of 2004 the total notional size of outstanding credit derivatives was $5 trillion.

occurs. In other words, in exchange for a payment or premium, protection buyers transfer credit risk to protection sellers, either up front or over time.[52] The CDS market has been controversial, in part because banks used CDSs to transfer hundreds of billions of dollars of credit risk to insurance companies, pension funds, and other institutions prior to the recent wave of corporate defaults. There is an active policy debate about the costs and benefits of CDSs, but it does not directly involve credit rating agencies.

Credit rating agencies enter the picture with respect to a second form of credit derivative, known as a collateralized debt obligation.[53] CDOs are structured, leveraged transactions backed by one or more classes of fixed-income assets.[54] In the mid-1990s, CDOs typically were based on portfolios of high-yield corporate bonds. During the past several years, CDOs have been based on other assets, including asset-backed securities, CDSs, and even other CDOs.[55]

At the core of a typical CDO is a special purpose entity (SPE) that issues securities to investors in several different classes, or tranches, most of which are rated by a credit rating agency. The SPE's proceeds are used to purchase a portfolio of fixed-income assets. If some of the assets default, the most junior of the SPE's securities takes the first loss. Payments to each tranche are governed by a stipulated priority of payments.

There are two broad categories of CDOs that are relevant to this discussion: cash flow CDOs and synthetic CDOs. Cash flow CDOs involve the actual purchase of real fixed-income assets whose cash flows are used to pay investors in the different tranches. Synthetic CDOs bundle the same kinds of credit risk exposure without real assets, by selling protection on the underlying assets using CDSs. Creation of cash flow CDOs was motivated both by reduction in bank capital charges and potential arbitrage opportunities. Because synthetic CDOs essen-

---

52. Note that a CDS also creates credit risk, because the parties are exposed not only to the underlying credit of the asset but also to the credit of their CDS counterparty. CDSs are now traded on exchanges, as well as in private counterparty transactions. There has been pressure to move to exchange trading of CDSs in order to standardize various contract terms.

53. See, generally, Tavakoli (2003).

54. See Standard & Poor's, Structured Finance, "S&P Global Cash Flow and Synthetic CDO Criteria," March 21, 2002, p. 4.

55. Recently the CDO markets have experienced some difficulties. In April and May 2005, market participants were surprised when equity tranches of CDOs suddenly became much cheaper, while mezzanine tranches became more expensive. Likewise, CDOs obviously performed poorly after the increase in corporate defaults during 2002. In 2003, S&P and Moody's downgraded 150 cash flow CDO transactions, 108 more than in 2001. See Anthony Currie, "Cool Heads Rule in CDO Land," *Euromoney*, April 2003, p. 114.

tially create new instruments instead of using assets on bank balance sheets, their creation was motivated primarily by arbitrage, not regulation.[56]

It is worth thinking about precisely how such "arbitrage" opportunities have arisen. According to S&P, "rating agencies played an important role in the development of the market since they were able to develop criteria to size default risk based on rates of the underlying obligors."[57] In other words, the rating agencies have developed methodologies for rating CDOs that result in the combination of the tranches being worth more than the cost of the underlying assets. The difference between the price that the investors in aggregate pay for CDO tranches and the cost of the underlying assets must be substantial, because it covers the high fees the various participants charge for structuring and arranging a CDO and for managing the underlying assets.

So how does such "arbitrage" arise? There are two views. The first is that actual value is created during the CDO process, either because the underlying assets are mispriced or because market segmentation otherwise prevents parties from buying the types of portfolios that CDOs create. It is difficult to test this view, but there are reasons to be skeptical. Investors who want to own diversified portfolios of fixed-income assets are not prohibited from doing so. Moreover, if markets were segmented by risk, one would expect market pressure to lead corporations that issue bonds to create capital structures that would be most attractive to particular market segments. Corporate bonds are not like home mortgages, which typically cannot be purchased individually or even in diversified classes. Economists know that arbitrage opportunities rarely persist unless there is a dominant information asymmetry or regulatory explanation. The purchasers of CDO tranches typically are sophisticated, and the regulatory rationales do not apply to synthetic CDOs. Moreover, the cost of this so-called arbitrage is enormous: if a trillion dollars of CDOs have been sold, financial intermediaries have earned billions of dollars in fees.

A second view is that because the methodologies used for rating CDOs are complex, arbitrary, and opaque, they create opportunities for parties to create a ratings "arbitrage" opportunity without adding any actual value. It is difficult to test this view, too, although there are reasons to find it persuasive. Essentially, the argument is that once the rating agencies fix a given set of formulas and variables

56. See Standard & Poor's, Structured Finance, "S&P Global Cash Flow and Synthetic CDO Criteria," March 21, 2002, p. 5; see also Standard and Poor's, "Structured Finance Ratings: Criteria for Rating Synthetic CDO Transactions," September 2003.

57. See Standard & Poor's, Structured Finance, "S&P Global Cash Flow and Synthetic CDO Criteria," March 21, 2002, p. 5.

for rating CDOs, financial market participants will be able to find a set of fixed-income assets that, when run through the relevant models, generate a CDO whose tranches are more valuable than the underlying assets. Such a result might be due to errors in rating the assets themselves (that is, the assets are cheap relative to their ratings), errors in calculating the relationship between those assets and the tranche payouts (that is, the correlation and expected payout of the assets appear to be higher and therefore support higher ratings of tranches), or errors in rating the individual CDO tranches (that is, the tranches receive a higher rating than they deserve, given the ratings of the underlying assets). These arguments are complex and subtle, and a complete analysis is well beyond the scope of this chapter.[58]

Nevertheless, it is possible to gain some insight by closely examining the CDO rating process. Consider S&P's methodology. S&P uses a proprietary model called CDO Evaluator, which simulates the loss distribution and time to default of the assets in the portfolio using Monte Carlo methods and determines whether in any of the simulations a loss trigger is breached. During the late 1990s, both S&P and Moody's developed early versions of such models with the close cooperation of the investment banks that created CDOs. S&P released the first version of CDO Evaluator in November 2001 and has released several updated versions since then.

Once a client has signed an engagement letter, S&P and the client use CDO Evaluator to run Monte Carlo simulations to establish the default level of each proposed pool of assets at each rating level. The model uses default estimates based on the existing ratings of the assets. For example, for a tranche to be rated AAA, S&P might require that it be able to withstand a default rate of 30 percent of the asset pool for a particular period of time, assuming a level of defaults based on the ratings of those assets. The default rate for lower credit ratings would be correspondingly higher. The model also incorporates assumptions about how much of the face value might be recovered after a default.

From a mathematical perspective, pricing the tranches of a CDO is a reasonably straightforward task. First, one calculates the expected cash flows of the underlying assets over time. Then one determines how those cash flows would be paid out to each tranche over time. The equity, or most junior, tranche absorbs losses up to the first "attachment point." Then the most junior mezzanine tranche absorbs losses up to the next attachment point, and so on. The rating agencies

---

58. The rating agencies are sensitive to these arguments. As S&P has described the CDO process, "This is not alchemy or turning straw into gold, but rather the implementation of structured finance to create different investment risk profiles, based on the structuring of credit support." See Standard & Poor's, Structured Finance, "S&P Global Cash Flow and Synthetic CDO Criteria," March 21, 2002, p. 14.

then give a credit rating to each of the tranches (but usually not to the junior tranche) based on assumptions about certain key variables, including expected default rates, recovery rates, and correlation rates among assets.

Although this process employs sophisticated mathematical techniques, the conclusions can be somewhat dubious. For example, a rating agency might run 100,000 computer simulations to determine the number of times a breach would occur—that is, how often a particular tranche would lose value beyond a certain level. However, the variable in this assessment is the number of breaches out of the 100,000 runs, not the magnitude of the breach or any qualitative analysis of the breach. For example, for a typical five-year synthetic CDO, S&P might establish a confidence interval for the AAA level of 0.284 percent, meaning that the particular tranche would be "breached" in 284 runs out of 100,000.

However sophisticated the techniques, they are subject to the limitations of "garbage in, garbage out." For example, S&P calculates a probability distribution of default rates for a portfolio and then calculates a set of scenario default rates (SDRs) in two steps.[59] First, for a given tranche to receive a particular rating, the probability of default in its portfolio cannot exceed the default rate for a corporate bond with that rating. Second, S&P multiplies the portfolio default rate by an adjustment factor depending on the tranche. This is basically an error factor that in S&P's judgment should adjust for the fact that actual defaults might be higher or lower.

But recovery rates and recovery time for assets vary depending on the nature of the asset, particularly its seniority. This is far from an exact science—recovery times vary by jurisdiction, legal framework, and debtor's rights—and there rarely is historical evidence of default rates for particular assets (especially rated assets). Yet the assumed recovery inputs that the rating agencies use necessarily must be precise ones.

The default probability estimates that S&P uses are fixed, based on default probability estimates within a given rating category. S&P has published assumptions about default rates to be used in certain CDO calculations, set forth in table 3-3 below.

If a CDO manager is able to purchase assets within a particular rating category at market prices that implied a lower default rate than the one suggested in the above table, the manager could create an "arbitrage" profit by achieving a higher rating. To the extent that purchasers of CDO tranches care primarily about ratings and yields rather than the analysis of the actual default probability of the

---

59. Standard & Poor's, "CDO Evaluator Applies Correlation and Monte Carlo Simulation to Determine Portfolio Quality," November 13, 2001.

Table 3-3. *S&P Default Rate Assumptions for CDOs*
Percent

Rating	ABS (all)	Corporate Year 4	Corporate Year 7	Corporate Year 10
AAA	0.25	0.19	0.52	0.99
AA	0.50	0.57	1.20	1.99
A	1.00	0.81	1.81	3.04
BBB	2.00	1.81	3.94	6.08
BB	8.00	9.49	14.20	17.47
B	16.00	21.45	26.15	28.45

Source: Standard and Poor's, "CDO Evaluator Applies Correlation and Monte Carlo Simulation to Determine Portfolio Quality," November 13, 2001.

assets, the CDO would add value. It is important to note that the agencies rate bonds within a particular rating category, say AAA, even though market prices imply different probabilities of default. They permit CDO managers to assume that the rating agencies' assumptions, not the market's implicit assumptions, are the relevant ones when evaluating tranches of CDOs. Put another way, credit rating agencies are providing the markets with an opportunity to arbitrage the credit rating agencies' mistakes (or, more generously, the fact that rating categories cover a broad range of default probabilities rather than offer just a point estimate).

The problems with how CDO pricing models incorporate various measures of correlation among assets are even more troubling. Clearly, the ratings of CDO tranches should be sensitive to the correlation of the underlying assets. Yet even as late as 2002, S&P's correlation inputs for corporate assets were simply 0.3 within a given industry and 0.0 between industry sectors. The correlation inputs for asset-backed securities were similar. S&P recognized that the inputs were flawed but used them nonetheless.[60] The Bank for International Settlements also has expressed concerns about this kind of model risk, particularly with respect to correlation.[61]

---

60. See Standard & Poor's, Structured Finance, "S&P Global Cash Flow and Synthetic CDO Criteria," March 21, 2002, p. 46: "As data becomes available, the correlation coefficients will be modified based on documented studies."

61. See Bank for International Settlements, "The Role of Ratings in Structured Finance," press release, January 17, 2005 (www.bis.org/press/p050117.htm). Some credit rating agency officials have echoed those concerns. See Bank for International Settlements, "BIS Vindicates Agencies, but Warns on Ratings Limitations, Correlation Risk," *Structured Finance International*, January 1, 2005, p. 56, quoting the head of CDOs at S&P in London as saying, "I'm not sure correlation risk has been fully understood by anyone. We try to be very clear to the market about what our assumptions are and how our models work."

Perhaps surprisingly, it is the investment bank structuring the CDO, not the rating agency, that typically performs these complex calculations.[62] The process of rating CDOs becomes a mathematical game that smart bankers know that they can win. A person who understands the details of the model can tweak the inputs, assumptions, and underlying assets to produce a CDO that appears to add value, though in reality it does not.

The mathematical precision of the models is illusory, because numerous subjective factors enter the process as well. For example, the rating agency evaluates the CDO asset manager, who has discretion to engage in trading. CDOs typically are not fully funded when they are first rated; instead, the manager has a set of parameters governing which assets he or she is permitted to buy or sell. There also are difficult questions about the documentation of CDOs, as well as recording and reporting requirements, which are not yet standardized.[63]

Even if these difficulties could be surmounted, consider the complexities associated with "CDO squared" transactions, whose assets consist of a reference portfolio of other CDOs and asset-backed securities (or, less commonly, "CDO cubed" transactions, whose assets consist of a portfolio of CDO squared transactions). Again, the models require assumptions about all of the variables stated above, but this time piled on to a second (or third) level with respect to the underlying CDOs, in addition to the underlying assets of those CDOs. Moreover, although a typical CDO squared transaction might involve 1,000 corporate names, there are only about 400 issuers of liquid corporate bonds.[64] That means that certain names must appear more than once. According to S&P, each corporate name appears in such transactions, on average, 4.17 times.[65]

Economists should ask why parties would do CDOs, given these complexities. If the problem is that bonds are mispriced, one would expect the CDS market to resolve that problem or at a minimum to provide lower-cost opportunities than high-fee CDOs to arbitrage the mispricing. If the problem is that bond purchasers

---

62. For example, S&P states that "[t]he transaction's sponsor or banker will generally perform the cash flow modeling and provide Standard & Poor's with the results and the model. The sponsor or the banker doing the cash flow modeling must also provide to Standard & Poor's an independent-accountant verification that the proprietary cash flow model is representative of the transaction structure, and that the dominant cash flow run results are as indicated by the party doing the modeling." See Standard & Poor's, Structured Finance, "S&P Global Cash Flow and Synthetic CDO Criteria," March 21, 2002, pp. 17–18.

63. Additional complications arise with regard to what are known as leveraged super senior notes, essentially tranches above the AAA-rated notes that take the last loss in a CDO transaction.

64. Standard & Poor's, "Drill-Down Approach for Synthetic CDO Squared Transactions," December 10, 2003.

65. Standard & Poor's, "Drill-Down Approach for Synthetic CDO Squared Transactions," December 10, 2003.

and issuers are in different market segments, one would expect issuers to take advantage of potential arbitrage opportunities by adjusting their capital structure or leverage to attract neglected segments of the market. Yet there is little evidence that CDOs are used to create new assets with underrepresented credit ratings; instead, the ratings of CDO tranches span the same range as those of corporate bonds.

If the mathematical models have serious limitations, how could they support a $5 trillion market?[66] Some experts have suggested that CDO structurers manipulate models and the underlying portfolio in order to generate the most attractive ratings profile for a CDO. For example, parties included the bonds of General Motors and Ford in CDOs before they were downgraded because they were cheap relative to their (then high) ratings.[67] The primary reason that the downgrades of those companies had an unexpectedly large market impact was that they were held by so many CDOs.[68]

Thus, with respect to structured finance, credit rating agencies have been functioning more like "gate openers" rather than gatekeepers. The agencies are engaged in a business, the rating of CDOs, which is radically different from the core business of other gatekeepers. No other gatekeeper has created a dysfunctional multi-trillion-dollar market, built on its own errors and limitations.[69]

66. Recent research in finance shows that asset pricing models of the variety used by credit rating agencies fail to explain real world data. See Nikola A. Tarashev, "An Empirical Evaluation of Structural Credit Spread Models," BIS Working Paper 179 (July 2005). For example, observed market spreads typically are much higher than those predicted by structural models, especially at the high-quality end of the rating spectrum. See Shuermann (2005), which cites numerous studies. These studies suggest that there are significant noncredit components to spreads on fixed-income instruments. Moreover, such models fail to take into account tail risk, and they are based on historical measures, which often are not good predictors. One would think that the collapses of firms such as Long-Term Capital Management and Askin Capital Management would have been sufficient warning to entities attempting to engage in arbitrage based on such models. See also Mark Whitehouse, "Slices of Risk: How a Formula Ignited a Market That Burned Some Big Investors," *Wall Street Journal*, September 12, 2005, p. A1.

67. Likewise, more than three-fourths of the pre-2002 CDOs that S&P rated in the United States contained WorldCom bonds, representing an average of more than 1 percent of the assets of synthetic CDOs. See Jenny Wiggins, "Growth of Structured Finance Sector Set to Slow Debit Markets," *Financial Times*, July 1, 2002, p. 26. Representatives of Moody's have stated that fifty-eight of the synthetic CDOs that it rated had exposure to WorldCom. See Rebecca Bream, "Moody's Expects Pressure on CDOs," *Financial Times*, July 10, 2002, p. 31.

68. See Henny Sender, Carrick Mollenkamp, and Michael Mackenzie, "Risky Strategies Take Toll on Traders," *Wall Street Journal*, May 11, 2005, quoting Janet Tavakoli, a prominent structured finance expert, as suggesting that "managers often game the portfolio."

69. One open question is the fate of the synthetic CDO market outside the United States, where it appears that transactions are driven more by "arbitrage," not regulatory capital motivations, particularly in Japan. See "From Crisis to Opportunity: The Evolution of CDOs in Japan," *Structured Finance International*, special report, June 2005, p. S4; see also Adams, Mathieson, and Schinasi (1999) assessing the role of the major credit rating agencies in various countries.

Why Credit Rating Agencies Are Not Like Other Gatekeepers

Given the differences between credit rating agencies and other gatekeepers, the next question is "Why?" Are there substantive economic differences between the function of rating credit and other gatekeeping functions that would lead one to expect credit rating agencies to differ from other gatekeepers in the way that they do? Or are the differences due to other factors?

The first reason for the differences between credit rating agencies and other gatekeepers is that many regulations depend on NRSRO ratings. It is difficult to argue that the function of providing credit ratings is much different, from an economic perspective, from the functions of other gatekeepers. Of course, credit rating agencies provide certification services only with respect to debt, while securities analysts provide certification services only with respect to equity. However, there is little reason to think that that distinction would generate the marked differences discussed earlier. Indeed, financial institutions also generate credit ratings, although they are used primarily for internal purposes. However, non-NRSRO credit ratings are not particularly valuable, because they do not entail any regulatory consequences.

A second reason for the differences is that credit rating agencies generally are not subject to civil liability for malfeasance. It is not surprising that the credit rating agencies would prefer to compare themselves not to gatekeepers such as securities analysts and auditors but to publishing companies. As an S&P official argued at a 2005 legislative hearing, "The very notion that a bona fide publisher—whether it be *BusinessWeek*, *The Wall Street Journal*, or S&P—can be required under the threat of penalty or other retribution to obtain a government license, adhere to government dictates about its policies and procedures, and/or submit to intrusive examinations before being permitted to disseminate its opinions is inconsistent with core First Amendment principles."[70]

Regulatory Licenses

I have argued elsewhere that the paradox of credit ratings—that they can be so valuable yet lack informational content—can be resolved by understanding the regulatory framework in which credit rating agencies operate.[71] I will not repeat the details of this argument here, except to note that this regulatory framework differs from that for other gatekeepers in important ways.

---

70. Rita M. Bolger, testimony before the House Subcommittee on Capital Markets, Insurance, and Government-Sponsored Enterprises, June 29, 2005.
71. See Partnoy (2002).

In particular, credit ratings are valuable not because they contain valuable information but because they grant issuers "regulatory licenses." In simple terms, a good rating entitles the issuer (and the investors in a particular issue) to certain advantages related to regulation. The regulatory license view of credit ratings illuminates some of the unique aspects of the role of credit rating agencies. Once regulation is passed that incorporates ratings, rating agencies will begin to sell not only information but also the valuable property rights associated with compliance with that regulation.

Moreover, if regulation enables only a few raters to acquire and transfer regulatory licenses or if it imposes costs on new raters, so raising the barriers to entry, the rating agencies will acquire market power in the sale of regulatory licenses. Unlike rating agencies selling information in a competitive market, rating agencies selling regulatory licenses under oligopolistic (or even monopolistic) conditions will be able to earn abnormal profits.[72]

The regulatory license view can be generalized beyond credit ratings, and it applies to a certain extent to other gatekeepers. For example, securities regulations set forth in great detail the minimum qualifications for certified and public accountants and for accountants' reports.[73] Federal regulations also require registered companies to file audited financial statements for the previous three fiscal years.[74] Other regulations cover the content and quality of accountant reports.[75] Section 404 of the Sarbanes-Oxley Act now requires certification of gatekeepers' internal controls.[76]

Since 1973 credit ratings have been incorporated into hundreds of rules, releases, and regulatory decisions, in various substantive areas including securities, pension, banking, real estate, and insurance regulation.[77] As noted above, the cascade of regulations began after the credit crises of the early 1970s, when the SEC adopted broker-dealer net capital requirements in rule 15c3-1, the first securities rule that formally incorporated NRSRO ratings. I have noted elsewhere the extensive credit rating–dependent rules and regulations promulgated under the Securities Act of 1933, the Securities Exchange Act of 1934, the Investment

---

72. For an assessment of the oligopolistic nature of NRSROs, see White (2002).
73. 17 C.F.R. 210 (1999). These qualifications depend on certification requirements specified by the relevant state licensing agency.
74. See 17 C.F.R. 210.3-01-02.
75. See 17 C.F.R. 210.2-02.
76. Section 404 has generated enormous controversy because of the high cost of implementation. It is not surprising that various gatekeepers have attempted to seek rents associated with section 404, which essentially is a scheme requiring that companies obtain regulatory licenses associated with their own internal controls.
77. See Partnoy (1999).

Company Act of 1940, various banking and insurance regulations and statutes, and other regulatory schemes.[78] More recently, international regulatory standards, including the Basel II capital accords, have depended on credit ratings.

Such extensive regulatory dependence on credit ratings is unique. For example, investors do not receive differential regulatory treatment when they purchase stocks with "buy" ratings from securities analysts. Investors might not buy the securities of an issuer without the relevant opinion letters from an audit firm, but that audit firm's opinion typically does not determine the level of the investors' compliance with government regulations.

To the extent that other gatekeepers are selling regulatory licenses, the problems are similar to those associated with credit ratings. Investment banking fairness opinions are unduly expensive, in part because they provide support for a due diligence defense for company directors who approve a merger or sale. The same is true of audit opinions, which similarly provide a legal defense. The very high fees associated with complying with Sarbanes-Oxley section 404 do not reflect the intrinsic market value of an accounting firm's substantive controls review, but rather the expense associated with being in compliance with the new law.[79]

The overriding message is that regulatory licenses are costly. They create oligopolistic pressure and exacerbate rent seeking among already concentrated industries. They might be necessary when a regulator is unwilling to or cannot make substantive decisions on its own and the risk of market failure is sufficiently serious to justify the cost. But as a general matter, regulators should be very careful not to create regulatory licenses, and once licenses are created regulators should take great care in policing them.

Unfortunately, regulators have taken no such care with respect to NRSRO ratings. Once NRSRO-based regulation became standard, market participants began to frame decisions in terms of ratings much more frequently. To the extent that financial market behavior is path-dependent, regulatory licenses have started parties down a suboptimal path, where dependence on ratings has generated behavioral influences. Once legal rules approve of reliance on credit ratings, it is only natural that individuals would come to rely heavily on such ratings as well.

Liability

The unique problems associated with credit rating agencies as gatekeepers stem from a second source: their lack of exposure to civil and criminal liability. Unlike other gatekeepers, rating agencies are explicitly immune to prosecution for certain

---

78. See Partnoy (2002).
79. See Carney (2005).

violations of securities law, including section 11 of the Securities Act of 1933 and Regulation FD.[80] Moreover, rating agencies have been unique among gatekeepers in their ability to argue that their function is merely to provide "opinions," which are protected by the First Amendment. Because of these differences, rating agencies have not paid substantial judgments or settlements resulting from the recent wave of corporate fraud.

The credit rating agencies claim that their core business is financial publishing.[81] Specifically, NRSROs have long argued that their core activities are purely journalistic pursuits: gathering information on matters of public concern, analyzing that information, forming opinions about it, and then broadly disseminating those opinions to the public. They have had some limited success in putting forth that argument in litigation.

As noted previously, Moody's financial statements show that it actually is engaged in a business that is entirely different from publishing, one that is much more profitable. In addition, in its most recent proxy statement, Moody's itself suggests that its business is not financial publishing. It notes that it "does not believe there are any publicly traded companies that represent strict peers."[82] For purposes of assessing the compensation paid to senior executives, Moody's looks instead to a "peer group" of "financial services companies with market capitalization comparable to the Company."[83] Interestingly, Moody's does not provide a list of the names of any of these companies, leaving it to investors to guess which

---

80. Rule 436(g)(1) of the Securities Act of 1933, 17 C.F.R. § 230.436(g)(1) provides for exemption of liability for NRSROs: "The security rating assigned to a class of debt securities, a class of convertible debt securities, or a class of preferred stock by a nationally recognized statistical rating organization . . . shall not be considered a part of the registration statement prepared or certified by a person within the meaning of sections 7 and 11 of the Act." NRSROs generally are shielded from liability under the securities laws for all conduct except fraud. See "Financial Oversight of Enron: The SEC and Private Sector Watchdogs," Report of the Staff to the Senate Committee on Governmental Affairs, October 8, 2002, p. 105.

81. Consider the following statement by Moody's: "As set forth more fully on the copyright, credit ratings are, and must be construed solely as, statements of opinion and not statements of fact or recommendations to purchase, sell or hold any securities. Each rating or other opinion must be weighed solely as one factor in any investment decision made by or on behalf of any user of the information, and each such user must accordingly make its own study and evaluation of each security and of each issuer and guarantor of, and each provider of credit support for, each security that it may consider purchasing, selling or holding." See Moody's ratings definitions (www.moodys.com/moodys/cust/AboutMoodys/AboutMoodys.aspx?topic=rdef&subtopic=moodys%20credit%20ratings&title=Introduction.htm [September 2, 2005]).

82. Moody's Corporation 2004 Proxy Statement Filing, March 23, 2005, p. 24. For the purposes of assessing its share price performance, Moody's compares itself to publishing companies, including Dow Jones and Reuters. As noted previously, Moody's is not comparable to those two companies from a financial perspective.

83. Moody's Corporation 2004 Proxy Statement Filing, March 23, 2005, p. 22.

financial services companies might provide relevant benchmarks for determining executive pay.

But even if one accepts the argument that credit rating agencies are financial publishers, that does not end the inquiry. Whether holding such a publisher or speaker liable for malfeasance would affect its freedom of expression remains a question.[84] The securities laws are predicated on the assumption that corporate speech can be regulated, and the Supreme Court has clearly indicated that "commercial speech" can be regulated to the extent that it is false or misleading.[85] Moreover, the securities laws provide for liability for false and misleading statements even if those statements are not made with the kind of malicious intent that is required to hold speakers liable for other forms of speech.[86] If speech by an issuer can be regulated, it should follow that speech by an agent of the issuer, whom the issuer has paid to speak, also can be regulated.

The Supreme Court has never ruled directly on the issue of whether gatekeepers are entitled to First Amendment protection of their opinions, and it is not clear what position it would take if it did. In one somewhat related case, *Dun & Bradstreet* v. *Greenmoss Builders*, the Supreme Court held that statements made in an individual's credit report are not a matter of public concern that would give a credit reporting agency (in this case, Dun & Bradstreet, the former parent of Moody's) special privileges under the First Amendment.[87] Although *Dun & Bradstreet* is not directly on point, the Court did note in that case that the market-driven nature of the speech made heightened First Amendment protection unnecessary. On the other hand, in a different case, also not directly on point, *Lowe* v. *SEC*, the Supreme Court noted in dicta that "it is difficult to see why the expression of opinion about a marketable security should not also be protected."[88]

In the lower courts, both S&P and Moody's have persuaded some judges to dismiss claims against them (Fitch has had less success) and to note that credit ratings were protected expressions of opinion.[89] However, the courts have distinguished

---

84. See *County of Orange* v. *McGraw-Hill Cos.*, 245 B.R. 154 (C.D. Cal. 1999): "S&P's status as a financial publisher does not necessarily entitle it to heightened protection under the First Amendment."
85. *Central Hudson Gas & Electric Corp.* v. *Public Service Commission*, 447 U.S. 557 (1980).
86. See *New York Times* v. *Sullivan*, 376 U.S. 254 (1964).
87. See *Dun & Bradstreet, Inc.* v. *Greenmoss Builders, Inc.*, 472 U.S. 749 (1985).
88. *Lowe* v. *SEC*, 472 U.S. 181, 210 n. 58 (1985).
89. See, for example, *Jefferson County School District No. R-1* v. *Moody's Investors Services, Inc.*, 175 F.3d 848, 856 (10th Cir. 1999), dismissing claims for tortious interference, injurious falsehood, and antitrust violations because Moody's credit ratings are "protected expressions of opinion"; *County of Orange* v. *McGraw-Hill Cos.*, 245 B.R. 151, 157 (C.D. Cal. 1999): "The First Amendment protects S&P's preparation and publication of its ratings."

situations in which credit rating agencies were merely acting as journalists or information gatherers from situations in which the agencies were playing a more significant role in the transaction. The most recent case was part of the Enron litigation in federal district court in Texas. In one of the numerous actions in *Newby v. Enron Corp.*, the consolidated litigation brought by various investors against numerous Enron-related entities, Connecticut Resources Recovery Authority (CRRA) sued to recover approximately $200 million of public funds it lost on a complex transaction it did with Enron in December 2000.

The transaction in effect was a $220 million loan from CRRA to Enron. Enron stopped making payments after it filed for bankruptcy protection on December 2, 2001, and CRRA sued S&P, Moody's, and Fitch, alleging that they were liable for negligent misrepresentation and violations of the Connecticut Unfair Trade Practices Act because they failed to exercise reasonable care or competence in obtaining and communicating accurate information about Enron's creditworthiness.[90] Specifically, at the time of the transaction between CRRA and Enron, all three agencies rated Enron's debt in the investment grade category. CRRA claimed those ratings were undeserved.[91]

The Newby court found opinion divided on the question of credit rating agency liability and concluded that any First Amendment protection for credit ratings was "qualified," not absolute.[92] In other words, credit ratings clearly can be regulated, the same as other corporate speech that is not entitled to absolute First Amendment protection. The court further observed that a potential conflict of interest is created by the compensation issuers pay to credit rating agencies.[93] However, the court ultimately dismissed the rating agencies from the case, in part because of the weak factual allegations made by CRRA.

Before the Enron litigation, various courts had reached a range of results in cases filed against the rating agencies. In the litigation surrounding the financial collapse of Orange County, the judge dismissed some but not all of the claims against S&P and ruled that S&P's constitutionally protected speech "was not absolutely privileged."[94] In *Commercial Financial Services v. Arthur Ander-*

90. *Newby v. Enron Corp.*, 2005 U.S. Dist. LEXIS 4494, * 174 (S.D. Tex., Feb. 16, 2005).
91. As of October 2000, S&P gave Enron a BBB+ rating, with "unsecured outlook stable"; Moody's gave Enron a Baa1 rating, with "no watch"; and Fitch gave Enron a BBB– rating.
92. *Newby v. Enron Corp.*, 2005 U.S. Dist. LEXIS 4494, * 03 (S.D. Tex., Feb. 16, 2005).
93. *Newby v. Enron Corp.*, 2005 U.S. Dist. LEXIS 4494, * 216 (S.D. Tex., Feb. 16, 2005).
94. See In re: County of Orange, debtor, *County of Orange* v. *McGraw-Hill Cos.*, D.C. Calif., SA CV 96-765 GLT, Bankruptcy No: SA 94-22272 JR, 3/16/98; see also "Orange County May Proceed with Claims against Standard and Poor's," BNA 444, March 20, 1998, p. 30. S&P settled the case with a payment of $140,000 to Orange County.

sen,⁹⁵ a case involving ratings of asset-backed securities, the court held that the First Amendment did not protect the credit rating agencies. The crucial distinction between the Commercial Financial Services (CFS) case and the Orange County litigation was that CFS had asked Moody's to rate its bonds and had in fact paid Moody's for rating them. (In *Jefferson County*, the unsolicited ratings case discussed above, Moody's had not been asked to rate the bonds and was not paid.) The court noted that although a journalist's speech might be protected, if CFS had hired that journalist to write a company report about the bonds, a different standard would apply.

Other cases have suggested that the question of whether credit rating agencies are liable depends on particular circumstances, such as the sophistication of the investor and the complexity of the transaction. In *Quinn v. McGraw-Hill*, the Seventh Circuit Court suggested that it was unreasonable for an investor to rely on an A rating from S&P, but it nonetheless permitted claims for negligent and fraudulent misrepresentation against S&P to go forward.⁹⁶ In *American Savings Bank v. UBS PaineWebber*, the court held that "the journalist privilege is a qualified one. Fitch is not primarily engaged in newsgathering generally, nor was it doing so when procuring the information sought by the subpoenas. The Court finds that Fitch is not entitled to the protections offered by the journalist privilege."⁹⁷ The transaction at issue in that case was a CDO.

Rating agencies have had success challenging subpoenas and refusing to turn over documents, although the courts generally have given them only a qualified journalist privilege, if any privilege at all. For example, in August 1992, Pan Am served a document subpoena on S&P seeking information about meetings between S&P and Delta as part of S&P's credit rating process. (Pan Am had alleged that it was forced to stop flying when Delta repudiated a commitment to fund Pan Am's reorganization.) S&P refused to produce the documents, claiming the journalist privilege. A bankruptcy court held a hearing and ruled that S&P was not acting as a journalist when it gathered the relevant information.⁹⁸ Judge Blackshear noted that S&P's activities were market driven and that it received fees for its ratings activity. Judge Loretta Preska reversed the ruling and

---

95. *Commercial Financial Services, Inc. v. Arthur Andersen LLP*, 94 P.3d 106, 109 (Okla. Civ. App. 2004): "The Rating Agencies' ratings fall somewhere between those opinions which receive constitutional protection and those that do not."

96. See *Quinn v. McGraw-Hill Companies*, 168 F.3d 331, 336 (7th Cir. 1999).

97. *American Savings Bank, FSB v. UBS PaineWebber, Inc.*, 2002 U.S. Dist. LEXIS 24102, * 2-3 (S.D.N.Y. Dec. 16, 2002).

98. In re Pan Am Corp., 161 B.R. 577 (S.D.N.Y. 1993).

found that S&P was protected by the First Amendment, noting that other journalists, including television reporters, newspaper publishers, and booksellers, all have received First Amendment protection even though their speech was profit motivated.[99]

What is one to make of these disparate decisions? The most that can be said is that to the extent that a credit rating agency played only the role of information gatherer and was not involved in structuring a transaction that it rated, courts have been more sympathetic to the claim that the agency is entitled to qualified protection.[100] However, the courts have been more skeptical of free speech claims when the rating agency played a significant role in structuring a transaction that it rated.[101] Obviously, this is an area that would benefit from some clarification.

Perhaps the reason credit rating agencies have been unique among gatekeepers in obtaining at least partial First Amendment protection for their certifications is that they have more clearly disclaimed the value of their opinions. Unlike equity analysts, who make buy, hold, or sell recommendations, credit rating agencies say that they are not providing investment advice.[102] In any event, credit rating agencies have used the privilege more effectively than any other gatekeeper, to avoid not only liability but also regulatory scrutiny.

Finally, it is interesting that the credit rating agencies seem to be worried that their First Amendment protections might be at risk. Moody's has noted in its financial statements that it "faces litigation from time to time from parties claiming damages relating to ratings actions. In addition, as Moody's international business expands, these types of claims may increase because foreign jurisdictions may not have legal protections or liability standards comparable to those in the U.S. (such as protections for the expression of credit opinions as is provided by the First Amendment)."[103] The SEC was hampered in its investigation of NRSROs by claims that the First Amendment shielded them from producing certain documents, and a legislative report on credit ratings was skeptical of the

---

99. But this argument creates problems for rating agencies that both argue that their ratings are speech and do not issue unsolicited ratings. Courts have based decisions in part on the fact that rating agencies rate all issuers, not merely those that pay them fees to do so. See In re Pan Am Corp., 161 B.R. 577 (S.D.N.Y. 1993): "The record is uncontradicted that S&P does not merely provide ratings to issuers who pay a fee." To the extent that the rating agencies provide ratings only to issuers who pay them for the ratings, the argument is weaker.

100. See *Compuware Corp. v. Moody's Investors Services, Inc.*, 324 F. Supp.2d 860 (E.D. Mich. 2004), in which Moody's was entitled to protection as a journalist under New York's reporter's privilege statute.

101. See In re Fitch, 330 F.2d 104, 111 (2d Cir. 2003), which found that such a relationship was "not typical of the relationship between a journalist and the activities upon which the journalist reports."

102. Although equity analysts' opinions typically are thoroughly disclaimed today, those disclaimers were weaker before 2001.

103. Moody's Corporation Form 10-K Filing, March 8, 2005, pp. 31–32.

First Amendment claims of credit rating agencies.[104] This difference between credit rating agencies and other gatekeepers might be short-lived, as judicial doctrine shifts and rating agency lobbying becomes less effective. In other words, the primary reason for the difference might be that no authoritative body has carefully considered the question of credit rating agency liability.

Proposals

It follows from the preceding discussion that policy solutions should address the reasons why credit rating agencies are not like other gatekeepers. The ideal proposals would reduce the benefits associated with regulatory licenses and impose a real threat of liability on credit rating agencies for malfeasance.

Reduce the Benefits of Regulatory Licenses

There are various ways to reduce the benefits associated with regulatory licenses. The simplest would be to remove the NRSRO designation. One preliminary question is whether the markets could function properly without the designation. They operated reasonably well prior to the 1970s, so there is reason to think that the markets and regulators could adapt to a system without NRSROs. It might be a difficult transition, as regulators would be forced to make the kinds of decisions that they made previously with respect to substantive regulation of financial market participants. They would no longer be able to delegate significant authority and responsibility to NRSROs. For example, the SEC would need to decide how to assess the net capital requirements of broker-dealers. Regulators would need to determine which bonds were appropriate for money market funds. The Basel II accords suggest that some regulators might have the ability to perform such tasks. Although Basel II relies in part on credit ratings, it also contains alternative mechanisms for determining bank capital requirements without reference to credit ratings.

However, while it might be a good idea to eliminate the NRSRO designation, it seems politically unlikely. A more plausible possibility is to find a replacement for NRSROs. There are three alternatives to the current regime. First, regulators

---

104. The report noted: "The fact that the market seems to value the agencies' ratings mostly as a certification (investment grade v. non–investment grade) or as a benchmark (the ratings triggers in agreements) and not as information, and the fact that the law, in hundreds of statutes and regulations, also uses their work that way, seems to indicate that their ratings are not the equivalent of editorials in the *New York Times*. The fact that the rating agencies have received First Amendment protection for their work should not preclude greater accountability." "Financial Oversight of Enron: The SEC and Private Sector Watchdogs," Report of the Staff to the Senate Committee on Governmental Affairs, p. 124, October 8, 2002.

could open the market to new NRSROs. Second, regulators could replace NRSROs with a market-based measure such as credit spreads or credit default swaps—or even an equity-based measure of credit risk. Third, regulators could replace the concept of recognition in the NRSRO regime with the concept of "registration," which is more familiar in securities regulation more generally. Recently introduced legislation has taken the last approach, and as of March 2006 both the United States Senate and House of Representatives had held hearings on legislative reform of credit rating agencies. Any of these approaches likely would be superior to the current regime.

OPEN THE MARKET TO NEW NRSROS. In April 2005, the SEC proposed new rules defining NRSROs, and it suggested that one regulatory solution might be simply to approve more NRSROs.[105] Moody's has indicated that it would support proposed new rules opening the market to competition from other agencies.[106]

One weakness of this approach is that simply adding NRSROs will not eliminate regulatory licenses. To the extent that there are natural monopoly pressures in the credit rating industry, those pressures would persist. It is worth remembering that twenty years ago there were many more NRSROs, but consolidation in the industry reduced that number to three. If the credit rating industry is a natural monopoly, even if the SEC approves new NRSROs, the market will consolidate, unless antitrust regulations or other pressures prevent it from doing so.

Moreover, opening the market to new NRSROs also raises the question of which credit rating agencies will qualify for designation. The criteria that the SEC has suggested for assessing new NRSROs are problematic, and they are likely to cement the current oligopoly structure.[107] Nor is it clear that opening the market to competition would generate any new informational value. Even without consolidation, there is an argument that opening the market to competition could make regulatory licenses more important, by creating incentives for rate shopping among issuers. The SEC appears willing to screen new NRSROs, but it could not possibly police the ratings of approved NRSROs to determine whether the conflicts of interest mentioned above were leading rating agencies to

---

105. "Definition of Nationally Recognized Statistical Rating Organization," SEC Release Nos. 33-8570, 34-51572; IC-26834; File No. S7-04-05 (April 19, 2005).

106. See Jeanne M. Dering, letter to the editor, *Financial Times*, July 15, 2005, p. 12: "Contrary to Professor Partnoy's implication, Moody's endorses market-based levels of competition in the provision of credit rating opinions."

107. Requiring that NRSRO ratings be "publicly available" or "generally accepted in the financial markets" would cement the oligopoly enjoyed by current NRSROs. See Frank Partnoy, letter to Jonathan G. Katz, Securities and Exchange Commission, June 9, 2005; see also Frank Partnoy, testimony before the House Subcommittee on Capital Markets, Insurance, and Government-Sponsored Enterprises, *Legislative Solutions for the Rating Agency Duopoly*, June 29, 2005.

issue inaccurate ratings. Nor has the SEC suggested that it should or would perform that function. Overall, opening the market to new NRSROs seems a weak and perhaps counterproductive choice, even if it would be superior to the current approach.

If regulators decided simply to open the market to competition, they might improve that approach by including among new NRSROs one or more credit rating agencies that rated debt issues using a market-based measure. For example, a credit rating agency might simply follow credit spreads or CDS prices and issue alphabetical ratings based on market prices. The algorithm for converting credit spreads or CDS prices could be straightforward and transparent, perhaps even automated, based on a rolling average of credit spreads, on the market prices of credit default swaps (which are becoming increasingly standardized), or even on one of the equity-based methodologies currently used by the rating agencies themselves.

REPLACE NRSROS WITH MARKET-BASED MEASURES. If regulators are attracted to the market-based approach, they might consider avoiding the problems associated with the NRSRO concept entirely by removing the NRSRO designation and replacing it with a market-based measure of credit risk. The SEC has been considering this proposal during recent years, although it has not yet endorsed it. The great advantage to a market-based measure is that it incorporates all available information into a rating, including the ratings of other credit rating agencies. Moreover, a market-based rating could be designed to be very timely or to lag, based on a rolling average of data.

Indeed, Moody's already has done much of the work to generate market-based ratings. Moody's publishes "market implied ratings" (MIRs), which reflect the market price of credit for various issues over time. Moody's argues that its ratings are superior to MIRs, but it is unclear whether the reason for the difference between a Moody's credit rating and an MIR is the market's inability to price credit risk accurately or Moody's inability to reflect the risks associated with a particular issue in its ratings in a timely manner. Moody's argues it is the former, but the latter seems more likely given the evidence set forth earlier in the chapter.

Three areas of criticism have surrounded the proposal to use credit spreads as a substitute for credit ratings. (Some of the same criticisms might be made regarding a proposal to use CDS or equity prices.) First, some critics have alleged that credit spreads would be more volatile than ratings.[108] It certainly is true that credit ratings are—and are intended to be—more stable than daily fluctuations in the

---

108. See SEC (2003); see also Hill (2004), suggesting a "pure market measure" should be used only after the additional NRSROs have been approved and the NRSRO designation reconsidered.

market. However, it is easy to limit the volatility of credit spreads simply by using a weighted average over time. Indeed, from the volatility perspective, credit spreads are superior to credit ratings, because they enable the regulator to make an explicit choice about volatility, instead of leaving that decision to a handful of credit rating agencies, which do not appear to be contemplating the consequences of volatility in ratings in any systemic way.

Instead, the current approach actually magnifies volatility, by creating and then unleashing a wave of selling pressure following downgrades.[109] Because the rating agencies approach downgrades in an ad hoc manner, they become trapped in a situation in which if they choose to downgrade an issue below investment grade, they potentially will force the insolvency of the issuer. Market-based ratings might avoid such problems, because market participants would be able to anticipate a downgrade with greater certainty in advance; such an approach might reduce the negative consequences associated with the human behavioral component of rating downgrades.

Moreover, information available in the market would be reflected more gradually through the use of credit spreads, so that institutional investors would be able to plan for when they might need to sell bonds for regulatory purposes. In contrast, credit rating changes are a discrete event that often come as a great surprise to investors (as was the case with Enron, for example—the single largest daily decline in Enron's share price, in percentage terms, was the drop immediately following its downgrade to below investment grade).

In any event, it is unclear why negative information for particular bonds should not be reflected in regulation if it is reflected in the market. As a policy matter, if NRSRO-based regulations make sense, they might as well be based on accurate ratings. If particular bonds are likely to be in default soon and various institutions will need to sell them when they are downgraded, why should that process not begin sooner rather than later? What advantage was gained by waiting for the credit rating agencies to downgrade Enron, abruptly throwing the company into bankruptcy?

The second objection is that credit spreads are backward looking.[110] This objection is, to be blunt, preposterous. Numerous academic studies have shown

---

109. Jon Macey has argued that issuers "capture" credit rating agencies, not because of these conflicts but because "issuers make it impossible for rating agencies to downgrade them." See Macey (2003), noting that a downgrade to below investment grade is especially significant because it can shut off a company's access to capital and calling such a downgrade "a corporate nuclear bomb."

110. See *The Current Role and Function of Credit Rating Agencies in the Operation of the Securities Markets*, Hearings before the U.S. Securities and Exchange Commission (November 15, 2002), testimony of Frank A. Fernandez (www.sec.gov/spotlight/ratingagency.htm): "Spreads are the reflection of the last trade

that credit ratings are backward looking, much more so than markets, and the agencies admit as much. The advantage of credit spreads is that the regulator can make a decision about how backward looking a measure to use. Moreover, the markets for bonds as well as the markets for CDSs and equities incorporate information about future expectations. To the extent that any measure is likely to be forward looking, it is a market measure, not an NRSRO rating.

The third objection is potentially more problematic: that the use of credit spreads or some other market-based measure would be limited to liquid securities. At the outset, it would be worth using such a measure for liquid securities or at least giving regulated entities that option, even if on a temporary or experimental basis. With the development of the CDS market, there now are market measures for many otherwise illiquid bonds. Critics are correct that there would be limitations regarding illiquid securities, although it would be a straightforward exercise to calculate reasonable market estimates of credit spreads even for illiquid bonds. Indeed, Moody's does precisely that with its market-based comparisons, and both Moody's and Fitch use equity-based measures when bonds are not sufficiently liquid.

Objectors argue that market participants would manipulate any market-based measure, using it to take advantage of either arbitrage opportunities or legal rules that depended on market-based ratings. However, it is unclear whether market participants would have greater incentives to manipulate market-based measures than NRSROs have to manipulate ratings. Moreover, if one market participant attempted to manipulate an issue through large amounts of buying or selling, that activity would both create liquidity and signal a potential arbitrage opportunity to other market participants. Market participants would not benefit from the NRSRO oligopoly and therefore would face competition from other firms that could profit from attempts at price manipulation. The bond, CDS, and equity markets are far more competitive than the current market for NRSRO ratings.

Perhaps most important, a market-based proposal would remove perverse incentives to engage in CDO transactions. If CDOs create value overall, parties would continue to do them under a market-based alternative to NRSROs. But if CDOs are merely a complex exercise in manipulating mathematical models based on inaccurate ratings, they should disappear or at least decline in number and importance.

Interestingly, Fitch has made several statements in its recent research that suggest that market-based measures might be a more viable option than anyone pre-

---

in the marketplace, and that market may be wrong on any given day about the long-term fundamental value, the probability of default or ultimate recovery value of any security."

viously had thought.[111] Both Fitch and KMV, a unit of Moody's, use equity prices to make calculations regarding debt ratings. A market-based measure based on equity prices—which the NRSROs already use—would not have many of the drawbacks that the critics have suggested might apply to a regime based on credit spreads or CDS prices. Certainly, equity markets are more liquid and less susceptible to manipulation. Policymakers who reject the credit spread and CDS alternatives might consider whether an equity-based bond credit rating measure would be an attractive market-based alternative.

REPLACE "RECOGNIZED" WITH "REGISTERED." The third alternative to the current regime, reflected in legislation introduced by Representative Michael G. Fitzpatrick (R-Penn.), is to replace the concept of recognition in the NRSRO regime with the concept of "registration" familiar in securities regulation more generally.[112] As initially proposed, this legislation would fundamentally alter the role of the SEC with respect to credit rating agencies. Instead of granting NRSRO designations, the SEC would oversee the registration of new credit rating agencies. It also would be involved in inspection, examination, and enforcement.[113]

S&P in particular has challenged this legislation on First Amendment grounds, repeating many of the arguments the rating agencies have made in private litigation. On June 29, 2005, at a House Financial Services Subcommittee hearing on the new credit rating agency legislation, Floyd Abrams, a well-known First Amendment lawyer, was present—and was recognized by the members of Congress—even though he was not scheduled to be a panelist and did not testify. Abrams's presence sent a clear message to members of Congress that the rating agencies likely would challenge the proposed legislation as unconstitutional. At the hearing, counsel for S&P argued that the bill would violate the First Amendment, because rating agencies are "members of the financial press."[114] And indeed

---

111. Consider the following from Fitch Ratings, Structured Finance, "Quantitative Financial Research Special Reports: A Comparative Empirical Study of Asset Correlations," July 14, 2005, p. 19 (www.fitchratings.com): "In the light of the empirical findings and the observations on methodological issues, we conclude that market-based methodologies are superior to solely ratings-driven methodologies in estimating asset correlations. Market-based methods address all of the aforementioned shortcomings of the latter category, and any possible systematic overestimation bias can easily be addressed with a calibration exercise"; and, on page 3 of the same report, "Correlations can be measured using credit spreads from either the bond market or the credit default swap market. One clear advantage of this approach, as in the case of equity-based correlations, is that the information is readily available in the market place" (citing limited universe of credit default swap market coverage and lack of historical data coverage and potential for liquidity and data quality concerns).

112. H.R. 2990, The Credit Rating Agency Duopoly Relief Act (2005), 109 Cong.

113. This legislation is in some tension with the SEC Staff Outline, in which the commission would continue to approve NRSRO status.

114. See Alec Klein, "Credit Raters Speak against Oversight," *Washington Post,* June 30, 2005, p. A08.

S&P recently sent a memorandum, written by Abrams, to the subcommittee staff arguing that the proposed legislation is unconstitutional.[115]

The legislation has many positive features, and perhaps most important is that it presents a unique opportunity to confront the First Amendment argument head on. The question of whether ratings are merely opinions protected by free speech doctrine is sufficiently important that it should be litigated properly and decided by the federal appellate courts. Unfortunately, private litigation has not yet generated any decisive cases and it remains unclear what protections credit rating agencies should receive. Whatever the courts decide, it is important to have some clarity, and this legislation appears to be the only possible route to that end.[116]

Another attractive feature of the legislation is that it would confront the regulatory license issue. Because the principal barrier to entry for credit rating agencies no longer would be SEC approval, market forces would be able to operate on NRSROs. Of course, to the extent that the rating business is a natural monopoly, the market structure arising from a registration regime might not be that different from the current structure under a designation regime. But to the extent that the overall securities system of registration makes sense, even if it reinforces some oligopolistic pressures, it ought to work equally well for credit rating agencies.

A registration system would be more consistent with the letter and spirit of the securities laws. In other words, the commission would take the same approach to NRSROs that it has taken in other areas, pursuant to and consistent with congressional authority. The legislation would permit the more than 130 non-NRSRO agencies to compete with current NRSROs, and it would create incentives for new rating agencies to enter the market. Perhaps most important is that it would encourage new rating agencies to use market-based measures in assessing companies.

Create a Threat of Liability for Rating Malfeasance

The final policy proposal is simple: make credit rating agencies liable for malfeasance and limit the extent to which the First Amendment is deemed to protect

---

115. This memorandum insists, incredibly, that Congress has no more power to regulate credit ratings than the publication of editorials in financial newspapers and magazines. See "A Constitutional Analysis of H.R. 2990," p. 2, 14–17 (2005) (www.standardandpoors.com/). It also wrongly suggests that the question of whether rating agencies are distinguishable from other financial market gatekeepers, such as accountants, is settled law, citing In re Scott Paper Securities Litig., 145 F.R.D. 366 (E.D. Pa. 1992). However, First Amendment experts have noted, to the contrary, that free speech protection in the securities area is narrow. See, for example, Schauer (2004), citing cases that narrowly interpreted free speech protections.

116. To the extent that a court followed the relatively narrow set of cases in which credit rating agencies are viewed exclusively as mere publishers, the legislation likely would survive any First Amendment scrutiny. Indeed, it would be difficult for a court to strike down a registration regime without calling into question the basis for securities regulation more generally.

their "opinions." This could be done in two ways. First, courts could reject the agencies' argument that their ratings are constitutionally protected speech. Here, the trends seem to be promising, notwithstanding the recent ruling in the Enron litigation. Judges are recognizing that the First Amendment protection of rating agencies depends on context; it is not qualified or absolute. At a minimum, CDO ratings do not appear to be protected.

The courts or Congress might mark the distinction emerging in some cases between agencies that play an active role and those that take a passive role, simply publishing an opinion. The argument for constitutional protection is strongest with respect to unsolicited ratings, for which an agency is not paid, and when the agency is not actively involved in either the structuring of an issue or an investigation of the issuer. In contrast, the agencies' role in the CDO market is far less likely to be protected speech. Agencies play an active role in structuring CDOs, and their "opinions" with respect to CDOs are less public.

Overall, this policy prescription is simple: treat credit rating agencies like other gatekeepers. During the past decade, credit rating agencies have become unique in various ways. That should not have happened. The simplest way to reverse course would be to amend section 11 and Regulation FD to include NRSROs and to make it clear—whether through legislation or judicial decision—that credit rating agencies' "opinions" are no different from the "opinions" of other gatekeepers.

Conclusion

Coffee has suggested a four-part typology of rules to govern gatekeeper behavior: structural rules, prophylactic rules, "empowerment" rules, and liability rules. Following this typology for credit rating agencies, structural rules could be designed to eliminate regulatory licenses by substituting alternatives, including market-based measures, for the current regime of NRSRO designation. Liability-enhancing rules could make credit rating agencies as liable as other gatekeepers for the same kinds of malfeasance, either by imposing negligence-based liability or a modified form of strict liability.[117] Prophylactic or empowerment rules seem less likely to improve the

---

117. Strict liability would have advantages over negligence liability, because it would give gatekeepers appropriate incentives to investigate issuers rather than prepare legal defenses, and it would force issuers, assuming gatekeepers passed on the costs, to bear the expected social cost of fraud. It also would avoid the thicket of ex post adjudication that creates incentives for dysfunctional gatekeeper behavior in the first place. See Coffee (2004a), Partnoy (2004), and Coffee (2004b).

current situation.[118] Proposals for new codes of conduct or voluntary approaches seem especially poorly suited to address the problems discussed here.[119]

In sum, credit rating agencies will continue to present unique difficulties until regulators address the ways in which the agencies differ from other gatekeepers. Credit rating agencies are more profitable than other gatekeepers and at least as subject to conflicts of interest, particularly in the CDO market. They benefit from regulatory licenses and limitations on liability more than other gatekeepers. This chapter suggests that reforms directed at credit rating agencies should reflect these differences between the agencies and other gatekeepers. Specifically, regulators should consider market-based alternatives to the NRSRO regime, as well as approaches that would make NRSROs liable for malfeasance, just as any other gatekeeper is.

---

118. Prophylactic rules might include prohibitions on self-dealing or other conflicts of interest. For example, regulation might preclude a rating agency from taking fees from issuers or rating firms that have a relationship with any member of the agency's board. The rating agencies have voluntarily implemented such prophylactic rules. It is hard to imagine that the credit rating agencies would be in need of "empowerment" rules, which would seek to give them greater leverage over issuers. Empowerment rules deal with the need for gatekeepers to be independent of the issuer's management if they are to be effective monitors of investors' interests. The Sarbanes-Oxley Act recognized this problem and transferred all responsibility for the hiring, supervision, retention, and compensation of auditors to the audit committee, whose own independence it also enhanced. This chapter has suggested that the power of S&P and Moody's over issuers already is too great and should be limited.

119. For example, in September 2004, S&P adopted a Code of Practices and Procedures. Unfortunately, self-regulation seems unlikely to solve the central problems associated with the differences between credit rating agencies and other gatekeepers. S&P's code is largely self-serving. It begins with a disclaimer, stating that "by making this Code available to the public Ratings Services does not assume any responsibility or liability to any third party arising out of or relating to this Code." Standard & Poor's Ratings Services, "Code of Practices and Procedures," September 2004. Its first set of provisions includes additional disclaimers and remarks that essentially are intended to protect S&P from civil and criminal liability. Section 1.1.1 of the code states that "[r]atings are current opinions regarding creditworthiness and not verifiable statements of fact"; section 1.1.2 states that "[r]atings do not constitute investment or financial advice. Ratings are not recommendations to purchase, sell, or hold a particular security"; section 1.1.3 states that "Ratings Services relies on the issuer, its accountants, counsel, advisors and other experts for the accuracy, completeness and timeliness of the information submitted in connection with the rating and surveillance process"; and section 1.1.4 states that "Ratings Services is not obligated to perform any due diligence or independent verification of information submitted to, or obtained by, Ratings Services in connection with the rating and surveillance process." Even the provisions directed at minimizing conflicts of interest are modest. Section 3.3.2 provides that analysts should not be involved in the negotiation of fees with issuers.

On December 23, 2004, the Technical Committee of the International Organization of Securities Commissions (IOSCO) published the voluntary Code of Conduct Fundamentals for Credit Rating Agencies (IOSCO Code). The IOSCO Code is not binding on credit rating agencies and does not carry the threat of sanction. It reflects two years of deliberation but does little more than what the agencies already have done with respect to conflicts of interest. The Committee of European Securities Regulators (CESR) has produced a similarly toothless set of recommendations.

References

Adams, Charles, Donald J. Mathieson, and Garry Schinasi. 1999. "The Role of Major Credit Rating Agencies in Global Financial Markets." In "International Monetary Fund," *International Captial Markets: Developments, Prospects, and Key Policy Issues,* pp. 185–212. Washington: International Monetary Fund (www.imf.org/external/pubs/ft/icm/1999/pdf/file05.pdf).

Carney, William J. 2005. "The Costs of Being Public after Sarbanes-Oxley." Emory Law and Economics Research Paper 05-4. (February).

Choi, Stephen. 1998. "Market Lessons for Gatekeepers." *Northwestern University Law Review* 92 (Spring): 916–66.

Coffee, John C., Jr. 1997. "Brave New World? The Impact(s) of the Internet on Modern Securities Regulation." *Business Lawyer* 52, no. 4: 1195–1233.

———. 2003. "The Attorney as Gatekeeper: An Agenda for the SEC." *Columbia Law Review* 103: 1293–1316.

———. 2004a. "Gatekeeper Failure and Reform: The Challenge of Fashioning Relevant Reforms." *Boston University Law Review* 84 (April): 302–364.

———. 2004b. "Partnoy's Complaint: A Response." *Boston University Law Review* 84: 377–382.

Cunningham, Lawrence. 2004."Choosing Gatekeepers: The Financial Statement Insurance Alternative to Auditor Liability." *UCLA Law Review* 52 (Winter): 413–75.

Dooley, Michael P. 1972. "The Effects of Civil Liability on Investment Banking and the New Issues Market." *Virginia Law Review* 58, no. 5: 776–843.

Fitch Ratings Structured Finance. "Quantitative Financial Research Special Report: A Comparative Empirical Study of Asset Correlations." July 14, 2005 (www.fitchratings.com).

Fitch Ratings, press release, "Survey Shows Majority of Structured Finance Executives Oppose Notching as Practiced by Moody's and S&P," March 27, 2002

"From Crisis to Opportunity: The Evolution of CDOs in Japan." Structured Finance International, June 2005, p. S4.

Gilson, Ronald J., and Reinier H. Kraakman. 1984. "The Mechanisms of Market Efficiency." *Virginia Law Review* 70, no. 4: 545–644.

Harold, Gilbert. 1938. Bond Ratings as an Investment Guide: An Appraisal of Their Effectiveness. New York: Ronald Press Company.

Hickman, W. Braddock. 1958. "Corporate Bond Quality and Investor Experience." National Bureau of Economic Research. Princeton University Press.

Hill, Claire A.. 2004. "Regulating the Rating Agencies." *Washington University Law Quarterly* 82, no. 1: 43–94.

Kraakman, Reinier H. 1984. "Corporate Liability Strategies and the Costs of Legal Controls." *Yale Law Journal* 93: 857–98.

———. 1986. "Gatekeepers: The Anatomy of a Third-Party Enforcement Strategy." *Journal of Law, Economics, and Organization* 82, no. 1: 53–104.

Macey, Jonathan R. 2003. "A Pox on Both Your Houses: Enron, Sarbanes-Oxley, and the Debate Concerning the Relative Efficacy of Mandatory Rules versus Enabling Rules." *Washington University Law Quarterly* 81, no. 2: 329–55.

Oh, Peter B. 2004. "Gatekeeping." *Iowa Journal of Corporation Law* 29 (Summer): 735–799.

Partnoy, Frank. 1999. "The Siskel and Ebert of Financial Markets: Two Thumbs Down for the Credit Rating Agencies." *Washington University Law Quarterly* 77, no. 3: 619–712.

———. 2001. "Barbarians at the Gatekeepers? A Proposal for a Modified Strict Liability Regime." *Washington University Law Quarterly* 79: 491–546.

———. 2002. "The Paradox of Credit Ratings." In *Ratings, Rating Agencies, and the Global Financial System*, edited by Richard M. Levich, Giovanni Majnoni, and Carmen M. Reinhart, pp. 65–84. Norwell, Mass.: Kluwer Academic Publishers.

———. 2004. "Strict Liability for Gatekeepers: A Reply to Professor Coffee." *Boston University Law Review* 84: 365.

Pinches, George E., and J. Clay Singleton. 1978. "The Adjustment of Stock Prices to Bond Rating Changes." *Journal of Finance* 33, no. 1: 29–44.

Pollock, Alex J. 2005. *End the Government-Sponsored Cartel in Credit Ratings*. Washington: American Enterprise Institute for Public Policy Research (January).

Schauer, Frederick. 2004. "The Boundaries of the First Amendment: A Preliminary Exploration of Constitutional Salience." *Harvard Law Review* 117, no. 6: 1765–809.

Schwarcz, Steven L. 2002. "Private Ordering of Public Markets: The Rating Agency Paradox." *University of Illinois Law Review* 14, no. 1: 1–28.

Securities and Exchange Commission. 2003. "Report on the Role and Function of Credit Rating Agencies in the Operation of the Securities Markets." January (www.sec.gov/news/studies/credratingreport0103.pdf).

———. 2005. "Staff Outline of Key Issues for a Legislative Framework."

Senate Committee on Governmental Affairs, press release, "Financial Oversight of Enron: The SEC and Private-Sector Watchdogs," October 8, 2002.

Shuermann, Til. 2005. "A Review of Recent Books on Credit Risk." *Journal of Applied Econometrics* 20, no. 1: 123–30.

Tarashev, Nikola A. 2005. "An Empirical Evaluation of Structural Credit Spread Models." Working Paper 179. Bank for International Settlements (July).

Tavakoli, Janet M. 2003. *Collateralized Debt Obligations and Structured Finance: New Developments in Cash and Synthetic Securitization*. Hoboken, N.J.: John Wiley & Sons.

Wakeman, L. Macdonald. 1981. "The Real Function of Bond Rating Agencies." *Chase Financial Quarterly* 1:19–25.

White, Lawrence J. 2002. "The Credit Rating Industry: An Industrial Organization Analysis." In *Ratings, Rating Agencies, and the Global Financial System*, edited by Richard M. Levich, Giovanni Majnoni, and Carmen M. Reinhart, pp. 41–64. Norwell, Mass.: Kluwer Academic Publishers.

Zacharias, Fred C. 2004. "Lawyers as Gatekeepers." Public Law and Legal Theory Research Paper Series no. 20. University of San Diego School of Law.

COMMENT BY

Justin Pettit

FRANK PARTNOY has produced an insightful and colorful contribution to the literature on rating agencies, which unfortunately are underrepresented in the corporate finance literature—surprisingly so, because of their importance in corporate finance decisionmaking.

I am going to take a capital markets perspective in touching on some of the points that Frank made, in large part because I am wholly incapable of taking a legislative perspective. Because I am an investment banker, my focus is on efficient markets and capital markets trying to become more efficient. What we have here is a case of growing, profitable businesses. They display tremendous capital and labor efficiency, as Frank's chapter shows—and certainly stock market success in the case of Moody's. We can only presume that S&P also would be doing very well if it were publicly traded.

Their achievements are shared by other companies. Certainly Dell Computers, Southwest Airlines, and many others would show similarly remarkable trends in their numbers. However, I think the real question here gets back to market efficiency and whether this success is an indication of superior execution or superior strategy or whether it is an indication of an imbalance—in effect, a general market failure—that raises the question of whether intervention is necessary.

I think the question of intervention always gets tricky once you start looking at successful businesses. Ultimately business strategy, in the Michael Porter sense of the word, is really all about deriving an economic advantage; it is about creating barriers to entry and superior bargaining power. In effect, all such strategies reduce market efficiency; business strategy focuses, if you will, on making the market less efficient in order to derive an economic advantage. To counter superior business skills with regulatory intervention seems, on the surface at least, somehow un-American. So I think we need to be careful about why we are considering intervention.

Coming back to Moody's, S&P, Fitch, and now also DBRS and AM Best, they clearly are sources of value. I would like to touch on what the financial community sees to be their value from a capital markets perspective. First, it is generally in primary issuance, not secondary trading. The point at which rating is most helpful is when a deal is being priced and taken to market, and frequently one will see cases in secondary market trading in which traders are pricing right through spreads associated with the rating. So over time, as the credit seasons, what you will find is that to some extent the actual rating loses its relevance.

New issuers, new issues, and speculative grades are where the ratings are most important, and that is also where market data are least helpful. As for using credit spreads as a proxy for ratings, that approach breaks down right where ratings are most helpful, on new issues and new issuers, when there is no history of spreads.

It also breaks down on the speculative grades where, unfortunately, spreads are notoriously unreliable. They are volatile, and also you'll find that the bid-ask is very wide and in many cases there is no volume behind the bid, so it is not a "real" bid. A good example of that is when investment bankers are advising, for example, a large German multinational on foreign direct investment in China and management wants to understand the sovereign risk associated with investing in China. If one looked at the yields on Chinese sovereign bonds, you would infer that there is a fairly low level of sovereign risk; the spreads are consistent with a weak AA or a strong A credit. Yet when you look at the rating agencies or even the *Economist* in its review of the sovereign risk of China, one would get the idea that more of a BBB kind of credit spread ought to be assumed for those bonds. So when bankers advise a corporate issuer with respect to foreign direct investment, I would suggest that they might want to think about the risk profile of that country being more consistent with the rating than with the spread. That is just one indication that spreads are not necessarily always the most useful piece of information, especially in cases in which the markets just are not as liquid as we would like them to be.

Better information content is another source of value from ratings, and it is the one area on which there has been some literature in financial economic circles. Unfortunately, in practice it is a bit of a chicken-and-egg question, because what is often found is a constant dialogue between the market and the agencies. When

Moody's bought KMV, it started to effectively incorporate the market perspective into their ratings. And the market is constantly looking at what the rating agencies are doing. So it is hard to say which one came first and whether there is real information content in either one without the other. It is a very circular reference.

The one area where the value of credit rating agencies may be suspect is their impact, or lack thereof, of issuers on corporate behavior—with respect to appropriate levels of leverage and how a company can achieve an investment grade rating. To some extent, ratings agencies can have an impact in this regard because their ratings take account of corporate cash balances, which companies can control. Dividends and buy-back decisions and recapitalization decisions also are corporate finance decisions that are made in the context of the implications of or impact on credit ratings.

On the merger and acquisitions side, I think probably the two most commonly asked questions at the board level—and this is not right or wrong, it is just the questions you get—is whether a particular deal is accretive (does it add value?), and how does it affect the company's rating? In my view, a fair amount of fiscal discipline is being imposed on corporate finance decisions because of concerns about ratings consequences.

There is a set of questions around market efficiency. Clearly, there are some areas in which market efficiency is not being supported by the status quo. For example, in the case of unsolicited ratings, if the customer is the issuer or if the source of the revenue is the issuer, then the question arises of why one would even have unsolicited ratings. If the source of the fees is a subscription service, then by all means one needs unsolicited ratings to support that business model. So we have a legacy from the past that has not yet been reflected in new fee models. In addition, the marketing of ancillary services could raise questions around moral suasion. I think Frank touched on that potential source of market inefficiency pretty well. Another potential inefficiency stems from supply-demand. We have legislated demand and legislative restriction of supply, and again, Frank did a nice job of touching on this potential supply-demand imbalance. To the extent that one can move to a more free market on the demand side of the equation and open things up on the supply side, then we would hope that one could move toward a more efficient market in the flow of ratings information.

ZOE-VONNA PALMROSE

Maintaining the Value and Viability of Auditors as Gatekeepers under SOX: An Auditing Master Proposal

It is both timely and necessary to consider the future role of auditors as financial gatekeepers in the United States. There have been many reforms over the last few years, of which the most radical for auditors was the shift from self-regulation to government regulation, when the Sarbanes-Oxley Act of 2002 (SOX) established the Public Company Accounting Oversight Board (PCAOB) to oversee auditors of companies registered with the U.S. Securities and Exchange Commission (SEC). Still, the scrutiny and criticism of auditors continues, and recent events have renewed the public debate over both the value of external audits and the viability of the largest firms performing these audits.[1] So, assessing

---

I would like to thank Bill Kinney for his comments and our many helpful discussions, along with Joe Brazel, George Fritz, Mark Nelson, Aulana Peters, Ralph Saul, Joe Schultz, participants at the Brookings–Tokyo Club Seminar, including Peter Wallison, and accounting research seminar participants at Arizona State University, the University of Georgia, North Carolina State, and University of California–Irvine.

1. Kinney, Botosan, and Palmrose (2006) provides some quantitative evidence on the benefits and costs of auditing for a large sample of public companies. As to viability, KPMG's problems from its past tax shelter services once again raised the specter that an audit firm might be rendered inoperable by a criminal indictment by the Justice Department. Any such result would further concentrate the market for accounting, auditing, and related services, constraining clients' choices among accounting firms. Proposals to break up or nationalize audit firms or to convert them to audit-only firms would be less speculative in such an environment. Certainly the future of privately owned accounting partnerships—whether limited liability partnerships (LLPs) or professional corporations (LLCs)—as external auditors for public companies is not ensured.

the consequences of reforms and considering where the auditing profession might be headed seem essential.

Yet taking stock is not an easy task. Companies and auditors are still adjusting to the requirements of SOX. Not all of the act's provisions have been fully implemented, but that has not prevented a backlash against parts of it, particularly the section 404 requirement for management to report on and auditors to attest to the effectiveness of company internal controls over financial reporting.[2] That requirement has engendered growing hostility from corporate America and a public relations nightmare for auditors.[3] Meanwhile, the PCAOB remains a work in progress, companies with significant accounting problems keep surfacing, the upward trend in financial restatements continues,[4] and auditors continue to be sued and investigated, even as they attempt to resolve litigation and regulatory investigations over services that they performed before SOX was enacted.

Given this environment, I decided to address what I consider to be an overarching concern: are post-SOX regulatory and legal forces undermining the continued value from and the viability of large external audit firms as financial gate-

---

2. The SEC formed the Committee on Smaller Public Companies primarily to address concerns over SOX and section 404 requirements. The committee recommended and the SEC approved a delay in the deadline for nonaccelerated filers to comply with section 404. The new compliance date is for fiscal years ending on or after July 15, 2007.

3. For example, see Powell (2005) and Smitherman (2005), and Neal L. Wolkoff, "Sarbanes-Oxley Is a Curse for Small-Cap Companies," *Wall Street Journal*, August 15, 2005, p. A13.

The backlash is not surprising. In unregulated markets, voluntary demand for financial statement audits is common, while demand for audits of the effectiveness of internal controls is not. Therefore imposing internal control reporting and auditing requirements—and the attendant costs—on *all* public companies as a response to instances in which auditors failed to detect fraudulent financial reporting is viewed by many clients as unjustly rewarding auditors by increasing their revenues and profits at their clients' expense.

For research on how private companies often provide audited financial statements, see Leftwich (1983), Strawser (1991), and Blackwell and others (1998). In addition, using data prior to the Securities Acts of 1933 and 1934, Chow (1982) reports that 79 percent of New York Stock Exchange (NYSE) and 48 percent of over-the-counter (OTC) industrial companies listed in the December 31, 1926, issue of the *Wall Street Journal* (with data available) had external audits. On the other hand, McMullen, Raghunandan, and Rama (1996), using 1993 data, document that the management of only fifty-five companies in their overall sample of 2,221 companies publicly reported on the effectiveness of their internal controls and that only twenty-five used COSO (Committee of Sponsoring Organizations of the Treadway Commission) criteria for doing so; moreover, it appears that few if any of them had an auditor attest to the effectiveness of their controls.

4. Interpreting this trend is difficult. Some see it as bad news because it indicates that quarterly (reviewed) and annual (audited) financial statements continue to be misstated after enactment of SOX. Others see it as good news because it indicates that SOX is working and that financial reporting problems are being cleaned up; that is, management is identifying and remedying financial reporting errors, perhaps as part of meeting the requirements of SOX sections 302 or 404 or both, and gatekeepers (both auditors and audit committees) are getting tough, and PCAOB inspections are working. Still others see it as "no news" because the upward trend has been driven by restatements over accounting technicalities (a recent example is lease accounting) and a tightening of materiality (Logue 2005).

keepers? I explore this concern by using a risk management framework. I discuss post-SOX risk management from the perspectives of both audit firms and the PCAOB. I identify a number of factors that complicate audit firms' risk management activities. Essentially, it appears that the PCAOB, rather than assuming or sharing risks, is transferring additional risks to audit firms. That has created new uncertainties for auditors, which now include PCAOB criticism for overauditing, while the critical risk of fraudulent financial reporting continues.

Under the fire-alarm approach to regulation, major instances of fraudulent financial reporting typically create the impetus for regulatory reform; enacting SOX in response to the Enron and WorldCom scandals is the latest example.[5] How much, if at all, SOX has mitigated the risk of fraudulent financial reporting (pre- or post-audit) by changing the behavior of management, boards, audit committees, auditors, regulators, users, and others is an open question. But regardless of whether SOX has reduced the risk of fraudulent financial reporting, it most certainly has not been eliminated.

Audit firms can bear some, but not all, of the risk of fraudulent reporting. Even the largest audit firms remain vulnerable when fraudulent financial reporting occurs on large clients with high market caps or significant amounts of debt and when it disguises fundamental problems with the viability of such companies. Under those circumstances, investors can lose billions of dollars. Yet audit firms *cannot* obtain insurance coverage for such large losses, and they are constrained in obtaining funds from alternative sources to otherwise cover a meaningful portion of those losses.[6] Moreover, the current legal system cannot be relied on to effectively sort out causal relationships and auditors' responsibilities from the limitations of generally accepted accounting principles (GAAP) and other factors.[7] That makes it difficult to match auditor conduct with appropriate sanctions in resolving private civil litigation and regulatory enforcement actions.

Now that government regulation of auditors by the PCAOB has supplanted self-regulation, it is appropriate that the audit regulator explicitly shares the risk of fraudulent financial reporting with audit firms. To do this, I propose establishing an auditing master's office under the PCAOB umbrella but independent

---

5. See Kinney (2005b). Political scientists describe the fire-alarm approach as one in which regulators take little action until constituents express complaints; regulators then respond by "answering the alarm" (McCubbins 1985).

6. State laws and professional codes of conduct preclude audit firms from operating as basic corporations and otherwise restrict them from having outside investors. Obtaining resources by charging higher fees to some or all existing clients based on predictions of future significant or catastrophic but low probability (albeit non–zero probability) events and their resulting costs is complex and further complicated by intergenerational allocation issues among partners joining and leaving a partnership.

7. See Kinney (2005b).

of the board and staff. This chapter provides some discussion of the rationale for and the role of such an office.

The chapter proceeds with a discussion of external auditors as gatekeepers, followed by a discussion of audit firm risk management. Background on the PCAOB as audit regulator, along with some commentary, is provided to give context to the discussion of risk management from a PCAOB perspective. Next, the chapter elaborates on fraudulent financial reporting as a central risk for audit firms (and for the PCAOB as audit regulator), using evidence from litigation against auditors. It finally proposes establishing an auditing master's office to help manage that risk and maintain the value and viability of external audit firms.

Auditors as Gatekeepers

Financial information is used to plan, control, and evaluate the activities and performance of companies and their managers. But to be useful in decisionmaking and contracting, the information needs to be relevant and trustworthy. Attestation by external auditors with expertise in accounting, auditing, systems, and client businesses helps give a company's financial information the requisite reliability and credibility even though the company's management provides the information. Essentially, managers use audited financial statements to inform themselves, to inform others, and to comply with laws and regulations.[8]

If auditors fail to detect and disclose material omissions or misstatements in financial statements, users of those statements can seek compensation from auditors, among others, for losses caused by that failure. Some studies describe these—that is, detection and disclosure and compensation—as the informational and insurance roles of auditing,[9] whereby attestation reduces information risk and, since investors have recourse against auditors for audit failures, "auditors provide investors with a means to indemnify losses."[10] However, as subsequently discussed, the insurance (indemnification) notion is fragile. Auditors cannot be asked or expected to insure financial statement users against losses in trillion-dollar capital markets.[11]

---

8. Kinney (2000).
9. For example, Dye (1993).
10. Mansi, Maxwell, and Miller (2004); also see Menon and Williams (1994), Baber, Kumar, and Verghese (1995), and Khurana and Raman (2004). However, in deciding the Dura Pharmaceuticals case, the Supreme Court recently reaffirmed that the purpose of permitting private lawsuits for securities fraud is not to provide investors with broad insurance against market losses but to protect them against those economic losses that misrepresentations actually cause (Greenhouse 2005).
11. Kinney (2005a). The Financial Accounting Standards Board (FASB) estimated that holders of public securities had $22.8 trillion invested at the end of 2003 (FASB 2005). About half of all SEC regis-

Because audited financial information—typically financial statements prepared in accordance with generally accepted accounting principles—is used in contracting, auditors represent one type of gatekeeper. In both free and regulated markets, auditors facilitate or inhibit companies' access to goods, services, debt, and equity for their operating, financing, and investing activities. While auditors are not the only party that functions as a gatekeeper, auditors are not viewed as bit players.[12]

Regulated markets, such as the U.S. public securities market, help emphasize the compliance role of auditor gatekeeping, given the need for companies to file audited GAAP financial statements with the SEC to comply with the Securities Acts. These acts grant independent public or certified accountants the exclusive right to perform audits and give the SEC some regulatory authority over the auditors. SOX extends the SEC's authority over public accounting firms and auditors, largely through the PCAOB. It also requires auditors to attest to management's assessment and reporting on internal controls over financial reporting, although material weaknesses in internal controls do not preclude SEC registrants from continuing to access the public capital markets.[13]

Unqualified opinions by auditors provide assurance that management-prepared financial statements are free of material misstatements, but auditors' fees for rendering such assurance are paid by client companies.[14] An audit firm may lose a client—and thus future fees—after identifying that the company's management does not follow GAAP or that it commits fraud. Audit firms do not receive private or public compensation for such revelations.[15] Indeed, investors

---

trants have a market capitalization of less than $100 million, and they represent about 1 percent of the total market cap; thus about half of all public companies make up 99 percent of the total market (*Securities Mosaic* 2005).

12. Kinney (2005a).

13. Since 1993, section 112 of the Federal Deposit Insurance Corporation Improvement Act has required the management of insured depository institutions with total assets of $500 million or more to annually assess and report whether their internal controls over financial reporting are effective and to provide an independent accountant's *attestation* report or management's assertion. Nonetheless, the American Banking Association told the PCAOB that proposed auditing standard no. 2 "goes beyond an attestation to require a full audit, which significantly alters the requirements under SOX and significantly increases the costs to companies" (Hamilton 2004a, p. 1).

In accordance with PCAOB auditing standard no. 2, auditors express two different opinions: one on management's assessment of the effectiveness of internal controls over financial reporting and another on the actual effectiveness of those controls.

14. SOX requires audit committees to assume responsibility for the appointment, compensation, retention, and oversight of the work of the external auditor, including resolution of disagreements between management and the auditor regarding financial reporting.

15. Kinney (2005b). Even so, audit firms can design partner and staff compensation arrangements to reward individual auditors for detecting and disclosing non-GAAP financial reporting.

and creditors often sue the audit firm for not detecting and disclosing fraud sooner. In the United States, clients can dismiss their audit firms at will. Assuming alternative audit firms are available, essentially, only the cost of changing auditors and the need for SEC registrants to disclose the change and some of the circumstances surrounding it constrain clients from dismissing auditors.[16] Further, confidentiality rules and restrictions preclude auditors from disclosing client information or discussing information disclosed by others, constraining auditors from defending their work. All of these factors contribute to some skepticism that auditors have adequate incentives to detect and disclose financial reporting problems.[17]

Yet there are a number of mechanisms (or countervailing forces) that do give auditors incentives to detect and disclose material misstatements.[18] Many of these mechanisms are economic and involve cost avoidance. Even so, it should not be overlooked that countervailing forces also include professional and societal standards. Some argue that there has been a gradual "deterioration in professional values" over time;[19] nonetheless, "As . . . professional, [auditors] recognize a responsibility to the public, to the client, and to fellow practitioners, including honorable behavior, even if that means personal sacrifice."[20]

In spite of the dearth of positive incentives, audit firms and auditors do face negative consequences if they fail to detect and disclose problems. Audit firms are highly regulated organizations, subject to a myriad of standards and regulations on auditing, quality control, independence, and professional conduct. Those constraints define a lower bound for auditors' actions and performance and require audit firms to maintain systems and processes to ensure compliance. Allegations of noncompliance can result in criminal action, civil litigation, regulatory enforcement by a variety of federal and state authorities (among them the PCAOB,

---

16. SEC registrants must disclose the end of their relationship with an auditor by filing Form 8K within five business days. The filing must disclose whether the auditor's report for either of the preceding two years contained an adverse opinion, disclaimer, or qualification. Other events reportable on Form 8K include disagreements, internal control weaknesses, inability of the auditor to rely on management representations, and unwillingness of the auditor to be associated with financial statements prepared by management.

17. Moore and others (2006) also argue that unconscious bias affects auditors' judgments and that auditors' lobbying activities prevent meaningful reform, but see Nelson (2006) for counterarguments and King (2002) for evidence on how any bias is neutralized in audit team settings because groups create social pressure to conform to group norms.

For evidence on whether the nature and extent of the auditor-client relationship (including non-audit services) create conflicts of interest that diminish the quality of audit services or users' perceptions of quality, see Kinney, Palmrose, and Scholz (2004), Larcker and Richardson (2004), and Myers and others (2005) and their discussions of extant research.

18. Nelson (2006).
19. Zeff (2003).
20. Arens and Loebbecke (1991, p. 75).

SEC, and state licensing bodies), and disciplinary action by professional organizations. Finally, allegations of an audit failure can diminish the reputation of both the audit firm and the individual auditors involved.

As an aside, audit firms typically have to defend themselves against multiple actions on any single alleged audit failure. Auditors may confront all types of actions, though typically actions involve civil lawsuits by numerous different plaintiffs (which may not all be consolidated in a class action) and regulatory investigations; only rarely do they face criminal investigation.[21] Further, since audits can be international in scope, an alleged audit failure on any one client with global operations can result in legal, regulatory, and professional disciplinary activities in both the United States and one or more foreign countries.

These mechanisms are intended to deter auditors from accidentally (erroneously) or intentionally compromising their services by attesting to financial statements with material misstatements or omissions. These mechanisms are economic in nature—they impose costs on auditors. Defending against allegations of audit failure, including the diversion of partner and staff time and effort, can be very costly, as can settlements, judgments, and other penalties. Holding auditors liable also is intended to help compensate users (plaintiffs) for their recoverable losses. It is this latter purpose that leads academics to attribute an insurance role to auditors. I will return to both of these issues after discussing risk management activities from the perspectives of audit firms and the PCAOB as audit regulator.

Audit Firm Risk Management

All organizations must manage risk; audit firms are no exception. Kinney (2000) provides a general framework for considering risk assessment and control activities. The first step is to identify risks and assess whether the risk-reward relationship is acceptable to the firm. If the answer is yes, the firm accepts the risk; if the answer is (unalterably) no, the firm prevents or avoids the risk. Between these two extremes, the firm's choices are to transfer the risk, share it, or design risk reduction processes to mitigate it or otherwise improve the risk-reward relationship. In all instances, the firm monitors the risks—whether accepted, transferred, shared, mitigated, avoided, or prevented—for exceptions and changes.

While a variety of mechanisms exist to transfer, share, or otherwise improve the risk-reward relationship—including hedging, derivatives, insurance, contracting, pricing, joint ventures, and alliances—laws and professional standards

---

21. In spite of criminal investigations of client personnel and the recent proceedings involving Andersen and KPMG, criminal actions against audit firms or individual auditors are rare.

(many of which address concerns over auditor independence) prohibit audit firms from using most of these mechanisms.[22] Moreover, even insurance appears to be unavailable at meaningful levels of coverage for larger audit firms. At least in the current environment, larger audit firms cannot obtain insurance against high-end claims for significant to catastrophic amounts.[23] And, as previously noted, "pricing-out" risks by raising the fees of either "more risky" or all existing clients is not a realistic option. Audit firms' risk management mechanisms therefore are limited. Still, auditors share a number of risks with the audit regulator, so some forms of risk sharing are possible.

But first, the discussion applies the risk management framework to audit firms, beginning with the question of what risks audit firms need to manage. Overall, an audit firm must assess and control its *business risk,* which is defined as the risk of lawsuits, regulatory action, diminishment of the firm's reputation, decline in the firm's viability, and the firm's failure from all sources, not just audit services, although audit services represent a major source of business risk.[24]

Focusing on audit services, auditors need to manage *engagement risk*—the risk of incurring losses from associating with a particular client.[25] To do that, auditors must assess and control the three elements of engagement risk: *financial misstatement risk* (also called *audit risk*), the risk that the auditor will unknowingly certify that the financial statements are free of material misstatement when in fact they are not;[26] *client business risk,* the risk of loss to the auditor from a decline in client performance, client financial distress, and client failure; and *client misconduct risk,* the risk of loss to the auditor from management fraud, illegal or unethical acts, excessive perks, shirking, and other acts of noncompliance by clients. Figure 4-1 illustrates these concepts and their interrelationship, including the intersections among financial misstatement risk, client business risk, and client misconduct risk.[27]

---

22. This includes contracting for alternative dispute resolution or indemnification, which the SEC precludes under most circumstances with regard to public clients. The Federal Financial Institutions Examination Council extended a similar preclusion to financial institutions (PCAOB 2006).

23. This statement is based on my private discussions with attorneys and general counsels.

24. For example, threats to the viability of KPMG involved tax services, and one way that the firm could have controlled that risk was not to have developed and sold the aggressive tax shelters at issue.

25. Huss and Jacobs (1991), AICPA (1992), and Kinney (2000).

26. Misstatement risk encompasses opinions rendered on annual (audited) financial statements, on interim (reviewed) financial statements, and on management assessments of internal control and its effectiveness. However, misstatement risk may no longer fully subsume internal control risk, given the separate audit of controls under section 404 of SOX. To the extent that it does not, internal control risk would be an additional risk for auditors (and regulators) to consider.

27. Figure 4-1 is not drawn to scale. However, a number of studies provide insights on these interrelationships (intersections) and their (ex post) frequency from litigation against auditors (for example, Palm-

Figure 4-1. *Audit Firm Business Risk and Engagement Risk*[a]

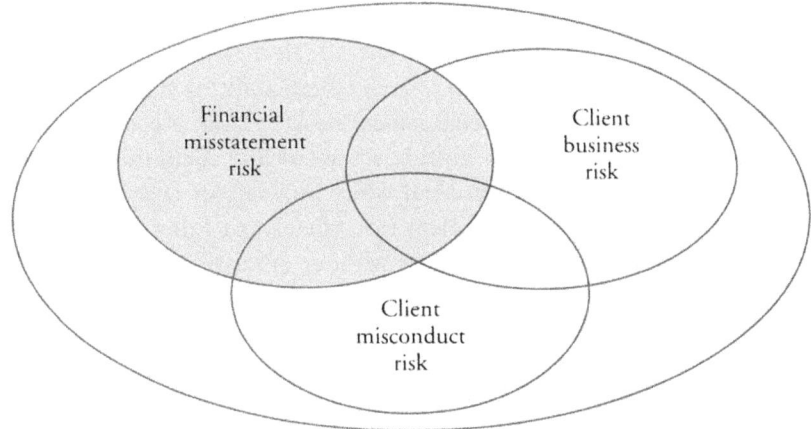

Audit firm business risk

Source: Adapted from Kinney (2000).
a. Engagement risk consists of financial misstatement risk (unknowing certification of materially misstated financial reports), client business risk (future decline in client performance), and client misconduct risk (management fraud, illegal or unethical acts, excessive perks, shirking, and noncompliance). Business risk consists of the risk of lawsuits, loss of reputation and viability, and failure. AuS and GAAP measurement and disclosure criteria apply.

Exploring the elements of engagement risk, note that both auditing and accounting (GAAP) standards have a role in the risk of financial misstatement.[28] GAAP provides the measurement and disclosure criteria that define misstatements, but it has some additional subtleties. For example, there is growing recognition that accounting standard setters can promulgate standards that

---

rose 1987, Carcello and Palmrose 1994, and Palmrose 1999) and restatements for non-GAAP accounting (for example, Palmrose and Scholz 2004).
   28. I use the term "auditing standards," while recognizing the complication and potential confusion from having three set of standards in the market: PCAOB audit standards (required by SOX for SEC registrants); generally accepted auditing standards (GAAS), promulgated for private companies, among others, by the Auditing Standards Board (ASB) of the American Institute of Certified Public Accountants (AICPA); and, from an international perspective, auditing standards promulgated by the International Auditing and Assurance Standards Board (IAASB). The ASB and IAASB are working together toward convergence, and the IAASB participates as an observer at the PCAOB's Standing Advisory Group meetings. However, with three sets of standards, auditors now must manage the risk that allegations of audit failure can involve questions regarding which auditing standards were applied and whether they were the appropriate ones to use (Rosario and Holl 2005).

facilitate misstatements,[29] in part because the standards are difficult to audit or even unauditable.[30]

While many assume that auditors would not encounter problems if they just did a better job of auditing, figure 4-1 makes it clear that an auditor can do a "perfect" audit (that is, comply with or even exceed auditing standards) and still not eliminate misstatement (or engagement) risk.[31] That is because misstatement risk does not coincide with client business risk and client misconduct risk, although it is influenced by both. And while increases in client business and misconduct risks increase misstatement risk, clients can suffer declines in performance, fail, or engage in misconduct without misstating financial information (or having weaknesses in internal control over financial reporting). Yet, if an auditor is associated with such clients, its reputation may be diminished or allegations may be made against it. And as previously noted, it is difficult for users and the legal system to sort out (ex post) the contributions to an alleged audit failure of GAAP, audit-related standards (for auditing, quality control, indepen-

---

29. Watts (2003 and 2005). The interplay between accounting standards and audit quality extends to earnings management. However, for earnings management, it is important to distinguish between non-GAAP reporting and aggressive reporting within GAAP, because the auditor's responsibilities differ with regard to each. Nelson, Elliott, and Tarpley (2002) provides useful insights on the role of GAAP from the perspective of auditors' experiences with earnings management.

30. See Carmichael (2004), Palmrose (2005), and Taub (2005). In particular, this issue has arisen as the FASB and International Accounting Standards Board (IASB) move more toward fair market value accounting (Carmichael 2004, Palmrose 2005, Taub 2005, and Watts 2005) and away from historical cost transaction-based accounting, traditional approaches to revenue recognition and expense measurement, and the concept of conservatism (Brown and Palmrose 2005 and Watts 2003).

The Panel on Audit Effectiveness (2000), the PCAOB's chief auditor (Carmichael 2004), and the Federal Reserve Board (Hamilton 2004b) have all recommended that the FASB consider the auditability of accounting standards before promulgating them. But tensions exist because the FASB considers auditors and the PCAOB just one of many sources of input into their standard-setting process. Since the SEC must adopt FASB pronouncements before they apply to financial reports issued by public companies, it remains to be seen whether the SEC will continue to adopt FASB accounting standards that involve auditability problems and that may increase the likelihood of misstatements.

31. Earnings management research, much of which relies on abnormal accruals, has contributed to the notion that auditors fall short in their role as financial gatekeepers. But while abnormal accruals may reflect a number of factors, including differences in performance or aggressive accounting, few studies actually distinguish between GAAP and non-GAAP reporting. Exceptions include DeChow, Sloan, and Sweeney (1995 and 1996), which documents statistically significant associations between non-GAAP reporting (using SEC enforcement actions) and abnormal accruals. Nonetheless, evidence in Bradshaw, Richardson, and Sloan (2001) demonstrates the limitations from an audit perspective of using abnormal accrual models to discriminate non-GAAP from GAAP reporting. Classifying a time series of companies on Compustat into ten accrual portfolios (with about 6,700 observations in each) and identifying those with subsequent SEC enforcement actions, Bradshaw, Richardson, and Sloan finds four enforcement actions in the lowest accrual portfolio and twenty-eight in the highest (that is, non-GAAP reporting rates that vary between .0006 and .004).

dence, and professional conduct), auditor performance, regulator performance, and various client characteristics.

Thus client business risk and client misconduct risk are among the reasons that client acceptance and retention decisions are important in managing auditors' engagement risk (and overall business risk). One way for auditors to avoid lawsuits or criticism of the quality of their work is to avoid clients with whom such results are likely. Further, client business risk and client misconduct risk are among the reasons that auditors cannot manage misstatement risk (or engagement and business risks) simply by doing better audits. Complying with accounting and auditing standards only partially protects an auditor.

Once the decision has been made to accept a client and the auditors have assumed engagement risk, they can audit more effectively to mitigate it and, accordingly, to mitigate misstatement risk.[32] Therefore it is not surprising that during 2004–05, when auditors were being closely monitored and scrutinized and were conducting first-time internal control audits, they would do more work, tighten materiality (and not waive adjustments of the misstatements detected), request advice and support from specialists within the firm (including through consultation) before making decisions, and make more conservative judgments and decisions on extant audit engagements. While such activities likely reduce misstatement risk, they also increase audit fees. Clients and the PCAOB have questioned whether these risk management activities are necessary (that is, whether the improved audit quality is worth the cost or whether an overauditing problem exists). However, assuming that the activities are necessary, an important question remains: are they sufficient, especially to detect collusive, actively hidden fraudulent financial reporting when management overrides internal controls?[33]

The Audit Regulator: The PCAOB

The question of whether activities to detect fraudulent financial reporting are sufficient extends the discussion to the question of whether the resulting risk-

---

32. An "audit risk" model forms the conceptual underpinning for financial statement audits. While the propriety of this model is not the focus of this chapter, there appears to be no economical alternative to a risk-based approach to auditing. Still, implementation issues do arise naturally and the Panel on Audit Effectiveness (2000) and Kinney (2005b) provide some discussion of those issues.

33. This is another reason, along with the lack of voluntary demand, that the Panel on Audit Effectiveness (2000) did *not* recommend that the SEC require management and auditors to report on the effectiveness of internal controls. Instead, the panel emphasized the need for greater audit committee involvement in internal control matters. AICPA (2005) provides guidance to audit committees in addressing the ever-present risk of management override of controls—the Achilles' heel of efforts to prevent fraudulent financial reporting.

reward trade-off is sufficient to maintain the value and viability of auditing in the post-SOX environment. To explore these issues requires considering the role of the PCAOB as audit regulator. This section provides background on the PCAOB and discusses risk management from the PCAOB's perspective.

PCAOB Statutory Authority

Section 101 of the Sarbanes-Oxley Act established the Public Company Accounting Oversight Board "to oversee the audit of public companies that are subject to the securities laws, and related matters, in order to protect the interests of investors and further the public interest in the preparation of informative, accurate, and independent audit reports for companies the securities of which are sold to, and held by and for, public investors." According to the PCAOB's website, it "has responsibility for improving the quality and transparency in financial reporting and independent audits, advancing corporate responsibility, and furthering the public interest."[34]

SOX gives the PCAOB the authority to register public accounting firms that prepare audit reports for issuers; establish or adopt (or both) auditing, quality control, ethics, independence, and other standards relating to the preparation of audit reports for issuers;[35] conduct inspections of registered public accounting firms; conduct investigations and disciplinary proceedings and impose appropriate sanctions when justified on registered public accounting firms and associated persons; perform other duties or functions that the board or the SEC determines to be necessary or appropriate to promote high professional standards and improve the quality of audit services; enforce compliance with SOX, rules of the board, professional standards, and securities law in the preparation and issuance of audit reports and the obligations and liabilities of accountants thereto; and set the budget and manage the operations of the board and its staff.

SOX gives the PCAOB statutory authority to make the rules, monitor and inspect for compliance with the rules, and otherwise enforce the rules, such as by

---

34. Probing the propriety of this broad statement and reconciling it with SOX is not the focus of this chapter. For example, some might suggest that it intrudes into the FASB's domain. However, a broad statement of responsibility recognizes external auditing as just one of the inputs into the quality of financial reporting and therefore appreciates the complexity of regulating audit-related matters.

35. The PCAOB has not attempted the monumental but arguably crucial task of rationalizing the current rule-oriented approach to and regulation of auditor independence. For example, the independence rules in conjunction with section 404 requirements and other documentation guidance have had a chilling effect on auditor-client communications and undermined the ability of clients to obtain accounting-related advice from their external auditors (Lumb 2005c). However, the PCAOB has issued independence rules on tax services and contingent fees (rules 3521, 3522, and 3523). Meanwhile the SEC continues to handle day-to-day inquiries that arise in practice when firms are trying to comply with the complexities of the various auditor independence rules.

bringing and deciding disciplinary actions for noncompliance.[36] Unlike self-regulatory standard-setting bodies, which include among their members currently practicing auditors who either implicitly or explicitly weigh the market (or personal) impact of their standards, the PCAOB is not constrained by market considerations (although political considerations matter, as discussed later). Moreover, SOX does not require the PCAOB to consider the costs and benefits of its rules and actions, although the board avows that it does so voluntarily.

Having standard setting, inspection, and enforcement under one umbrella has the advantage, in theory at least, of allowing for timely feedback between auditors and the regulator. Thus it has the potential for facilitating more current, seamless, and continuous improvements in standards and performance (by both auditors and regulators) and thereby for improving the quality of auditing and financial reporting. However, improvement cannot occur without open communication between practicing auditors and regulators; that in turn requires a high level of mutual trust and respect, which may take some time and experience to develop.[37] Unfortunately, the design and implementation of the PCAOB may impede this development. For example, the general exclusion of practicing auditors from and their disempowerment in the PCAOB's regulatory activities, the natural uncertainties that attend regulatory inspections, and the risk of enforcement may be among the impediments.

While in concept inspections allow the PCAOB to maintain confidence in the underlying quality of audits, the inspection process really focuses on areas for improvement in practice. The public portions of the inspection reports discuss problems, deficiencies, and defects in audits and criticisms of audit firms and the work of their partners and staff. Neither the inspection process nor the public portions of the inspection reports are intended to provide a balanced assessment of the overall effectiveness of the audits of public companies by each of the registered firms.

---

36. SOX allows the PCAOB, through the SEC's subpoena powers, to compel testimony and production of documents. SOX also requires the PCAOB to notify the SEC of pending board investigations involving potential violations of securities law and to coordinate its work with that of the SEC's enforcement division as necessary to protect an ongoing SEC investigation (section 105).

37. Still, when communications occur, the PCAOB must agree to resolve practice issues. For example, the SEC's recent reform of rules on new securities offerings, which took effect December 2005, raises issues for ASB Statement on Auditing Standards (SAS) no. 72, which applies to comfort letters. Since the "matter is not a high priority on the PCAOB's agenda, the AICPA and a group of industry participants developed a framework for discussions between underwriters and auditors and shared their white paper with the PCAOB" (Lumb 2005d, p. 3).

Another impediment may be the lack of checks and balances within the SOX-designed regulatory structure.[38] The only designated check and balance on the PCAOB is another regulator—the SEC. SOX gives the SEC overall authority over the PCAOB. For example, the SEC appoints board members, approves the PCAOB's budget, approves all standards promulgated by the PCAOB before they take effect, and reviews disciplinary actions of the PCAOB upon an auditor's application to do so. While SOX is silent on the need for the PCAOB to consider costs and benefits, the SEC is required to assess costs and benefits before promulgating rules. Nonetheless, the SEC's regulatory mandate and enforcement orientation, along with some evidence of tensions between auditors and the SEC (see Panel on Audit Effectiveness 2000), demonstrates that the SEC may not always prove an ideal solitary system of checks and balances.

PCAOB Expertise Issues

To give proper consideration to the PCAOB's risk management activities, it must be recognized that the PCAOB is a board of non-experts. SOX specifies that the PCAOB shall consist of five members, only two of which can be or can have been certified public accountants.[39] To qualify for appointment to the PCAOB, a candidate must be "among prominent individuals of integrity and reputation who have demonstrated commitment to the interests of investors and the public and an understanding of the responsibilities for and nature of the financial disclosures required of issuers under the securities laws and the obligations of accountants with respect to the preparation and issuance of audit reports with respect to such disclosures" (SOX, section 101).

These SOX provisions are intended to ensure that auditors do not dominate or control the regulatory process, but they also minimize the involvement on the board of people with recent, relevant auditing and accounting experience and therefore essential expertise.[40] None of the current board members has any sub-

---

38. The Panel on Audit Effectiveness (2000) recommended a governance structure that provided checks and balances by recognizing important roles for a self-regulatory body or bodies (for example, a more empowered Public Oversight Board and, if it had been supported, an Independence Standards Board), the SEC, audit firms, and any other professional standard-setting body (for example, the ASB) and related organizations (for example, the AICPA).

39. SOX specifies that the chairperson cannot have been a practicing CPA for at least five years prior to appointment to the board.

40. This discussion is not a criticism of any member of the PCAOB or its staff. I believe that they are extremely dedicated individuals, and I have the utmost respect for them. However, the design and implementation of the PCAOB has been subject to very little analysis and debate; for rare exceptions see Wallison (2005) and Kinney (2005b). Given the importance of the change from a self-regulated to a government-regulated auditing profession, it seems essential to analyze the usefulness and limitations of government

stantive experience actually auditing financial statements. It is somewhat ironic that SOX requires greater financial expertise for audit committees (section 407) than it does for the PCAOB.

The lack of accounting and auditing expertise within the PCAOB goes beyond having a non-expert board. Most holders of the fourteen major staff positions listed on the PCAOB's website as of August 2005 lacked meaningful experience in auditing financial statements. Having such experience may be less important or even unimportant for some staff positions, but not for all.

The PCAOB can help mitigate expertise problems by including currently practicing auditors in a number of activities. For example, the PCAOB elected to establish auditing standards itself by relying on the Office of the Chief Auditor rather than delegate this important task to an outside professional group, like the Auditing Standards Board, as it is allowed to do under SOX (section 103).[41] The board describes its process for developing standards as an open, public one; therefore auditors and the accounting profession can provide input for the PCAOB's consideration.

The board formed its Standing Advisory Group (SAG) to offer advice on establishing auditing and related professional practice standards. In 2005, the SAG was composed of about thirty people, of whom only six held audit-related positions with firms that audit public companies. Indeed, the same number held positions in public companies being audited, while another five were lawyers. Not only is SAG hampered by a lack of deep, current, audit-related expertise, it also is currently limited to four two-day meetings per year and its agenda is full. Still, the board and staff can and should bring the requisite expertise to the standard-setting process by using other formal and informal means, such as ad hoc task forces. Apparently they are doing this, although little transparency attends these activities. It therefore is not surprising to find concerns that auditor expertise is lacking in the regulatory process.[42]

Inspection is another PCAOB activity that requires extensive accounting and auditing expertise. The Public Oversight Board (POB), the previous, self-regulatory body, relied on a peer review process that used practicing audit partners

---

regulation. Moreover, the PCAOB's reach extends to foreign auditors of SEC registrants, and anecdotal evidence suggests that the PCAOB is not recognizing self-regulated (rather than government-regulated) bodies as satisfactory for overseeing and inspecting those auditors.

41. The Office of the Chief Auditor had twelve employees at the end of 2004 (PCAOB 2004, p. 23), in contrast to the number of experts involved in audit standard setting by the ASB. For example, to develop and draft a single standard, ASB Statement on Auditing Standard (SAS) no. 99, *Consideration of Fraud in a Financial Statement Audit* (October 2002), the fourteen (expert) members of the ASB used a core group of at least seventeen people to serve on a task force and subgroup and as liaisons and technical staff.

42. Wallison (2005).

and more senior managers from an outside audit firm to conduct reviews. That made sense given the need for broad, deep, current expertise in accounting, auditing, internal controls, audit firm practices and methodologies, client industries, and so forth. However, because it did not use paid employees who had severed all ties to their former accounting firms, the POB peer review process was criticized for lacking at least the appearance of independence. While the PCAOB decided to hire its own inspectors, it has traded off expertise for perceived independence. That is a very significant trade-off. The PCAOB's 2004 annual report disclosed that it had 120 inspectors in seven domestic offices and that "inspection teams are composed of accountants who have an average of 12 years of auditing experience."[43] Twelve years is likely well below the average for POB peer reviewers.[44] In addition, anecdotal evidence suggests that the board is having difficulty hiring and retaining people with extensive and high-level audit experience (including recently retired audit partners). While that raises concerns, there is not enough publicly available information to allow a realistic assessment of the expertise of the inspectors employed by the PCAOB and how that expertise is being maintained over time.

The one group that is not in short supply at the PCAOB is lawyers. In 2005, the majority of board members were lawyers, as were a number of their aides and nearly half of the holders of the major staff positions. In addition, many members of the board and staff have prior associations with the SEC. Lawyers and prior SEC affiliates occupy more than 60 percent of the board and major staff positions. Together, they imbue the PCAOB with an enforcement perspective, whether in perception or in fact.[45]

---

43. PCAOB (2004, pp. 23, 10). In comparison, the SEC chairman reported in 2004 that 400 inspectors monitored and oversaw 8,000 funds and 7,000 brokerage firms (*AccountingWeb.com* 2004). SOX requires annual inspections of registered firms that audit more than 100 public companies, of which there were eight U.S. firms in 2004 (PCAOB 2004, p. 10). Other firms require inspection at least once every three years, and the PCAOB conducted ninety-one of those inspections in 2004 (p. 10). At the end of 2004, 1,423 audit firms were registered with the PCAOB, including 530 non-U.S. firms based in seventy-six countries (p. 8). (However, 585 of the 1,423 firms had no SEC registrants as clients.) The PCAOB adopted oversight rules that provide a model for inspections of non-U.S. firms so that the board may rely on the work of a home-country regulator. In addition to the required inspections, the board can use the Office of Registration and Inspections to conduct special inspections.

44. In a recent audit judgment study (Nelson, Smith, and Palmrose 2005) that gathered data from audit partners and managers of one B5 firm, audit partners averaged twenty-one years of experience and audit managers averaged 8.3 years.

45. The inspection process, including the use of inspections as a source for both PCAOB and SEC discipline and enforcement, reinforces this perception. It is further exacerbated in the post-SOX environment by the emphasis on documentation in PCAOB standards—including standard no. 2, which implements section 404—and the notion that if it is not documented, then auditors (issuers) did not do it. While the

Furthermore, a legalistic focus may be contributing to making the operations and activities of the PCAOB more opaque. Certainly the board is restricted from disclosing confidential audit firm and client information (for example, see SOX sections 102, 104, and 105). But, as discussed, a number of PCAOB activities seem to lack transparency. Indeed, there appears to be less publicly available information for gaining insight into the practice of auditing under government regulation than under self-regulation.[46] And, under pre-SOX self-regulation, the Panel on Audit Effectiveness (2000) even recommended that both the POB and SEC consider expanding their disclosures.

PCAOB Risk Management

I now turn to risk assessment and control activities from a PCAOB perspective. Here, arguably, the risks to be managed include all those described in figure 4-1 and previously discussed from an auditor's perspective. In addition, the PCAOB must assess and control its own form of business risk, namely the risk of loss of confidence in the board itself. The PCAOB must manage its own reputation to maintain confidence in the current SOX-created regulatory regime. To do that requires the board to consider the media, the SEC, and Congress, along with market participants and the diverse groups that represent them. But the PCAOB must avoid the tipping points at either end of the spectrum—that is, from too much or too little regulation. Creating a reputation as a tough and unreasonable regulator risks a loss of confidence through overregulation. Perhaps paradoxically, to maintain its own reputation, the PCAOB must maintain the reputation of the auditing profession. Most of the risks to be managed by the PCAOB are risks that it shares with auditors.

For example, a central focus of the PCAOB is misstatement risk related to audits of annual financial statements, reviews of interim financial statements, and auditor reports on management assessments of internal controls. This is similar to misstatement risk from the perspective of auditors. Misstatement (audit) risk is clearly shared by the PCAOB and auditors.

Audit standards are one mechanism to help mitigate misstatement risk. But they can be crafted by the regulator to either share or transfer risk, as illustrated by considering two different conceptual approaches to setting audit standards.

Panel on Audit Effectiveness (2000) recognized the need for appropriate documentation, it also emphasized the importance of qualitative information and the usefulness of interviews in the peer review (inspection) process.

46. For example, see Kinney (2005b), which explains that this has inhibited both audit scholarship, particularly research on audit practices, and audit education.

On one hand, the board can promulgate output standards, which explicitly make the auditor responsible for detecting misstatements, and so attempt to transfer misstatement risk to auditors.[47] On the other hand, the board can promulgate auditing standards (whether based on rules or principles) that provide guidance or specify procedures for auditors to perform (audit inputs). This approach assumes that performing a particular procedure increases the likelihood of detecting misstatements, but the standard setter bears the risk of that assumption. At least implicitly, it makes the auditor responsible for performance, not detection, and thereby the board shares some misstatement risk with the auditor.

The board could go even further and make risk sharing explicit. For example, through its inspection process, the PCAOB could find that an auditor adhered to audit, quality control, and independence standards and that, even though the auditor did not detect a misstatement, no discipline (or liability) would be appropriate. I will return to this point later; for now, it is worth emphasizing that while the PCAOB's broad powers regarding standards, inspections, and enforcement may allow it to reduce audit failures, the PCAOB has responsibility for the residual risk of failing to detect material misstatements when all of its standards have been followed.[48]

Other risk-sharing activities also can mitigate misstatement risk. For example, the board could facilitate continuous improvements in auditor performance by identifying and communicating "best practices" to auditors, thereby reducing misstatement risk by promoting more effective auditing.

Because they share misstatement risk, auditors and regulators can and should work cooperatively to reduce it. Again, audit standards are one way of doing that. Ideally, both groups would communicate and cooperate on emerging practice issues and the need for additional standards, guidance, or risk alerts. There are indications that such a process has not yet evolved and that it may be complicated by inspection lags, lack of expertise, and other issues previously discussed. Such a process could have avoided the disruption of auditor-client communications and the strained relations resulting from implementation of PCAOB auditing stan-

---

47. For example, the PCAOB could specify that auditors perform certain procedures—for example, to detect management fraud—and then "any other procedures that would be necessary under the circumstances to detect fraudulent financial reporting." Or, in the extreme, an output standard could specify just the latter. Output standards impose strict liability on auditors indirectly through audit standards rather than directly through law. Another perhaps more subtle way to ensure strict liability by using standards is to remove extant protective (exculpatory) language from auditing standards, which has been suggested in speeches by some board members.

48. Kinney (2005b).

dard no. 2 (March 2004), which apparently did not get to the PCAOB's attention until a roundtable on section 404 in spring 2005.[49]

The board's reaction to criticisms of attestation on internal controls (under section 404) also illustrates that even though the PCAOB and auditors share misstatement risk, the board can mitigate the risk for the PCAOB by trying to transfer more of it to auditors. The board declined to reconsider auditing standard no. 2 (AS no. 2),[50] claiming that auditors misinterpreted its requirements, failed to exercise reasonable judgment, applied a checklist rather than tailored and flexible approaches, and generally overaudited.[51] The board framed it as an auditor problem, not a regulatory problem.[52]

Moreover, having standards, inspections, and enforcement under one umbrella may increase the incidence of risk transfer rather than encourage risk sharing by the PCAOB. To maintain the PCAOB's reputation, the board and staff have an incentive to label any detected deficiencies as performance problems (as occurred with AS no. 2) rather than as standard or inspection problems. Furthermore, the PCAOB is considering a proposed rule (rule 3502) that would establish a *negligence* standard of secondary liability for individual accountants and that appears to be inconsistent with the Securities Acts and seems not to have been contemplated by SOX.[53] In such an environment, it is difficult for auditors to rely on public statements by the board that "the staff will not second-guess good faith audit judgments," particularly during private and nontransparent inspection and enforcement processes.[54]

But recall from figure 4-1 that misstatement risk is just one component of engagement risk. The PCAOB also needs to consider engagement risk because client business and misconduct risks influence misstatement risk. The PCAOB appears to be doing this for some tasks. For example, the board's Division of Registrations and Inspections relies on risk assessment to identify which audit firm engagements to inspect, with the goal of identifying the engagements that may

---

49. Lumb (2005a).
50. The board did issue a policy statement and a series of questions and answers, which could be interpreted as acknowledging a problem with AS no. 2. Nonetheless, the policy statement reinforces the message that "it is an auditor problem" and states that a failure to apply the concepts of the policy may reflect poor audit planning and result in unnecessary costs (Lumb 2005b).
51. Lumb (2005b).
52. This is somewhat surprising considering that the crafting of AS no. 2 required the PCAOB staff to have expertise not just in financial statement auditing but in control process auditing as well as in the integration of the two (Kinney 2005b).
53. Hamilton (2005).
54. Lumb (2005b, p. 1).

pose the most significant and consequential auditing challenges.[55] Division staff consider general economic, industry, and issuer-specific factors. Further, inspections encompass the audit firm's quality control system, which includes client acceptance and retention decisions. So the PCAOB's engagement risk considerations do overlap with those of auditors.

In addition, the board has established the Office of Research and Analysis to monitor, analyze, and report on world and U.S. events that affect the capital markets and that present risks to U.S. public company financial reporting. The office intends to provide the board with continuous and contemporaneous assessments of risks to identify trends and anomalies, assist the staff in selecting audit engagements for inspection and enforcement, and identify issues for standard setting. Because this office is just being organized, it is too new to assess. But rather than using the office only to inform itself and the staff, the board could also use the office to alert auditors to issues affecting misstatement risk (and overall engagement risk) and even to develop and disseminate tools for doing so.

Perhaps more controversial is that the PCAOB also needs to consider auditor business risk. One of the objectives of the Federal Reserve is to maintain the credibility of the banking system and the public's confidence in it. Likewise, one objective of the SEC and PCAOB is to maintain confidence in the U.S. capital markets. To do that requires the PCAOB to maintain confidence in the firms that audit SEC registrants.[56] Auditor business risk is a risk shared by auditors and regulators alike. In the long run, the PCAOB cannot manage its own business risk by undermining confidence in the value of audits and the viability of the firms that audit public companies.

But, so far, the PCAOB appears reluctant to recognize audit firm business risk as a risk it shares; it may even be exacerbating audit firm business risk as it manages its own business risk.[57] For example, the PCAOB ignored early warnings that AS no. 2 went beyond SOX requirements and would be very costly,[58] and when those warnings proved true, the board publicly aligned itself with clients complaining about audit fees.[59] Recently, the PCAOB chairman said: "In a liti-

---

55. PCAOB (2004, pp. 10–11).
56. American Assembly (2003).
57. An exception is the press release issued in response to the KPMG deferred prosecution agreement with the Justice Department, in which the board stated: "The PCAOB previously performed a limited inspection of KPMG's auditing work . . . and based on the[se] inspection[s], the Board remains confident in KPMG's ability to perform high-quality audits of public companies" (PCAOB 2005).
58. Hamilton (2004a).
59. Even though SOX assigns audit committees the responsibility for overseeing auditor compensation, early on board member Kayla Gillan assured registrants that the PCAOB would be on the lookout for any evidence of "price gouging" (Hamilton 2004c). Historically, the Federal Trade Commission and the Anti-

gious society, there's no question that some auditors may be protecting themselves by doing work that all of us might think objectively is excessive. . . . That I want to see eliminated."[60]

Unfortunately, as the PCAOB, SEC registrants, and the media question the extent of post-SOX audit effort, sight has been lost of a more fundamental issue—the effect of this new government regulatory regime on reducing the risk of fraudulent financial reporting, which was the primary motivation for SOX. Users expect auditors to detect fraudulent financial reporting, and SOX has certainly increased that expectation.[61] However, users have little appreciation for the fact that management can override controls in any company, even those with controls that appear to be operating effectively under section 404; users have little appetite for the limitations of auditing in detecting intentional misstatements, even when management works collusively and actively to conceal the misstatements from the auditors; and users have little tolerance for a non-zero defect rate, which is implicit in the notion of "reasonable assurance."

Moreover, in the face of future instances of major financial fraud, the PCAOB, as the direct regulator of auditing, does not have the options for deflecting criticism and avoiding responsibility that were available to previous overseers of self-regulation, like the pre-SOX Securities and Exchange Commission. The PCAOB cannot fall back on lack of funding and inadequate resources as a rationale for regulatory failures. Even though the PCAOB's annual budget requires SEC approval, approval is not conditioned on congressional funding or limited by the SEC's own budgetary considerations. SOX (section 109) instituted annual support fees from SEC registrants and registered audit firms to cover the PCAOB's budget.

Fraudulent financial reporting therefore represents an overarching risk for both auditors and the PCAOB. The next section discusses this risk in the context of the legal liability system, explains why it threatens the viability of audit firms, and proposes a risk-sharing mechanism to mitigate the threat.

Trust Division of the Justice Department have focused on competitive conditions within all the professions, including competitive pricing in the accounting profession (Kinney 2005b). Audit regulators like the POB and SEC have focused on audit quality and, in that regard, have been concerned about fees being too low, thus creating budget and time pressures that might compromise audit quality (Panel on Audit Effectiveness 2000). In testimony before the House Committee on Financial Services, the PCAOB chair said that in the future the board would be as critical of auditors that it discovered had done too much "unnecessary" work as those that had done too little. "Audit Firms Urged to Cut Fees," *Financial Times*, April 25, 2005.

60. "Mr. McDonough, You Have the Floor: The Accounting Watchdog on Sarbanes-Oxley, Excessive Auditing, and Investor Trust," *Business Week*, August 1, 2005, p. 56.

61. See, for example, Solomon and Peecher (2004); Kinney (2005b).

Fraudulent Financial Reporting and Legal Liability

Fraudulent financial reporting increases the likelihood and severity of auditor litigation.[62] To illustrate the threat to audit firm viability from fraudulent financial reporting, table 4-1 uses a sample of fifty-one securities class action suits filed and resolved between 1996 and mid-2002 (that is, since the 1995 Reform Act but before enactment of SOX). The sample consists of securities class actions with auditor defendants in which both the total class settlement amount and the auditor's contribution, if any, are publicly available.[63] All but one of these actions involved the largest audit firms (that is, the B6, B5, or B4 or the three next-largest firms), and the sample represents at least 25 percent of the class actions filed against the largest audit firms during the period.[64] The table gives an overview of the sample (panel A), summarizes total and auditor resolutions (panel B), and provides selected characteristics for each total resolution category (panel C).

Panel A shows that the median decrease in the market value of the equity of the public companies over the class period was slightly less than $473 million, although the decreases ranged from $12 million to almost $23 billion (not shown in the table).[65] The median total settlement was $14.5 million (3.6 percent of equity decrease), and the median auditor payment was $1.8 million (with medians of 0.4 percent for the percent of equity decrease and 21.5 percent for the percent of the total settlement amount).

The matrix in panel B of table 4-1 places auditor resolutions in three categories (auditor dismissed or no contribution, auditor contributed 100 percent of the total resolution, and auditor contributed less than 100 percent), and it places total resolution amounts in four categories (under $5 million, $5 to $19.5 million, $20 to $100 million, and more than $100 million). Amounts of more than $100 million are called *mega-settlements*.

Auditors were dismissed or made no contribution in 23 percent (twelve of fifty-one) of the class actions, and that occurred most frequently with total resolutions of less than $5 million (that is, in seven of twelve actions, or 58 percent).

---

62. For example, see Palmrose (1987), Carcello and Palmrose (1994), and Scholz and Palmrose (2004).
63. These resolution amounts do not consider defense costs, which can be considerable.
64. The percentage was estimated from numbers disclosed by the POB, based on information reported to the POB's Quality Control Inquiry Committee.
65. This computation reflects the difference between the highest value of market capitalization during the class period and the market capitalization on the day after the class period ended. This represents a proxy for legally compensable losses, which likely are less because other factors unrelated to the allegations may also have caused companies' stock prices to decline. However, the computation does not reflect losses by other types of plaintiffs, including debt holders.

Table 4-1. *Sample of Fifty-One Class Actions with Auditor Defendants*[a]

Panel A. Overview

Result	Median (N = 51)
Decrease in equity over class period[b]	$472.9 million
Total settlement	
Amount	$14.5 million
As percent of equity decrease	3.6
Auditor payment	
Amount	$1.8 million
As percent of total settlement	21.5
As percent of equity decrease	0.4

Panel B. Resolution

		Total resolution amount (millions)			
Auditor contribution	Total (N = 51)	Under $5 (N = 16)	$5–$19.5 (N = 15)	$20–$100 (N = 11)	Over $100 (N = 9)
None or dismissed					
(number)	12	7	3	1	1
100 percent					
Median amount	...	$0.9	...	...	...
Number	3	3	...	...	...
Less than 100 percent					
Median amount	...	$0.7	$2.6	$11.7	$75
Number	36	6	12	10	8
Total	51	16	15	11	9

Panel C. Total Resolutions, Comparing Circumstances

Circumstance					
Decrease in market value over $3 billion					
(number/percent)	10 (20)	0	1 (7)	0	9 (100)
Mean class period (days)	622	530	612	592	837
Fraud (number/percent)	23 (45)	5 (31)	4 (27)	6 (55)	8 (89)
NYSE listed					
(number/percent)	15 (29)	1 (6)	4 (27)	3 (27)	7 (78)
Bankrupt					
(number/percent)	19 (37)	5 (31)	7 (47)	6 (55)	1 (11)
Restatement					
(number/percent)	36 (71)	10 (63)	9 (60)	9 (82)	8 (89)

a. Filed 1996–2001 and resolved by 2002, with data on both total and auditor resolution amounts.
b. Computed as the difference between the highest value of market capitalization during the class period and the market capitalization on the day after the class period.

In a few instances (three of fifty-one, or 6 percent), auditors contributed 100 percent of the settlement amount, and all of those cases involved total settlements of less than $5 million. In the majority of actions (thirty-six of fifty-one, or 71 percent), auditors contributed less than 100 percent. Panel B shows that the median auditor resolution jumped to $75 million in the mega-settlement category, an important detail. Although the defendant audit firms managed each of those cases without compromising their firm's viability, the cases likely posed the greatest risk to the firm before being resolved.

Panel C describes some distinguishing characteristics of these cases, revealing frequencies (or means) for selected client circumstances for each total resolution category. These circumstances include the class period, decreases in market value over the class period that exceeded $3 billion, fraudulent financial reporting, NYSE listing, bankruptcy, and restatements. Restatements appear to have been common across all resolution categories. Only one company with a mega-settlement declared bankruptcy. All of the mega-settlements involved decreases in market value during the class period of more than $3 billion, while only one non–mega-settlement did. Other distinguishing (and interrelated) circumstances for mega-settlements were much longer class periods (mean 837 days), NYSE listing (78 percent), and fraudulent financial reporting (89 percent). All but one of the mega-settlements involved fraudulent financial reporting, and the one without fraud involved no auditor contribution (panel B).[66]

While these data highlight how failing to detect fraudulent financial reporting, particularly on large clients with high cap values, puts audit firms at risk in the litigation process, the data do not reflect resolutions for most lawsuits resulting from the bear market of 2000–02—a number of which likewise involved fraudulent financial reporting—and the data precede SOX.[67] Not only the dollar amount of subsequent securities class action settlements but also the number and magnitude of mega-settlements have increased.[68]

---

66. While the client acceptance and retention decision failed to filter out all the cases that eventuated in litigation against audit firms, note that the mega-settlements tended to involve large companies listed on the NYSE. These are among the characteristics that can otherwise distinguish desirable audit clients, which helps make the client acceptance and retention decision an imperfect risk management mechanism, especially at the upper end of the risk distribution.

67. In addition to other changes, post-SOX auditor litigation exposure has increased because of section 404 and AS no. 2. For example, before SOX a restatement did not equate to a failure in the financial statement audit or review (see Palmrose and Scholz 2004). But since SOX, a restatement presumes an unidentified material weakness in controls on financial reporting and therefore hinders defending the audit of internal control effectiveness.

68. Buckberg and others (2005).

These trends likewise apply to auditor litigation, and the data suggest that current unresolved and potential "mega" cases can threaten the stability of even the largest audit firms. For example, consider data on auditor resolutions in excess of $100 million. The first auditor settlement of that magnitude occurred in the 1980s, when there were two.[69] Similarly, there were two in the late 1990s (ignoring global settlements in the early 1990s by several firms over audits of multiple financial institutions). But, so far, from 2001 to 2005, there have been eight auditor settlements of U.S. litigation that exceeded $100 million, and all but two involved fraudulent financial reporting.[70]

Auditor legal liability is intended to both deter audit failures and compensate users for auditors' proportionate share of losses caused by such failures. If auditors fail to detect misstatements, including those due to fraudulent financial reporting, users expect to be compensated for their losses. Nonetheless, audit firms cannot cover user losses for significant or catastrophic amounts and remain viable businesses, especially since audit firms cannot obtain insurance to cover such amounts. For example, net U.S. revenues from all sources for the four largest audit firms totaled about $20 billion for their 2003 fiscal years,[71] while almost $23 trillion was invested by holders of public securities at the end of 2003.[72]

Furthermore, to succeed as deterrence mechanisms, civil litigation and regulatory enforcement cannot be random. That is, actual auditor liability and penalties need to reflect the merits of the claims against auditors, including the degree of the auditor's departure from standards of due care, other applicable professional standards, and PCAOB rules. Obtaining a reasonable evaluation within the legal system of the merits of claims of alleged audit failures and the monetary worth, if any, of such claims continues to be a vexing problem, even a decade after passage of the 1995 Reform Act.

The legal system is premised on the option of trial. However, that premise is acknowledged to be highly problematic for defendants in securities class actions.[73]

---

69. For the purposes of this illustration, auditor resolution data over time are not adjusted for inflation (Palmrose 1999). One of these cases involved payments of up to $163 million over audits of ESM. At that time the audit firm was reported to have adequate insurance coverage.

70. The two without fraud involved failed financial and financial services institutions, representing another characteristic that appears in some large auditor resolutions.

71. "Top 100 for 2004: America's 100 Largest Public Accounting Firms," *Public Accounting Report*, August 31, 2004, p. 6.

72. FASB (2005).

73. Alexander (1991) explains that this is partly due to directors' and officers' insurance, which is available to fund settlements, but not necessarily to fund trial judgments, where findings of fraud can trigger fraud exclusions and nullify coverage. More than 1,700 federal securities class actions were filed between

Decades ago non-jury (judge) trials were available in accounting and auditing litigation, but they no longer occur unless agreed to by both plaintiff and defendant.[74] Although judges may lack expertise in accounting and auditing matters, it is certain, with limited exceptions, that juries do. That makes it difficult for the legal system to determine the merits of users' claims and the relative contribution to users' losses from misstated financials, if any, due to GAAP, audit-related standards, auditor performance, (now) regulator performance, the actions of various other parties, and client characteristics (including declines in performance or failure).

So, even though defense lawyers "have become more sophisticated about honing their cases before mock juries,"[75] trial itself is not really a viable option for auditors when users claim billions of dollars in losses, even when the probability of plaintiffs' winning is very low. This is especially true when fraudulent financial reporting or large unexpected business failures occur.[76] These circumstances engender great jury sympathy for plaintiffs and exacerbate jury unwillingness or inability to appreciate complex and technical responses to the essential question: Where were the auditors? Audit firms cannot take the risk of trying cases to verdict that "bet the entire audit firm." It is important to note that these conditions also push settlement amounts upward and contribute to the mega-settlement trend just described.[77]

Currently, when audit firms are sued for failing to detect or disclose misstated financials (including from fraudulent financial reporting), the firms have to fully assume the risks and manage the limitations and disadvantages of the legal process. In fact, so far the PCAOB has only added a new layer of potential discipline and enforcement. A report by the American Assembly recognizes this disconnect and proposes that the PCAOB share some risk (that is, misstatement, engagement, and business risks) with audit firms. It suggests the following:

—When the PCAOB's inspection and evaluation of auditors finds that an auditor has satisfactory quality control, that auditor could be given a measure of protection from civil liability.

1996 and 2004 (MacLean 2005); about half had some accounting-related allegations, the majority of which involved claims of misstated interim or annual financial statements, and a subset of those had auditor defendants. In spite of indications, more cases may be going to trial (MacLean 2005); since the 1995 Reform Act, only four federal securities class actions with post–Reform Act claims (claims filed after 1995) have been tried to verdict (Tu 2005). Two of those trials had auditor defendants, who "won" in both cases.

74. Palmrose (1991).
75. MacLean (2005).
76. Note that these represent large ex post realizations on client business risk and client misconduct risk described in figure 4-1.
77. For example, see Alexander (1991) and Palmrose (1991).

—The PCAOB plans to scrutinize audits of companies deemed to have a higher risk profile. When these examinations find the audits satisfactory, the auditors could receive an additional measure of protection.[78]

These suggestions are worthwhile, and I modify and extend them by proposing establishment of an auditing master's office under the PCAOB umbrella but independent of the PCAOB.

Auditing Master Proposal

Before describing the auditing master proposal, I summarize below some of the major points discussed in the previous sections:

—The PCAOB, as the SOX-mandated government regulator, shares a number of risks with audit firms and therefore could be allocated some responsibility for any audit failures.

—The PCAOB is not an "objective" regulator. It has an incentive to maintain its operations, it lacks checks and balances, and it has problems related to expertise and transparency.

—Audit firms are highly regulated businesses. Regulations and market conditions prevent audit firms from using most risk-transfer and -sharing mechanisms (including insurance against significant and catastrophic claims).

—The client acceptance and retention decision is an important risk management tool. But if the client has been retained, only misstatement risk can be mitigated by more effective auditing. Moreover, even effective audits will not detect on a timely basis all instances of fraudulent financial reporting or prevent client misconduct and unexpected declines in client performance or failure (figure 4-1).

—The legal system currently cannot effectively assess the merits or determine the monetary worth of claims involving accounting and auditing issues.

—Trial is not a viable option for auditor defendants in cases claiming multibillion-dollar damages (especially those involving fraudulent financial reporting). Without the option of going to trial, the defendant is forced to settle, and the resulting settlement amount is higher than damages would have been if trial had been an option.

—Current (unresolved) and potential future mega-cases may undermine the stability of even the largest audit firms.

An auditing master, similar to the master occasionally used to advise the court in a legal proceeding, is one way to address a number of the issues raised in this chapter and to respond to the overarching need for independent, objective

78. American Assembly (2003, p. 17).

accounting and auditing expertise to inform participants in the legal process. An auditing master's office could be created under the PCAOB umbrella but independent of PCAOB supervision and control. Broad and deep accounting and auditing expertise would be a prerequisite for office staff.[79]

The purpose of the office would be to assess auditor compliance with GAAP and with PCAOB auditing standards following allegations of audit failure resulting from litigation and regulatory enforcement on audit clients that are SEC registrants. The office would be able to determine the merits, if any, of the allegations and the relative role of the various contributing factors, whether auditor performance, audit firm quality control systems and methodologies, standards (auditing, quality control, independence, and professional standards and so forth), other regulatory processes (for example, PCAOB inspections and risk assessment), GAAP, or client characteristics.[80] That determination would then be available to audit firms (to use in the legal process to resolve the allegations) and to the PCAOB (to use in the regulatory process to improve its standards, inspections, and so forth).

To avoid violating confidentiality requirements imposed on the PCAOB by SOX, defendant audit firms would voluntarily furnish assessments by the auditing master's office to the court as part of the legal process. Input from the auditing master's office would represent "friend of the court" advice on the merits and reasonable worth of plaintiffs' claims, based on the facts and circumstances of the specific case and on how those facts and circumstances compare with those in resolved cases (and with the resolution amounts in such cases).[81] Of course, declining to voluntarily disclose any information would be an indication of its potential negative content and might put a defendant audit firm at a disadvantage in a legal proceeding.

Establishing an auditing master's office under the PCAOB umbrella has several advantages. It should avoid the need to obtain congressional approval to establish the office, because the PCAOB should be able to do so under its existing SOX authority, with SEC concurrence. The PCAOB umbrella would give the auditing

---

79. The office should also be able to hire part-time staff and consultants with special expertise.

80. This determination could also distinguish between U.S. and foreign audit firm affiliates and between the PCAOB and foreign regulators.

81. Currently plaintiffs and defendants hire experts to conduct assessments. However, these experts do not necessarily have detailed knowledge of all the accounting and auditing facts and circumstances of the particular case (and certainly not of how they compare with those of other auditor litigation cases). Moreover, among the experts' tools for settlement negotiations are "high-level" regression models that explain variances in past settlements (Buckberg and others 2005). These models rely on variables that, at best, represent very crude proxies for accounting and auditing matters and the merits of allegations against auditors over departures from accounting and auditing standards.

master's office access to all necessary confidential data, with appropriate legal protections. On the other hand, making the office independent of the PCAOB would give it the incentive and objectivity to evaluate the regulator.[82] Also, such an office would relieve the PCAOB of some of its current inspection workload and allow it to better focus its efforts.

There is a precedent for establishing an auditing master's office within the regulatory structure. The office would actually modify and redirect the POB's Quality Control Inquiry Committee (QCIC) process.[83] Under the POB's self-regulatory system, member firms were required to report to the QCIC, within thirty days of being served a complaint, all matters of alleged audit failures involving SEC clients arising from litigation or regulatory investigations, including criminal indictments. The QCIC reviewed the allegations to determine whether there were deficiencies in the reporting firm's quality control system, its compliance with the system, or its professional standards. The QCIC made no determination concerning guilt, innocence, or liability of the reporting firm.[84] The PCAOB has not created a function that duplicates the QCIC process, although parts of it occur through registration, inspections, and enforcement.

Finally, an auditing master's office represents a feasible incremental change within the existing structure. It does not require radical changes in long-standing contractual and market arrangements based on theoretical, controversial, and untested proposals, such as proposals for financial statement insurance,[85] or on major reform initiatives, such as proposals for liability caps.[86]

In the current climate, audit firms can be expected to engender little sympathy and support for enacting radical changes. But an auditing master's office is one example of what can be done to address audit firm risk management and viability problems, which are rooted mostly in regulatory restrictions and market

---

82. The board created the Office of Internal Oversight and Performance Assurance (IOPA) to conduct internal reviews and examinations to help ensure the efficiency, effectiveness, and integrity of PCAOB programs and operations. While the purpose of the IOPA differs from that of the auditing master, the IOPA also reports to the board and so lacks the requisite independence to objectively evaluate the role of the regulator in instances of audit failure. Finally, the IOPA as currently constituted would not have the necessary expertise to function as an auditing master. Similar issues, previously discussed, arise with both the PCAOB inspections and enforcement offices.

83. An auditing master's office also would incorporate elements of the National Transportation Safety Board (NTSB) (POB 1993). The NTSB is an independent agency that determines the probable cause of transportation accidents and promotes transportation safety through publication of safety recommendations. For some aviation accidents, the NTSB delegates the actual investigation to the Federal Aviation Administration.

84. Panel on Audit Effectiveness (2000, p. 193).

85. Ronen (2002).

86. "Called to Account: The Future of Auditing," *Economist*, November 18, 2004.

constraints. While a more limited proposal by the American Assembly (2003) has found no traction within the PCAOB, the burden is on the PCAOB to suggest reasonable alternatives.

In conclusion, there has been little consideration of the usefulness and limitations of the SOX-created government regulatory system of the PCAOB. Hopefully, proposals such as that for an auditing master's office will encourage further discussion and research on the impact of government regulation on external (independent) auditing and the future role of large, privately owned audit firms as financial gatekeepers.

References

AccountingWeb.com. 2004. "SEC Chairman: Find Solutions before Problems Explode." *AccountingWeb.com* (September 30) [www.accountingweb.com].
Alexander, Janet C. 1991. "Do the Merits Matter? A Study of Settlements in Securities Class Actions." *Stanford Law Review* 43 (February): 497–598.
American Assembly. 2003. *The Future of the Accounting Profession*. Columbia University, 103rd American Assembly, November 13–15.
American Institute of Certified Public Accountants (AICPA). 1992. *Audit Risk Alert: 1992*. New York.
———. 2005. *Management Override of Internal Controls: The Achilles' Heel of Fraud Prevention (The Audit Committee and Oversight of Financial Reporting)*. New York.
Arens, Alvin A., and James K. Loebbecke. 1991. *Auditing: An Integrated Approach*. Englewood Cliffs, N.J.: Prentice-Hall.
Baber, William R., Kishna R. Kumar, and Thomas Verghese. 1995. "Client Security Price Reactions to the Laventhol and Horwath Bankruptcy." *Journal of Accounting Research* 33, no. 1: 385–95.
Blackwell, David W., Thomas R. Noland, and Drew B. Winters. 1998. "The Value of Auditor Assurance: Evidence from Loan Pricing." *Journal of Accounting Research* 36, no. 2: 57–70.
Bradshaw, Mark T., Scott A. Richardson, and Richard G. Sloan. 2001. "Do Analysts and Auditors Use Information in Accruals?" *Journal of Accounting Research* 39, no. 1: 45–75.
Brown, Mike and Zoe-Vonna Palmrose. 2005. *Thog's Guide to Quantum Economics: 50,000 Years of Accounting Basics for the Future*. Duvall, Wash.: MAC Productions.
Buckberg, Elaine, and others. 2005. *Recent Trends in Shareholder Class Action Litigation: Bear Market Cases Bring Big Settlements*. New York: NERA Economic Consulting (Marsh & McLennan Company) (February).
Carcello, Joseph, and Zoe-Vonna Palmrose. 1994. "Auditor Litigation and Modified Reporting on Bankrupt Clients." *Journal of Accounting Research* 32 (supplement): 1–30.
Carmichael, Douglas R. 2004. "The Accounting and Auditing Connection." Presentation at the Third Annual Financial Reporting Conference, Baruch College (CUNY), April 29.
Chow, Chee W. 1982. "The Demand for External Auditing: Size, Debt and Ownership Influences." *Accounting Review* 57, no. 2: 272–91.
DeChow, Patricia M., Richard G. Sloan, and Amy P. Sweeney. 1995. "Detecting Earnings Management." *Accounting Review* 70, no. 2: 193–225.

———. 1996. "Causes and Consequences of Earnings Manipulation: An Analysis of Firms Subject to Enforcement Actions by the SEC." *Contemporary Accounting Research* 13, no. 1: 1–36.

Dye, Ronald. 1993. "Auditing Standards, Legal Liability, and Auditor Wealth." *Journal of Political Economy* 101, no. 5: 877–914.

Financial Accounting Standards Board (FASB). 2005. "Elevating Investor Input." FASB Presentation. Norwalk, Conn. (July).

Greenhouse, Linda. 2005. "Securities Fraud Standards Upheld by Supreme Court." *NYTimes.com* (April 20).

Hamilton, James. 2004a. "Banking Group Urges PCAOB to Narrow Auditor Internal Control Standard." *CCH PCAOB Reporter* 2 (February 17): 1, 7.

———. 2004b. "Federal Governor Cautions against Quick Move to Fair Value Accounting." *CCH PCAOB Reporter* 2 (October 25): 6, 13.

———. 2004c. "Gillan Advises Company Management on Internal Control Audits." *CCH PCAOB Reporter* 2 (November 8): 3, 8.

———. 2005. "Accounting Industry Troubled by Board Proposal on Secondary Liability." *CCH PCAOB Reporter* 3 (March 14): 6, 13–14.

Huss, H. Fenwick, and Fred A. Jacobs. 1991. "Risk Containment: Exploring Auditor Decisions in the Engagement Process." *Auditing: A Journal of Practice and Theory* 10, no. 3: 16–32.

Khurana, Inder K., and K. K. Raman. 2004. "Litigation Risk and the Financial Reporting Credibility of Big 4 versus non-Big 4 Audits: Evidence from Anglo-American Countries." *Accounting Review* 79, no. 2: 473–95.

King, Ronald R. 2002. "An Experimental Investigation of Self-Serving Biases in an Auditing Trust Game: The Effect of Group Affiliation." *Accounting Review* 77, no. 2: 265–84.

Kinney, William R., Jr. 2000. *Information Quality Assurance and Internal Control for Management Decision Making*. Boston: Irwin McGraw-Hill.

———. 2005a. "The Auditor as Gatekeeper: A Perilous Expectations Gap," in *Restoring Trust in American Business*, edited by J. W. Lorsch, L. Berlowitz, and A. Zelleke. Cambridge, Mass.: MIT Press and American Academy of Arts and Sciences: 99–108.

———. 2005b. "Twenty-Five Years of Audit Deregulation and Re-regulation: What Does It Mean for 2005 and Beyond?" *Auditing: A Journal of Practice and Theory* 24 (supplement): 89–109.

Kinney, William R., Jr., Christine Botosan, and Zoe-Vonna Palmrose. 2006. "Do Issuer Benefits from Mandated Audits Exceed Audit Firm Fees?" Deloitte/KU Audit Symposium (April).

Kinney, William R., Jr., Zoe-Vonna Palmrose, and Susan Scholz. 2004. "Auditor Independence, Non-Audit Services, and Restatements: Was the U.S. Government Right?" *Journal of Accounting Research* 42, no. 3: 561–88.

Larcker, David F., and Scott A. Richardson. 2004. "Fees Paid to Audit Firms, Accrual Choices, and Corporate Governance." *Journal of Accounting Research* 42, no. 3: 625–58.

Leftwich, Richard. 1983. "Accounting Information in Private Markets: Evidence from Private Lending Agreements." *Accounting Review* 58, no. 1: 23–43.

Logue, Ann C. 2005. "Materiality Threshold Drops to 'Zero' for Restatements." *Compliance Week* (June 28).

Lumb, Jacquelyn. 2005a. "PCAOB Announces Next Actions at SEC's Roundtable on Internal Controls." *CCH PCAOB Reporter* 3 (April 25): 1, 10–14.

———. 2005b. "PCAOB Issues Policy Statement on the Implementation of Auditing Standard No. 2." *CCH PCAOB Reporter* 3 (May 23): 1, 8–9.

———. 2005c. "Panelists Discuss Experiences with Section 404: Small Business Panel." *CCH PCAOB Reporter* 3 (June 20): 10–11.

———. 2005d. "Panelists Review Impact of Securities Offering Reform Rules on Auditors." *CCH PCAOB Reporter* 3 (August 29): 3.

MacLean, Pamela A. 2005. "Securities Class Action Trials on the Rise: Larger Settlements, Savvy Lawyering Key." *National Law Journal* (August 9).

Mansi, Sattar A., William F. Maxwell, and Darios P. Miller. 2004. "Does Auditor Quality and Tenure Matter to Investors? Evidence from the Bond Market." *Journal of Accounting Research* 42, no. 4: 755–93.

McCubbins, Mathew. 1985. "The Legislative Design of Regulatory Structure." *American Journal of Political Science* 29, no. 4: 721–48.

McMullen, Dorothy A., Kannan Raghunandan, and Dasaratha V. Rama. 1996. "Internal Control Reports and Financial Reporting Problems." *Accounting Horizons* 10, no. 4: 67–75.

Menon, Krishnagopal, and David D. Williams. 1994. "The Insurance Hypothesis and Market Prices." *Accounting Review* 69, no. 2: 327–342.

Moore, Don A., and others. 2006. "Conflicts of Interest and the Case of Auditor Independence: Moral Seduction and Strategic Issue Cycling." *Academy of Management Review* 31, no. 1 (January): 10–29.

Myers, James N., and others. 2005. "The Length of Auditor-Client Relationships and Financial Statement Restatements." Working Paper. Texas A&M University (June).

Nelson, Mark W. 2006. "Ameliorating Conflicts of Interest in Auditing: Effects of Recent Reforms on Auditors and Their Clients." *Academy of Management Review* 31, no. 1 (January): 30–42.

Nelson, Mark W., John A. Elliott, and Robin L. Tarpley. 2002. "Evidence from Auditors about Managers' and Auditors' Earnings Management Decisions." *Accounting Review* 77 (Quality of Earnings Conference Supplement): 175–202.

Nelson, Mark W., Steven D. Smith, and Zoe-Vonna Palmrose. 2005. "The Effect of Quantitative Materiality Approach on Auditors' Adjustment Decisions." *Accounting Review* 80 (July): 897–920.

Palmrose, Zoe-Vonna. 1987. "Litigation and Independent Auditors: The Role of Business Failures and Management Fraud." *Auditing: A Journal of Practice and Theory* 6 (Spring): 90–103.

———. 1991. "Trials of Legal Disputes Involving Independent Auditors: Some Empirical Evidence." *Journal of Accounting Research* 29 (Supplement): 149–85.

———. 1999. *Studies in Accounting Research 33: Empirical Research in Auditor Litigation: Considerations and Data.* Sarasota, Fla.: American Accounting Association.

———. 2005. "The FASB's Move toward Fair Value Accounting: Is It Auditable?" Presentation at the American Accounting Association Annual Convention, August 8, 2005.

Palmrose, Zoe-Vonna, and Susan Scholz. 2004. "The Accounting Causes and Legal Consequences of Non-GAAP Reporting: Evidence from Restatements." *Contemporary Accounting Research* 21, no. 1: 139–80.

Panel on Audit Effectiveness. 2000. *The Panel on Audit Effectiveness: Report and Recommendations.* Stamford, Conn.: Public Oversight Board (August 31).

Powell, Scott S. 2005. "Costs of Sarbanes-Oxley Are Out of Control." *Wall Street Journal* (March 21): op-ed.

Public Company Accounting Oversight Board (PCAOB). 2004. *Annual Report.* Washington.
———. 2005. "Board Issues Statement Regarding Oversight of KPMG." PCAOB Press Release (August 29).
———. 2006. "Emerging Issue: The Effects on Independence of Indemnification, Limitation of Liability, and Other Litigation-Related Clauses in Audit Engagement Letters." Standing Advisory Group Meeting Discussion Paper (February 9).
Public Oversight Board (POB). 1993. *A Special Report by the Public Oversight Board of the SEC Practice Section, AICPA.* Stamford, Conn. (March 5).
Ronen, Joshua. 2002. "Post-Enron Reform: Financial Statement Insurance and GAAP Revisited." *Stanford Journal of Law, Business, and Finance* 8, no. 1: 39–68.
Rosario, Ric R., and Suzanne M. Holl. 2005. "Stay out of Trouble." *Journal of Accountancy* 200, no. 2: 67–73.
Securities Mosaic. 2005. "SEC Committee Begins to Shape Its Vision of Enforcement and Market Caps." *Securities Class Action: Weekly News.* Stanford Law School Securities Class Action Clearinghouse (August 12, 2005).
Smitherman, Laura. 2005. "Corporations Protest Cost to Comply with Law." *Baltimore Sun,* March 15.
Solomon, Ira, and Mark Peecher. 2004. "Sox 404: A Billion Here, a Billion There . . ." *Wall Street Journal* (November 9): B1.
Strawser, Jerry R. 1991. "The Role of Acountant Reports in Users' Decision-Making Processes: A Review of Empirical Research." *Journal of Accounting Literature* 10: 181–208.
Taub, Scott. 2005. "SEC Update and Developments." Speech at the American Accounting Association Annual Convention, Auditing Section Luncheon, San Francisco, August 8.
Tu, Michael C. 2005. "Ten Years after the Reform Act: Trends in Securities Class Action Trials." *Securities Reform Act Litigation Reporter* 19, no. 4: 475–79.
Wallison, Peter J. 2005. "Rein in the Public Company Accounting Oversight Board: Guest Article." *AccountingWeb.com* (January 31).
Watts, Ross L. 2003. "Conservatism in Accounting Part I: Explanations and Implications." *Accounting Horizons* 17, no. 4: 207–21.
———. 2005. "The FASB's Move toward Fair Value Accounting: Is It Auditable?" Presentation at the American Accounting Association Annual Convention, San Francisco, August 8.
Zeff, Stephen A. 2003. "How the U.S. Accounting Profession Got Where It Is Today: Part II." *Accounting Horizons* 17, no. 4: 267–86.

COMMENT BY
Peter Wallison

NOT ONLY DOES this terrific chapter recognize a very significant problem, it also develops a very practical solution. I question whether the agency involved will follow Zoe-Vonna's suggestion, but I do think that she has identified a real problem and worked hard to find a solution that might actually work, under the right kind of leadership at the Public Company Accounting Oversight Board (PCAOB).

I'd like to reinterpret a bit the argument that Zoe-Vonna makes. As I see it, the main problem is that auditors cannot detect or discover fraud unless they stumble on it. I have always understood that accountants never claim that they can discover fraud.

The WorldCom case is a great example of the problem. If Arthur Andersen's auditors had looked at more of the company's accounting, they might have been lucky enough to have stumbled on the way that WorldCom was treating its leases, but they didn't. Fraud is, by definition, concealed. The purpose of fraud is to put something over on someone; if you're management and you control the financial statements and you're halfway clever, you ought to be able to do it—whether or not the gatekeepers involved, in this case auditors, have any conflict of interest.

However, that is not, as I see it, a perspective that is shared by the public, by the media, or most important, perhaps, by Congress. I think that, in general, those groups assume that when fraud occurs, auditors should discover it. That is essentially what Congress and the media have been assuming about the Sarbanes-

Oxley Act—that the directors, the audit committee, or the auditors would discover fraud if they weren't conflicted in their relationships with management. As a result, it has become impossible, I think, for counsel representing an audit firm in a fraud case to make the argument to the jury that the failure to discover fraud was not the fault of the auditor.

The legal system simply does not work anymore to allocate losses according to malfeasance when there has been a fraud. Auditors, who couldn't possibly have discovered a fraud, are now charged with malfeasance and, therefore, now run tremendous risks when they certify financial statements. As Zoe-Vonna points out, many of those risks are so large that they cannot be adequately insured against. So we are in some jeopardy of losing one or more of the Big Four accounting firms. Recently, KPMG was saved by prosecutorial discretion, probably because the prosecutors had already destroyed Arthur Andersen and had realized their mistake. We cannot expect that kind of sympathy from a plaintiff's counsel or from a principal plaintiff, such as New York state comptroller Allan Hevesi, who has an accounting firm over a barrel.

So how do we address these risks? Zoe-Vonna's suggestion is excellent. She points out that the PCAOB also shares some of the risks, and having the imprimatur of the government, it could go into court or at least allow the accounting firm involved to go into court and say, "We complied with all of the requirements of an audit and we did everything required by our professional standards, but we still could not discover this fraud." That might provide some real practical defense. The author has gone one step further to suggest a very smart refinement—establishment of an independent auditing master's office within the PCAOB that would have the responsibility for making a declaration to a court that the auditing firm has carried out a thorough audit, even if they did not find a fraud. That is a very good idea.

The need for such a reform was demonstrated just a couple of months ago, when the SEC and the PCAOB held a roundtable on the cost of section 404 of the Sarbanes-Oxley Act. They listened to all the complaints about section 404. In the end, they concluded that they were not at fault; it was the accountants: "They're just focusing on too many details." That declaration, if it were really based on a lack of knowledge about what is happening in the accounting profession, might be excusable. But it cannot be based on ignorance; it has to be disingenuous. The SEC and PCAOB must understand that accounting firms go through a detailed process under section 404 because they are subject to lawsuits on the basis of hindsight. If they miss one small detail in the audit of some internal control, and the plaintiff's attorney shows that there is a logical connection between that missing detail and the eventual fraud, the auditing firm is likely to be held responsible. From that perspective, creating a separate auditing master's office is a great idea. As I see it, the audit masters at the PCAOB would provide some support to accounting firms trying to defend themselves against liability for failing to discover fraud. The audit masters would declare to a court that all the rules were followed—the audit was proper.

So I like that idea quite a lot. I want to mention one more way that this issue could be addressed. On November 13–15, 2003, the American Assembly held a conference on the future of the accounting industry where a lot of suggestions were made about how the accounting industry could be saved from its troubling situation. One of the most interesting ideas was that the auditor's certification—that the financial statements are materially correct—is quite misleading. Many things that go into the preparation of GAAP financials are management estimates, and auditors cannot really assess the quality of those estimates. One example is the collectibility of receivables. Management always estimates the collectibility of receivables, and the auditors have very little ability to assess whether these estimates are correct or not. Yet these estimates have a major effect on earnings.

So the conference report suggested that the auditors' certification statement be changed. Accountants would certify the things that they can actually see, record, and vouch for—things such as cash, items that have an actual market value, or even items whose value is based on cost less some kind of verifiable depreciation—but they would state that everything else in their certification statement was based on management estimates, for which they would not be responsible.

The central problem, as I see it, is that people tend to think that when accountants certify financial statements, they are certifying their accuracy—that the statements are in fact an accurate representation of the real world—whereas ultimately auditors are doing nothing more than endorsing what management said was happening within the company. So that is another way, if I may suggest it, that we might approach the issue of attempting to protect accounting firms from the liabilities to which they have been increasingly subject.

As I said at the beginning, I think this is an excellent piece of work because Zoe-Vonna has not only identified the issue but also proposed a very practical kind of solution that might actually work in the real world. Whether the PCAOB has the courage to do what has been recommended is another matter, but the proposal makes a lot of sense to me.

LESLIE BONI

5

Analyzing the Analysts after the Global Settlement

On April 28, 2003, U.S. securities market regulators held a press conference to announce the completion of the Global Settlement Agreement with ten of the largest investment banking firms. The agreement settled enforcement actions that alleged that those firms "engaged in acts and practices that created or maintained inappropriate influence by investment banking over research analysts, thereby imposing conflicts of interest on research analysts." The firms agreed to make organizational changes, to increase disclosure, and to make payments totaling $1.39 billion for penalties, independent research, and investor education. New York attorney general Eliot Spitzer stated at the press conference that these "wide-ranging structural reforms to firms' research operations will empower investors to use securities research in a practical and meaningful way when making investment decisions."[1] Now that several years have passed since the settlement, it seems appropriate to analyze the extent of the progress made toward that objective.

Typically, investment banks provide brokerage services for investors in addition to investment banking services—such as securities underwriting, commercial

---

1. The settlement was reached with the U.S. Securities and Exchange Commission, the State of New York, the North American Securities Administrators Association, the National Association of Securities Dealers (NASD) and the New York Stock Exchange (NYSE), and state securities regulators. For more information, see U.S. Securities and Exchange Commission, press release, "Ten of Nation's Top Investment Firms Settle Enforcement Actions Involving Conflicts of Interest between Research and Investment Banking," April 28, 2003 (www.sec.gov/news/press/2003-54.htm [March 2006]).

loans, and merger and acquisition advice—to corporations. The securities research referred to by the Global Settlement is the product of analysts employed by the brokerage arm within each investment bank. This research, which is provided to the firm's brokerage clients, takes the form of detailed reports about companies and industries as well as earnings forecasts and investment advice, such as recommendations to buy, sell, or hold securities.

Within each investment bank's brokerage research operation, individual analysts are assigned to cover one or more industries. They are expected to be experts on the factors that drive the profits of companies in those industries, such as technological developments, competition, the regulatory environment, and the impact of economic factors such as interest rates, energy prices, and world supply and demand. The analysts are expected to gather and synthesize information from a variety of sources, including company management, financial statements and other filings, suppliers and customers, industry and trade publications, and regulators. Brokerage firm analysts are referred to as "sell-side" analysts to distinguish them from "buy-side" analysts, who are employed by mutual funds and other investment management firms to perform similar securities analysis.

Research is provided to the firm's brokerage clients in the expectation that it will increase brokerage revenue in the form of commissions. Typically, brokerage clients are categorized as either institutional investors or retail investors. Institutional investors are professional money managers, such as managers of mutual funds, pension funds, hedge funds, and insurance company portfolios. Retail ("individual") investors usually generate less trading volume and lower total brokerage commissions per account.

In the summer of 2001, Congress held hearings during which market participants and regulators voiced concerns that sell-side analysts faced conflicts of interest that resulted in their sometimes being overly optimistic about stock investment values.[2] Conflicts might result from pressure exerted by the management of the company whose stock is being covered, by institutional clients hoping to protect their holdings, by the investment banking operation within the analyst's firm, by the firm's proprietary trading operation, or even by the analyst, to protect his or her own trading positions.[3]

Polls of institutional investors conducted prior to the Global Settlement indicated that they were largely savvy to the conflicts of interest faced by sell-side analysts. As a result, many read the analysts' detailed research reports—lengthy

---

2. Testimony from the hearings can be found at Subcommittee on Capital Markets, Insurance and Government Sponsored Enterprises, *Analyzing the Analysts*, June 14, 2001 (http://financialservices.house.gov/Hearings.asp?formmode=detail&hearing=54 [December 5, 2005]).

3. See Boni and Womack (2002a).

and infrequently issued assessments of a company's future profits as well as the factors and assumptions behind those assessments—but largely ignore analysts' investment recommendations.[4] The Global Settlement therefore was aimed primarily at addressing concerns about the generally less experienced, more vulnerable retail investor. Of the settlement, $80 million was earmarked for investor education. The settlement also required firms to disclose their research analysts' historical recommendation ratings to "enable investors to evaluate and compare the performance of analysts."[5]

This chapter examines the recommendations made by the analysts at the ten firms before and after the Global Settlement to analyze whether the research provided by the firms now offers individual investors "a practical and meaningful way" to make decisions. It asks the following questions:

—Did the nature of analysts' recommendation ratings (for example, the distribution across best to worst ratings categories and frequency of changes in recommendations) differ before and after the settlement?

—Did investors differ in how they reacted to analysts' recommendation announcements before and after the settlement?

—What gains and losses were to be made from trading on analysts' recommendations before and after the settlement?

—What can one conclude about the settlement's effectiveness with regard to educating and protecting investors?

In summary, the chapter presents the following major findings and conclusions:

—Whether the result of reduced trading commissions or the disentanglement of investment banking and research, the ten firms on average appear to have reduced their research coverage. The number of stocks that received research coverage by those firms by 2004 dropped an average of 14 percent relative to the number in 2000 and 20 percent relative to the number in 2001. Ironically, academic research has shown that stocks covered by fewer analysts may present greater investment opportunities for investors.[6]

—Both before and after the Global Settlement, 99 percent of the stock recommendations by the ten firms could be partitioned into three simple categories, which I define as "high" (strongest recommendation), "medium," and "low" (least strong recommendation). As measured by their recommendations, analysts were *more* optimistic after the Global Settlement: low recommendations decreased as

---

4. Boni and Womack (2002b).
5. See U.S. Securities and Exchange Commission, press release, "Ten of Nation's Top Investment Firms Settle Enforcement Actions."
6. See Hong, Lim, and Stein (2000), Jegadeesh and others (2004), and Boni and Womack (2006).

a percentage of total recommendations while high recommendations remained about constant.

—Conflict-of-interest arguments suggest that analysts at the large investment banks tended to congregate at recommendation levels. For example, if positive recommendations are attempts to favorably impress the management of companies considering secondary offerings, one should observe the strongest recommendations for those companies from all ten firms. Interestingly, analysts at firms did not tend to cluster on recommendation categories, either before or after settlement. On average, only two to three firms shared a given recommendation level for stocks before and after.

—Both before and after the Global Settlement, on average analysts issued changes in recommendations infrequently for most firms. Recommendation changes occurred an average of once every few years per firm per company covered. As a result, any new information that led to the change was usually quite stale for most of the life of the recommendation.

—After the Global Settlement, the market showed less short-term reaction to analysts' recommendation changes. In the three-day window around recommendation changes, stock prices increased less on upgrades and decreased less on downgrades than they did before the settlement.

—Stocks that received analysts' strongest investment recommendations outperformed the market index (Standard and Poor's 500 index) both before and after the Global Settlement. But so did stocks that received the worst ratings. In fact, more often than not, stocks that received analysts' worst ratings outperformed those that received analysts' strongest investment recommendations, both before and after the Global Settlement.

—Both before and after the Global Settlement, recommended stocks that outperformed the Standard and Poor's 500 index did so at least in part because on average they were riskier.

The finding that post-settlement stock prices reacted less in the three-day window around recommendation changes is consistent with investors' becoming savvier about recommendations. In summary, however, I conclude that the Global Settlement has done little if anything to change the recommendations made by the ten settlement firms or their long-term investment value for investors. The Global Settlement, as well as the new analyst rules effective in 2002, requires sell-side analysts to publish the historical price performance of recommendations that they have made for a stock along with the current recommendation rating of the stock. But as highlighted in this chapter, those disclosures do not provide investors with a complete picture. The stocks that analysts recommended outperformed the S&P 500 index because, on average, they took more risk. And on average, analysts' low-ranked stocks outperformed their high-ranked stocks more often than not.

A far better tool for educating retail investors on the relative value (or lack thereof) of analysts' recommendations would be to disclose on an ongoing basis the aggregate performance of each firm's recommendations, as suggested in this chapter. Specifically, a historical chart would be provided for each firm that compares the performance of the portfolio of stocks that carry the firm's strongest investment recommendations to the performance of those that carry the firm's lowest recommendations. In addition, various measures of the risk that the portfolios carry would be reported. Given the empirical findings reported here, it is unlikely that aggregate comparative reports will be provided voluntarily by the firms, but the data probably could be easily obtained by regulators, who could automate the monthly calculation of aggregate statistics. The websites of regulatory agencies might be an appropriate means of getting the information to investors.

The Global Settlement

The Global Settlement was jointly announced by the Securities and Exchange Commission, the State of New York, the North American Securities Administrators Association, the National Association of Securities Dealers, the New York Stock Exchange, and state securities regulators. The ten investment banking firms involved agreed to pay penalties, disgorgement, and funds for independent research and investor research, shown in table 5-1.

The ten firms were named as part of the Global Settlement, announced on April 28, 2003. On August 26, 2004, two additional firms, Deutsche Bank and Thomas Weisel Partners, settled similar enforcement actions. Deutsche Bank agreed to pay a total of $87.5 million ($25 million for disgorgement, $25 million for conflict-of-interest penalties, $25 million to fund independent research, $5 million for investor education, and $7.5 million for "failing to promptly produce all e-mail and thereby delaying over a year the investigation"). Thomas Weisel Partners agreed to pay a total of $12.5 million ($5 million for disgorgement, $5 million for conflict-of-interest penalties, and $2.5 million to fund independent research).[7] Because the Deutsche Bank and Thomas Weisel Partners settlements were agreed to more than a year after the Global Settlement, they are excluded from this analysis.

7. See U.S. Securities and Exchange Commission, press release, "Deutsche Bank Securities Inc. and Thomas Weisel Partners LLC Settle Enforcement Actions Involving Conflicts of Interest between Research and Investment," August 26, 2004 (www.sec.gov/news/press/2004-120.htm [March 3, 2005]).

Table 5-1. *Allocation of Payments of the Ten Original Global Settlement Firms*[a]

Firm	Penalty	Disgorgement	Independent research	Investor education	Total
Bear Stearns	25	25	25	5	80
Credit Suisse First Boston	75	75	50	0	200
Goldman Sachs	25	25	50	10	110
J. P. Morgan	25	25	25	5	80
Lehman Brothers	25	25	25	5	80
Merrill Lynch	100	0	75	25	200
Morgan Stanley	25	25	75	0	125
U.S. Bancorp Piper Jaffray	12.5	12.5	7.5	0	32.5
Citigroup/Salomon Smith Barney	150	150	75	25	400
UBS Warburg	25	25	25	5	80
Total	487.5	387.5	432.5	80	1,387.5

Source: U.S. Securities and Exchange Commission, press release, "Ten of Nation's Top Investment Firms Settle Enforcement Actions Involving Conflicts of Interest between Research and Investment Banking," April 28, 2003 (www.sec.gov/news/press/2003-54.htm [March 2006]).

a. In millions of dollars.

Data

Data on analyst recommendations of the Global Settlement firms were obtained from I/B/E/S© International (IBES) through September 2004.[8] Recommendations are for ordinary shares and American depository receipts (ADRs) listed on the New York Stock Exchange, the American Stock and Options Exchange (AMEX), and the NASDAQ Market System. To supplement the data, stock prices, investment returns, and shares outstanding were obtained from the Center for Research in Security Prices (CRSP).

The IBES data indicate for each recommendation the date that it was issued and the name of the analyst and the analyst's firm. Typically, each brokerage firm (or the brokerage arm of the investment bank) chooses its own recommendation nomenclature and the number of different categories that it uses when issuing recommendations. Historically, naming conventions and number of categories have

---

8. I/B/E/S© International began providing data on brokerage analyst earnings forecasts in the 1970s. Many institutional investors purchase its data services for real-time analyses. IBES also makes historical data available (with a delay) to academic researchers. The IBES data include recommendations made by sell-side research analysts employed by stand-alone brokerage firms as well as investment banks with brokerage arms.

varied from the simplest three-category set-up ("buy," "sell," and "hold") to more finely partitioned designs, such as one firm's nine-level framework ("outperform/overweight," "outperform/market weight," "outperform/underweight," "peer perform/overweight," "peer perform/market weight," "peer perform/underweight," "underperform/overweight," "underperform/market weight," and "underperform/underweight"). IBES data indicate for each recommendation observation the nomenclature assigned by the firm. Because these naming conventions sometimes confuse those who are not clients of the brokerage firm, IBES maps each firm's naming convention to IBES's own five-level system: "strong buy" (IBES code 1), "buy" (IBES code 2), "hold" (IBES code 3), "underperform" (IBES code 4), and "sell" (IBES code 5). When performing empirical studies of analyst recommendations with the IBES data, academic researchers typically partition recommendation data simply by using the IBES five-level assignments, not the brokerage firms' naming systems. The complications created when a firm's three-level system is mapped to IBES's five-level system are discussed later in the chapter.

Although each recommendation observation in the IBES dataset indicates the date and level of the recommendation, the observation does not indicate the analyst's prior recommendation for the stock. However, it is necessary to determine any prior recommendation in order to examine whether analysts changed their approach to making recommendations (for example, frequency and ratio of upgrades to downgrades) and how investors reacted to upgrades and downgrades. To determine the prior level, I simply searched the dataset for the most recent observation by the analyst for that stock.

There is no prior recommendation in some cases, as, for example, when a brokerage firm is initiating its coverage of a stock. Prior recommendations also may be absent if the brokerage firm has issued recommendations before but has not yet contributed any recommendation information to IBES. Brokerage firms themselves decide whether to contribute their information to IBES.[9] Although many firms provided IBES with data as early as 1993, at least one of the Global Settlement firms did not contribute until 1998. I chose 1999 as the starting point of my study so that I can not only analyze the recommendations made by all the Global Settlement firms but also determine prior recommendations.

As a final step in creating the dataset, I constructed a dataset for each of the Global Settlement firms that shows the recommendation outstanding for each

---

9. It is understood that once a brokerage firm begins contributing recommendation data to IBES, all recommendation changes it issues are provided to IBES, not just a self-selected subset of the recommendations it issues.

stock for any day from January 1, 1999, through September 30, 2004. For example, suppose Brokerage Firm X initiated coverage on Amazon on May 2, 2000, with a "strong buy" recommendation and downgraded Amazon to a "buy" on January 15, 2001. For any day from May 2, 2000, to January 14, 2001, the dataset would show Brokerage Firm X with a "strong buy" for Amazon. This is referred to as the standing recommendation dataset.[10]

The ten settlement firms must be examined individually because firms' reaction to the settlement were not necessarily uniform, nor did their clients necessarily respond uniformly to the firms' recommendations after the settlement. However, IBES data are made available to academic researchers with the proviso that individual brokerage firms' identity will be masked in studies. Therefore, for this study, each of the ten firms has been assigned a number from 1 to 10 in a random fashion.

The Nature of Analysts' Recommendations

First, the stock recommendations that firms made to their investor clients were examined, and recommendations made before and after the settlement were compared to determine whether the firms changed any of the following:

—the number of companies for which they issued research coverage in the form of recommendations to buy, sell, or hold

—the percentage of the covered companies that received the highest and the lowest recommendations

—the frequency of changes in recommendations

—the extent to which, for each company covered, the analysts at each of the ten firms maintained the same recommendation level as the analysts at the other nine firms.

Recommendation statistics are provided in table 5-2. Statistics are reported by year. Eight of the ten firms changed the naming system that they used for recommendations in the year 2002. To address the impact of the name changes, table 5-2 reports data before the name change as for year "2002A" and after the name change as for year "2002B." Name changes are discussed in further detail below.

The Global Settlement requires that "firms' senior management will determine the research department's budget without input from investment banking and

---

10. IBES provides a "stop file" that indicates if an analyst discontinues his or her recommendation without issuing a new recommendation for that stock. Data from this file are incorporated to adjust the standing recommendation dataset as appropriate.

without regard to specific revenues derived from investment banking." Furthermore, "analysts' compensation may not be based, directly or indirectly, on investment banking revenues" and research management, not investment bankers, "will make all company-specific decisions to terminate coverage."[11] In sum, these requirements could result in lower post-settlement brokerage research budgets and coverage of fewer companies. In fact, as shown in table 5-1, the average number of companies covered ("standing recommendations") dropped from a high pre-settlement total in 2001 of 996 a year to lows of just 800 companies covered in 2003 and 799 companies covered in 2004.[12] While that pattern is true for most firms, three of the firms (Firms 7, 8, and 9) showed little change or even an increase in the number of companies that they covered before and after the settlement.

It is worth noting that in 2002, the self-regulatory organizations of the NYSE and NASD issued new rules for all sell-side analysts, not just those at the ten settlement firms. Among their provisions, the rules required firms to disclose the meanings of their recommendations; to break down all their recommendations into simple buy, sell, and hold categories; and to report the performance of past recommendations by using price charts.[13] As noted by Madureira, eight of the ten Global Settlement firms changed their recommendation ranking systems in 2002 as the new rules became effective and when settlement negotiations were already well under way.[14] For example, before settlement, some of the settlement firms used a four-category system for recommendations (that is, a recommendation would be one of four possible recommendations, such as a strong buy, buy, hold, or sell). During 2002, these firms changed to three-category systems. Perhaps more interestingly, some firms that used a three-category system before settlement continued to use a three-category system afterward, but they used different categories. For example, some firms that used categories that IBES mapped to 1 ("strong buy"), 2 ("buy"), and 3 ("hold") before the settlement changed naming conventions so that their recommendations were mapped to IBES categories 2 ("buy"), 3 ("hold"), and 4 ("underperform") after the settlement.

For each of the firms, most if not all recommendations fell within one of three IBES categories, even before the name changes, when some firms allowed their analysts to use more than three categories. The discussion can be simplified by

11. See U.S. Securities and Exchange Commission, press release, "Ten of Nation's Top Investment Firms Settle Enforcement Actions."
12. "Standing recommendations" were calculated from the standing recommendation dataset described earlier in the chapter. Standing recommendations were calculated for each of the settlement firms at the end of each month and then averaged for each year.
13. These rules are NYSE rule 472 and NASD rule 2711. See Boni and Womack (2002b) for additional background on the development of these rules.
14. Madureira (2004).

Table 5-2. *Recommendations of the Ten Global Settlement Firms, Pre- and Post-Settlement*[a]

Firm and recommendations	1999	2000	2001	2002A	2002B	2003	2004
Average of all ten firms							
Standing recommendations	845	930	996	971	881	800	799
Recommendation level[b]							
High	36.6	39.8	32.2	28.4	34.5	31.8	39.0
Medium	36.8	35.8	38.3	38.0	45.6	48.8	48.2
Low	26.2	24.1	29.0	32.4	19.6	18.8	12.8
Other	0.4	0.4	0.5	1.3	0.3	0.6	0.1
Upgrades[b]	24.5	18.2	19.3			32.2	38.6
Downgrades[b]	22.6	28.5	34.8			33.0	27.6
Cluster measure average							
High	2.6	2.9	2.9			3.1	3.4
Medium	2.3	2.4	2.6			3.1	3.2
Low	2.2	2.4	2.7			2.1	2.1
Firm 1							
Standing recommendations	1,140	1,130	1,195	1,165	1,075	848	838
Recommendation level[b]							
High	40.8	44.9	35.6	30.5	31.4	32.8	36.5
Medium	29.1	28.1	33.2	34.1	40.9	43.6	49.2
Low	29.6	26.6	30.4	34.3	27.6	23.5	14.1
Other	0.5	0.4	0.8	1.1	0.1	0.1	0.2
Upgrades[b]	28.9	19.8	22.3			42.1	42.5
Downgrades[b]	23.6	27.3	37.7			39.4	33.7
Cluster measure average							
High	2.5	2.9	2.9			3.1	3.4
Medium	2.4	2.5	2.7			3.1	3.2
Low	2.2	2.5	2.7			2.1	2.1

(continued)

redefining recommendation categories as "high," "medium," and "low." For each firm, the three categories within which most of the firm's recommendations fell were determined by pre- and post-settlement name changes. For each period, the category with the lowest IBES number (that is, the best rating) is defined for that firm as "high." Similarly, the category with the worst rating of the three most commonly used (per IBES) is defined for the firm as "low." The most often used category that is neither high nor low is defined as "medium." Table 5-2 shows for each of the ten firms, as well as the average of all ten firms, the percentage of standing recommendations that fall into these high, medium, and low categories.

Table 5-2. *Recommendations of the Ten Global Settlement Firms, Pre- and Post-Settlement (continued)*

Firm and recommendations	1999	2000	2001	2002A	2002B	2003	2004
Firm 2							
Standing recommendations	949	1,169	1,283	1,202	1,009	875	820
Recommendation level[b]							
High	12.7	17.0	11.6	9.0	40.2	37.4	41.2
Medium	54.3	52.3	51.0	52.6	40.3	46.6	46.6
Low	32.6	30.1	36.7	37.9	19.5	16.0	12.2
Other	0.4	0.6	0.7	0.5	0.0	0.0	0.0
Upgrades[b]	22.4	20.9	18.2			30.6	28.0
Downgrades[b]	23.8	29.5	33.2			30.3	23.7
Cluster measure average							
High	2.8	3.2	3.2			3.0	3.4
Medium	2.2	2.3	2.4			3.1	3.3
Low	2.3	2.3	2.5			2.1	2.1
Firm 3							
Standing recommendations	1,366	1,496	1,503	1,373	1,161	1,066	1,107
Recommendation level[b]							
High	21.0	26.6	22.7	24.4	43.0	40.3	44.2
Medium	49.3	46.7	41.0	32.5	49.7	53.8	51.5
Low	29.2	26.3	35.1	39.0	6.6	5.6	4.3
Other	0.5	0.4	1.2	4.1	0.7	0.3	0.0
Upgrades[b]	37.7	27.2	26.6			37.3	28.5
Downgrades[b]	24.8	34.7	40.8			31.5	34.0
Cluster measure average							
High	2.7	3.0	2.9			2.8	3.0
Medium	2.2	2.2	2.5			2.9	2.9
Low	2.1	2.3	2.4			2.5	2.4

(continued)

For example, in 1999, 40.8 percent of Firm 1's recommendations fell into its highest ("high") category. Table 5-1 also shows the recommendations that fall outside these three categories as "other." For the average of the ten firms, the redefinition successfully partitions, at worst, all but 1.3 percent of recommendations ("2002A"). The worst the redefinition does is for Firm 7 in 2003, when 5.2 percent of recommendations fall outside the three categories.

During the *Analyzing the Analysts* congressional hearings held in 2001, market participants and regulators voiced concerns that sell-side analysts, as a result of conflicts of interest, issued too many positive recommendations and too few negative

Table 5-2. *Recommendations of the Ten Global Settlement Firms, Pre- and Post-Settlement (continued)*

Firm and recommendations	1999	2000	2001	2002A	2002B	2003	2004
Firm 4							
Standing recommendations	912	940	925	900	910	794	698
Recommendation level[b]							
High	21.2	21.3	14.8	13.6	31.7	28.1	31.0
Medium	43.5	45.3	43.0	39.6	48.0	50.8	48.1
Low	35.1	33.1	41.8	45.9	20.2	21.1	20.9
Other	0.2	0.3	0.4	0.9	0.1	0.0	0.0
Upgrades[b]	28.3	19.0	21.7			25.1	23.5
Downgrades[b]	28.6	30.2	40.3			30.2	26.2
Cluster measure average							
High	3.0	3.5	3.5			3.4	3.7
Medium	2.5	2.6	2.9			3.2	3.4
Low	2.3	2.4	2.7			2.1	2.0
Firm 5							
Standing recommendations	1,011	1,119	1,004	979	856	738	739
Recommendation level[b]							
High	30.4	32.8	27.7	24.0	23.2	22.9	23.8
Medium	40.4	40.1	41.0	40.5	56.4	57.6	58.2
Low	28.1	26.3	30.7	34.1	20.3	19.3	17.8
Other	1.1	0.8	0.6	1.4	0.1	0.2	0.2
Upgrades[b]	22.7	16.6	13.3			26.7	21.7
Downgrades[b]	19.7	25.0	21.5			26.7	22.6
Cluster measure average							
High	2.8	3.2	3.2			3.7	4.2
Medium	2.3	2.4	2.9			3.3	3.4
Low	2.3	2.5	2.5			2.3	2.1

(continued)

recommendations.[15] Table 5-1 shows that before name changes (that is, 2002A and earlier), the stocks with the best recommendations ("high") made up from 28.4 percent (in 2002A) to 39.8 percent (in 2000) of all recommendations on average across the ten firms. After the Global Settlement, the percentage of high recommendations did not decrease. Top recommendations made up 31.8 percent

---

15. See U.S. Securities and Exchange Commission, press release, "Ten of Nation's Top Investment Firms Settle Enforcement Actions."

Table 5-2. *Recommendations of the Ten Global Settlement Firms, Pre- and Post-Settlement (continued)*

Firm and recommendations	1999	2000	2001	2002A	2002B	2003	2004
Firm 6							
Standing recommendations	826	922	856	812	733	684	720
Recommendation level[b]							
High	41.7	44.7	39.3	35.6	38.3	37.3	38.3
Medium	30.7	29.2	32.1	33.4	44.8	48.7	49.5
Low	27.0	25.5	27.9	30.0	16.9	13.9	12.0
Other	0.6	0.6	0.7	1.0	0.0	0.1	0.2
Upgrades[b]	18.8	14.0	11.2			23.1	22.8
Downgrades[b]	18.9	23.8	19.3			24.7	18.5
Cluster measure average							
High	2.4	2.7	2.6			3.1	3.4
Medium	2.3	2.3	2.7			3.1	3.0
Low	2.2	2.3	2.6			2.3	2.2
Firm 7 (Firm 7 did not change ratings systems in 2002, so "2002A"= "2002B".)							
Standing recommendations	335	428	455	495	495	448	465
Recommendation level[b]							
High	38.7	40.0	24.7	19.8	19.8	14.0	56.8
Medium	43.0	44.3	47.9	44.4	44.4	41.3	38.7
Low	18.2	15.8	27.3	33.6	33.6	39.5	4.4
Other	0.1	0.0	0.1	2.2	2.2	5.2	0.1
Upgrades[b]	34.6	18.2	23.1			36.8	133.0
Downgrades[b]	37.6	47.2	56.5			35.0	30.7
Cluster measure average							
High	2.0	2.1	2.3			2.8	2.7
Medium	1.8	2.0	2.3			2.5	2.6
Low	1.7	1.7	2.1			1.5	1.5

(continued)

(in 2003) to 39.0 percent (in 2004) of all recommendations on average across the ten firms.

Perhaps even more interesting, the percentage of recommendations in the most negative category ("low") actually decreased. On average, the percentage of most negative recommendations went from a pre-settlement range of 24.1 percent (in 2000) to 32.4 percent (in 2002A) to a post-settlement range of 18.8 percent (in 2003) to just 12.8 percent (in 2004). It is worth noting that in all but two of the firms the percentage of negative recommendations decreased after the settlement.

Table 5-2. *Recommendations of the Ten Global Settlement Firms, Pre- and Post-Settlement (continued)*

Firm and recommendations	1999	2000	2001	2002A	2002B	2003	2004
Firm 8							
Standing recommendations	564	607	935	945	766	868	976
Recommendation level[b]							
High	51.5	53.6	45.0	40.0	30.2	31.5	34.1
Medium	14.0	12.2	24.3	26.1	46.1	46.0	46.3
Low	33.8	33.9	30.4	32.9	23.5	22.4	19.6
Other	0.7	0.3	0.3	1.0	0.2	0.1	0.0
Upgrades[b]	16.1	13.7	23.3			35.1	29.6
Downgrades[b]	18.8	26.5	38.5			36.3	32.0
Cluster measure average							
High	2.8	3.1	2.6			3.2	3.4
Medium	2.7	2.9	2.7			3.2	3.1
Low	2.4	2.6	2.7			2.0	1.9
Firm 9							
Standing recommendations	731	820	883	936	900	944	922
Recommendation level[b]							
High	43.4	47.6	38.8	30.9	31.2	34.4	40.6
Medium	29.5	29.9	31.6	33.9	42.7	45.1	44.4
Low	26.9	21.9	29.0	34.3	26.1	20.5	14.8
Other	0.2	0.6	0.6	0.9	0.0	0.0	0.2
Upgrades[b]	20.8	19.8	15.2			27.4	21.5
Downgrades[b]	15.6	22.0	32.0			17.2	20.0
Cluster measure average							
High	2.6	2.9	2.9			3.2	3.4
Medium	2.5	2.5	2.7			3.1	3.1
Low	2.4	2.5	2.8			2.0	1.9

(continued)

The exceptions were Firm 7, which decreased the percentage radically in 2004, to just 4.4 percent of its recommendations, but not in 2003; and Firm 10, which increased its percentage from less than 2 percent before settlement to a still remarkably low 6 to 8 percent after settlement.

These results are disappointing. One might have hoped that if, as a result of various conflicts of interest, analysts issued too many positive and too few negative recommendations before settlement, the post-settlement ratios of positive to negative recommendations would decrease. It is possible, however, that rather than reflecting an optimism bias resulting from various potential conflicts of

Table 5-2. *Recommendations of the Ten Global Settlement Firms, Pre- and Post-Settlement (continued)*

Firm and recommendations	1999	2000	2001	2002A	2002B	2003	2004
Firm 10 (Firm 10 did not change ratings systems in 2002, so "2002A"= "2002B".)							
Standing recommendations	620	671	917	901	901	739	709
Recommendation level[b]							
High	64.6	69.1	62.1	56.0	56.0	39.2	43.3
Medium	34.3	29.8	37.4	42.5	42.5	54.3	49.0
Low	1.1	1.0	0.5	1.5	1.5	6.5	7.7
Other	0.0	0.1	0.0	0.0	0.0	0.0	0.0
Upgrades[b]	15.0	13.1	17.8			37.8	34.4
Downgrades[b]	14.7	18.6	28.5			58.3	35.0
Cluster measure average							
High	2.4	2.7	2.4			3.1	3.5
Medium	2.2	2.2	2.6			3.3	3.5
Low	2.5	2.8	3.5			2.4	2.5

a. This table reports the standing recommendations of the ten Global Settlement firms. Individual firms' identities are masked, with firms randomly assigned a number of one through ten. Standing recommendations are calculated at the end of each month and then averaged for the year. Most of the firms renamed their recommendation categories *during* the year 2002; therefore, separate statistics are provided for 2002, before (2002A) and after (2002B) the firm's change in naming system. Each firm's three most frequently used recommendation levels are divided into "high" (most favorable recommendation), "medium" (next most favorable), and "low" (least favorable). Recommendation levels are then reported as a percent of standing recommendations for that year. As some firms used more than three recommendation categories, the percentage of recommendations that do not fall into the three most frequently used categories is also reported ("other"). The table also reports the changes in recomendation levels ("upgrades" and "downgrades") each year, as a percent of standing recommendations. "Cluster measure" is the number of Global Settlement firms that have the same standing recommendation level for the company covered, averaged across the companies that the firm covers with that recommendation level. Percentage of upgrades and downgrades and cluster measures are not shown for 2002 because firms changed category names during different months of the year.

b. Percent.

interest, the smaller percentage of recommendations in the most negative category reflects analysts' accurate and unbiased expectation of the investment value of stocks for the post-settlement period. For example, the analysts cover only a fraction of all U.S.-listed stocks, and perhaps after settlement they intentionally skewed their coverage to stocks that they expected to outperform the market. Perhaps the more important question when analyzing the impact of the Global Settlement for retail investors is whether analysts' relative rankings reflect an accurate assessment of future investment value. That question is examined later in this chapter.

The Global Settlement requires firms to disclose analysts' historical rankings so that investors can measure analysts' track records as stock pickers. As a result, analysts might have issued changes in recommendation rankings more frequently after settlement. Table 5-1 reports the frequency of upgrades and downgrades as a percentage of standing recommendations each year. Both before and after settlement, recommendation changes were fairly infrequent. On average, before settlement, a company's stock would be upgraded by each firm only once every four to five years and downgraded only once every three to four years. After settlement, although recommendation changes were more frequent on average, only 32.2 percent to 38.6 percent of stocks per firm were upgraded on average each year. The rate of downgrades also was relatively infrequent.[16]

Finally, I was interested in examining the extent to which, for each company covered, the analysts at each of the ten firms maintained the same recommendation level as the analysts at the other nine firms. If, before settlement, analysts were driven by investment banking operations to be more optimistic regarding companies that were expected to generate more banking revenues for the firm, recommendations of analysts across firms might have been more likely to cluster together. For example, if AT&T were about to pick an investment bank to lead a $30 billion bond offering, all ten firms might be expected to maintain the highest possible recommendation for AT&T's stock. After the Global Settlement's disentanglement of investment banking and brokerage operations, analysts' recommendations for each stock across firms might be more diffuse or varied.

I calculated a "cluster measure average" for each recommendation level for each firm as well as the average of all the firms to examine that possibility, as reported in table 5-2. The cluster measure indicates the number of the ten firms that share the same recommendation level for the stocks in a particular recommendation category. For example, suppose Firm 1 had a high recommendation for Intel at the end of January 1999 and only one of the other nine settlement firms also gave Intel a high recommendation. The cluster measure for Intel for January 1999 for Firm 1 would be 2. Similarly, the cluster measure average for all of the stocks that Firm 1 ranked "high" for January 1999 was calculated. This procedure was repeated for all months in 1999, and the average cluster measure for "high" for 1999 was reported for Firm 1. Similarly, cluster measures were calculated for "medium" and "low," firm by firm, year by year.

16. For 2004, recommendations issued only for the first three quarters were observed. Therefore, to calculate upgrades and downgrades as a function of outstanding recommendations in 2004, I extrapolated the rate of upgrades and downgrades and the average number of standing recommendations from the first three quarters of 2004 to arrive at estimates for fourth quarter 2004.

If all firms covered the same stocks, the highest possible value that the cluster measure could have would be 10. In any event, 1 is the lowest possible value; it was observed if the firm was alone in its recommendation for all the stocks that it assigned that particular recommendation level. Table 5-1 shows that on average, analysts at the ten settlement firms, both before and after settlement, did not tend to cluster on the high, medium, and low recommendation categories. On average, only two to three firms shared a given recommendation level for stocks before and after settlement.

Investors' Reactions to Analyst Recommendation Announcements

Next, I look at whether investors reacted differently to analysts' recommendation announcements before and after the Global Settlement. Typically, clients of a brokerage firm are alerted to an analyst's change in recommendation before the beginning of the U.S. trading day. During the day, the recommendation change becomes public information as word leaks from clients to non-clients and the news media report the change. Green reports that about 75 percent of the recommendation changes in his 1999–2002 data sample were reported by the Bloomberg news service after the market closed on the day that the recommendation was made to the brokerage firm's clients.[17]

Previous research documents that investors react very quickly to recommendation changes. Using data from the year 2000, Busse and Green show that traders responded to televised analysts' recommendations within a minute of their broadcast.[18] Green finds that for his 1999–2002 data sample of NASDAQ stocks, prices fully incorporated the information contained in the recommendation change announcement (that is, the price increased for upgrades and decreased for downgrades) within two days of the announcement.[19]

I compared investors' reactions to analysts' recommendation announcements before and after the Global Settlement by comparing the price reactions to analysts' upgrades and downgrades. I examined a three-day window around the recommendation change "event" to allow for the reaction of the public plus the possibility that clients learned of the recommendation a day before it was reported publicly. Specifically, I examined the three-day event excess return from the day before to the day after the recommendation change event, which was calculated

17. See Green (2004).
18. Busse and Green (2002).
19. Green (2004).

using stock prices at the close of the trading day (and stock dividends if paid within the three-day window) as follows:

Three-day event excess return =
  Three-day event return − Three-day market return, where

Three-day event eeturn =
  $\dfrac{(Stock\ price\ day\ after\ +\ Dividend\ -\ Stock\ price\ day\ before)}{Stock\ price\ day\ before}$

and the *Three-day market return* is the return from investing in an equal-weighted index of all same-market-cap decile stocks listed on NYSE, AMEX, and NASDAQ.

The adjustment for the market return helps in differentiating the price response due to the analyst's announcement from price changes due to movements in the stock market as a whole, such as interest rate changes and so forth. Of course, large single-day price changes can result from information from sources other than a change in an analyst's recommendation, the most common being company announcements of quarterly earnings. Perhaps not surprisingly, sell-side analysts quickly incorporate that information and many of their recommendation changes occur within a day or two of earnings announcements. Ivkovic and Jegadeesh show that about 15 percent of the recommendation changes in their 1990–2002 data sample occurred on the same date as the company's earnings announcement or the following day.[20] For these recommendation changes, it is impossible from the data to differentiate the amount of a price reaction that is a response to analyst recommendation changes from the amount that is a response to the company's earnings announcement. Therefore, I partitioned recommendation changes into those that were made within a day of the earnings announcement and those that were not.

Three-day event excess returns for the possible upgrade and downgrade categories are shown in table 5-3, which reports for each category the average of the recommendation changes in the category made by all ten settlement firms. Returns for recommendation changes that were not made within a day of the company's earnings announcement are shown in panel A. Recommendation changes that were upgrades to "high" from a prior recommendation of "medium" were associated with an average three-day event *excess* return of 3.51 percent for the pre–Global Settlement period and 2.81 percent for the post–Global Settlement period. Both are significantly different from zero at the 5 percent level, and a *t* test of these averages indicates that they are different before and after the set-

---

20. See Ivkovic and Jegadeesh (2004, p. 444, figure 3).

tlement. In other words, investors reacted less to analysts' upgrades from a medium rating to a high rating after the Global Settlement. In fact, for each category of recommendation change in panel A, after the settlement investors showed less inclination on average to buy on upgrades and sell on downgrades. The exception is the three-day event returns average for upgrades from "low" to "high," which is 3.95 percent before and 4.48 percent after settlement. However, there were relatively few of these observations of analysts skipping a ratings level, and a t test of the averages indicates that they are not significantly different from each other at the 5 percent level.

As shown in panel B of table 5-2, three-day event excess returns are of an even greater magnitude of increase for upgrades and of decrease for downgrades when the recommendation change coincides with the company's earnings announcement. For each category, after the settlement investors again showed less inclination on average to buy on upgrades and sell on downgrades. It is worth noting that although the market reaction (that is, three-day event excess returns) for upgrades from "low" to "high" (6.01 percent before and 3.42 percent after) and downgrades from "high" to "low" (–15.34 percent before and –13.24 percent after) were smaller after settlement, there were relatively few of these observations and the pre- and post-settlement averages are not statistically different from each other at a 5 percent significance level.

Unfortunately, although the results indicate that market participants on average responded less to recommendation changes made by the ten settlement firms after the Global Settlement, it is possible that retail investors reacted as they did before but institutional investors responded less. As noted previously, perhaps the more important question for retail investors is whether analysts' relative rankings reflect an accurate assessment of future investment value for a longer-term investment window than the three-day event examined here.

Gains and Losses from Trading on Analysts' Recommendations

Previous studies have documented that predictable and economically significant returns can be earned from trading on analysts' recommendation changes. Such trading strategies generally require relatively frequent trading, however, as most of the profits to be made from buying upgrades and selling downgrades occur in the first days to several months, at most, following recommendation changes.[21] As

---

21. Stickel (1995), Womack (1996), Jegadeesh and others (2004), Jegadeesh and Kim (2004), and Boni and Womack (2006) document that returns for upgraded stocks continued to increase (after appropriate market and risk adjustments) and those for downgraded stocks continued to decrease for a month

Table 5-3. *Initial Market Reaction around Recommendation Upgrades and Downgrades by the Ten Global Settlement Firms Pre- and Post-Settlement*[a]

Panel A: Three-day event excess returns, excluding recommendation changes made within a day of the company's earnings announcement

Pre-settlement

From recommendation:		To recommendation:		
		High	Medium	Low
	High	—	-5.98	-10.18
	Medium	3.51	—	-7.86
	Low	3.95	3.33	—

Post-settlement

From recommendation:		To recommendation:		
		High	Medium	Low
	High	—	-2.93	-4.79
	Medium	2.81	—	-3.77
	Low	4.48	1.80	—

Panel B: Three-day event excess returns for recommendation changes made within a day of the company's earnings announcement

Pre-settlement

From recommendation:		To recommendation:		
		High	Medium	Low
	High	—	-8.64	-15.34
	Medium	6.50	—	-11.09
	Low	6.01	6.82	—

Post-settlement

From recommendation:		To recommendation:		
		High	Medium	Low
	High	—	-5.53	-13.24
	Medium	5.21	—	-8.97
	Low	3.42	5.06	—

a. This table reports the initial market reaction around recommendation changes made by the ten Global Settlement firms. Data are reported separately for the "pre-settlement" and "post-settlement" periods, using data from 1999 through third quarter 2004. Panel A reports market reaction for recommendation changes, excluding those made within a day of the recommended company's report of quarterly earnings. Panel B reports market reaction when recommendation changes are made within a day of that company's report of quarterly earnings. Each firm's three most frequently used recommendation levels are divided into "high" (most favorable recommendation), "medium" (next most favorable), and "low" (least favorable). Columns indicate the recommendation level that the firm gives the company's stock when it issues a change in recommendation, and rows indicate the recommendation level immediately prior to the change in recommendation. Initial market reaction is defined as the three-day event excess return. The three-day event return is the geometrically cumulated return for the day before, day of, and day after the recommendation. The excess return is the stock return less the appropriate size-decile return of the equal-weighted CRSP NYSE/AMEX/NASDAQ index. The table reports the mean of the excess return for each change category. All excess return means are significantly different from zero at the 5 percent level.

reported earlier in table 5-1, each of the ten settlement firms changed the recommendation for each stock it covered only once every three to five years on average. Thus, although gains may be had by trading short term on recommendation changes, most of the ranking levels that investors observe at any given time were issued much earlier and may be too stale to offer investment gains.

To measure what retail investors observe, I constructed for each firm at the beginning of each month the portfolio of all the stocks ranked "high" by the firm at that time. Stocks were included whether the high recommendation was announced just the day before or several years before and had not changed since. This approach is consistent with what a retail investor would learn when asking his or her broker what the firm recommended most highly each month. I assumed that portfolios were equal-weighted—that is, each month dollars were invested equally across all the stocks in the portfolio—and that at the end of the month, the investor earned the average return of all the stocks in the portfolio and then rebalanced the portfolio as necessary for the next month. Similarly, I also formed portfolios each month for each firm's medium- and low-ranked stocks.

It is worth noting that the market capitalizations of stocks covered by firms varied widely. For example, in 2004, about 5,800 companies were listed on U.S. stock exchanges, but the twenty largest companies accounted for more than 40 percent of the total market capitalization of all 5,800 companies.[22] It may be more reasonable therefore to assume that investors will "value-weight" the portfolios. In other words, they might invest more dollars in stocks with greater market capitalizations. Therefore, I constructed another set of portfolios that are identical to the equal-weighted portfolios described above, except that dollars are invested in each stock according to its relative market capitalization.

The average monthly returns for the equal-weighted portfolios are show in table 5-4. The high recommendation portfolio had an average return across all ten firms of 1.8 percent per month in 1999, or about 21.6 percent annualized. In 2002, it lost 2.0 percent, or about –24 percent annualized. Table 5-3 also reports average monthly returns for each individual firm's portfolios. No firm averaged positive monthly returns every year. Almost every firm averaged positive monthly returns after the Global Settlement (in 2003 and 2004), however.

Of course, investors could have ignored analysts' recommendations and instead invested every month in stocks through a broadly diversified mutual fund, such as one that replicates the Standard and Poor's 500 index. Therefore it is

---

or more after an analyst recommendation change. Green (2004) reports that most gains were earned for NASDAQ stocks within the first few days following changes.

22. Calculated using data provided by the Center for Research in Security Prices.

Table 5-4. *Investment Value of Recommendations by the Ten Global Settlement Firms, Pre- and Post-Settlement (Equal-Weighted Portfolios)*

Firm and recommendations	1999	2000	2001	2002	2003	2004
Average of all ten firms						
High recommendations	1.8	0.8	−1.1	−2.0	3.6	0.4
High recommendations minus S&P 500 index	1.0	0.9	0.3	0.1	1.2	0.4
Medium recommendations	1.6	1.2	−0.4	−1.7	4.0	0.4
Medium recommendations minus S&P 500 index	0.8	1.3	1.0	0.4	1.6	0.4
Low recommendations	1.6	1.8	−0.3	−1.5	5.1	−0.1
Low recommendations minus S&P 500 index	0.8	1.9	1.2	0.7	2.8	−0.1
High minus low recommendations	0.2	−1.0	−0.8	−0.6	−1.5	0.5
Firm 1						
High recommendations	1.5	0.9	−1.1	−1.9	3.8	0.5
High recommendations minus S&P 500 index	0.7	0.9	0.3	0.2	1.4	0.5
Medium recommendations	1.3	1.7	−0.1	−1.2	3.8	0.8
Medium recommendations minus S&P 500 index	0.5	1.7	1.3	0.9	1.4	0.8
Low recommendations	0.8	1.9	0.1	−1.5	4.7	0.3
Low recommendations minus S&P 500 index	0.0	1.9	1.6	0.6	2.3	0.3
High minus low recommendations	0.7	−1.0	−1.3	−0.4	−0.9	0.2
Firm 2						
High recommendations	2.6	1.3	−2.3	−2.0	3.4	0.0
High recommendations minus S&P 500 index	1.8	1.3	−0.9	0.2	1.0	0.0
Medium recommendations	2.3	0.9	−0.7	−1.5	3.9	0.6
Medium recommendations minus S&P 500 index	1.5	0.9	0.8	0.6	1.6	0.5
Low recommendations	0.5	2.2	0.7	−1.4	4.8	0.1
Low recommendations minus S&P 500 index	−0.3	2.3	2.1	0.7	2.4	0.1
High minus low recommendations	2.1	−0.9	−3.0	−0.6	−1.4	−0.1

(continued)

Table 5-4. *Investment Value of Recommendations by the Ten Global Settlement Firms, Pre- and Post-Settlement (Equal-Weighted Portfolios) (continued)*

Firm and recommendations	1999	2000	2001	2002	2003	2004
Firm 3						
High recommendations	1.1	0.9	−0.6	−1.9	3.4	0.4
High recommendations minus S&P 500 index	0.3	0.9	0.8	0.2	1.0	0.4
Medium recommendations	1.5	1.5	−0.6	−0.7	4.3	0.4
Medium recommendations minus S&P 500 index	0.7	1.5	0.9	1.5	1.9	0.4
Low recommendations	1.2	1.8	0.0	−1.2	5.1	−0.6
Low recommendations minus S&P 500 index	0.4	1.8	1.4	1.0	2.7	−0.6
High minus low recommendations	−0.1	−0.9	−0.6	−0.8	−1.7	1.0
Firm 4						
High recommendations	1.6	1.4	−1.0	−1.8	3.5	1.0
High recommendations minus S&P 500 index	0.8	1.5	0.4	0.3	1.1	1.0
Medium recommendations	1.6	1.4	−0.6	−1.8	4.0	0.1
Medium recommendations minus S&P 500 index	0.8	1.5	0.8	0.3	1.6	0.1
Low recommendations	2.0	2.0	0.1	−2.0	4.3	0.7
Low recommendations minus S&P 500 index	1.2	2.1	1.5	0.1	1.9	0.7
High minus low recommendations	−0.4	−0.6	−1.1	0.2	−0.7	0.3
Firm 5						
High recommendations	1.7	0.8	−1.6	−2.0	3.2	0.7
High recommendations minus S&P 500 index	0.9	0.8	−0.2	0.2	0.8	0.7
Medium recommendations	1.4	0.7	−0.5	−1.8	3.9	0.4
Medium recommendations minus S&P 500 index	0.6	0.8	1.0	0.3	1.5	0.4
Low recommendations	1.2	2.5	0.9	−1.7	5.0	−0.1
Low recommendations minus S&P 500 index	0.4	2.6	2.3	0.5	2.6	−0.1
High minus low recommendations	0.5	−1.8	−2.5	−0.3	−1.8	0.8

(continued)

Table 5-4. *Investment Value of Recommendations by the Ten Global Settlement Firms, Pre- and Post-Settlement (Equal-Weighted Portfolios) (continued)*

Firm and recommendations	1999	2000	2001	2002	2003	2004
Firm 6						
High recommendations	1.8	0.2	−0.7	−2.4	3.6	0.7
High recommendations minus S&P 500 index	1.0	0.2	0.7	−0.2	1.2	0.7
Medium recommendations	2.1	1.2	0.0	−1.7	3.8	0.5
Medium recommendations minus S&P 500 index	1.3	1.3	1.4	0.4	1.4	0.5
Low recommendations	0.9	1.9	−0.1	−0.9	5.7	0.0
Low recommendations minus S&P 500 index	0.1	1.9	1.3	1.3	3.3	0.0
High minus low recommendations	0.9	−1.7	−0.6	−1.5	−2.1	0.7
Firm 7						
High recommendations	2.6	−0.7	−0.9	−2.5	4.2	−0.1
High recommendations minus S&P 500 index	1.8	−0.7	0.6	−0.4	1.8	−0.1
Medium recommendations	2.6	0.6	−1.2	−3.2	4.3	−0.6
Medium recommendations minus S&P 500 index	1.8	0.7	0.2	−1.1	1.9	−0.6
Low recommendations	3.2	1.6	0.4	−2.3	6.2	−2.0
Low recommendations minus S&P 500 index	2.4	1.7	1.8	−0.2	3.8	−2.0
High minus low recommendations	−0.6	−2.3	−1.3	−0.2	−2.0	1.9
Firm 8						
High recommendations	1.1	0.5	−1.5	−2.2	3.9	0.5
High recommendations minus S&P 500 index	0.3	0.6	−0.1	−0.1	1.5	0.5
Medium recommendations	1.0	0.0	−0.3	−2.5	3.9	0.6
Medium recommendations minus S&P 500 index	0.3	0.1	1.2	−0.4	1.5	0.6
Low recommendations	1.0	1.9	0.6	−1.2	5.3	0.5
Low recommendations minus S&P 500 index	0.2	2.0	2.1	0.9	2.9	0.5
High minus low recommendations	0.1	−1.4	−2.1	−1.0	−1.4	0.0

(continued)

Table 5-4. *Investment Value of Recommendations by the Ten Global Settlement Firms, Pre- and Post-Settlement (Equal-Weighted Portfolios) (continued)*

Firm and recommendations	1999	2000	2001	2002	2003	2004
Firm 9						
High recommendations	2.4	1.1	−1.0	−1.7	3.4	0.3
High recommendations minus S&P 500 index	1.6	1.2	0.5	0.4	1.0	0.3
Medium recommendations	1.5	1.3	−0.6	−1.7	4.3	0.2
Medium recommendations minus S&P 500 index	0.7	1.4	0.8	0.5	1.9	0.2
Low recommendations	2.3	2.2	−0.1	−1.5	5.0	0.7
Low recommendations minus S&P 500 index	1.5	2.3	1.3	0.7	2.6	0.7
High minus low recommendations	0.1	−1.1	−0.9	−0.3	−1.6	−0.4
Firm 10						
High recommendations	1.8	1.9	−0.1	−1.9	3.9	0.2
High recommendations minus S&P 500 index	1.0	1.9	1.3	0.2	1.5	0.2
Medium recommendations	0.8	2.9	0.1	−1.3	3.8	0.7
Medium recommendations minus S&P 500 index	0.0	2.9	1.5	0.8	1.4	0.7
Low recommendations	2.8	0.3	−5.2	−1.1	5.5	−0.1
Low recommendations minus S&P 500 index	2.0	0.4	−3.8	1.0	3.1	−0.1
High minus low recommendations	−1.0	1.5	5.1	−0.8	−1.6	0.3

This table reports the investment value of recommendations of the ten Global Settlement firms. Individual firms' identities are masked, with firms randomly assigned a number of one through ten. Each firm's three most frequently used recommendation levels are divided into "high" (most favorable recommendation), "medium" (next most favorable), and "low" (least favorable). Standing recommendations are calculated at the end of each month, and then portolios are formed as shown below. Stocks are equal-dollar weighted ("equal weighted") within portfolios. Portfolios are rebalanced monthly. This table reports the mean monthly return each year (percent) from these investment portfolio strategies. Results are shown separately for each firm's recommendations along with the results equally averaged across all ten firms. Portfolio performance compared with the Standard and Poor's (S&P) 500 index provides a measure of the recommendations' relative investment value compared with investing in a mutual fund that replicates the S&P 500 index. The last line ("High minus low recommendations") provides a measure of how well analysts' high-ranked stocks performed compared with their low-ranked stocks.

worthwhile to examine how the analyst portfolios compare with that index. Table 5-4 shows that the high recommendation portfolios of most of the firms averaged higher monthly returns than did the index in most years and that the portfolios of three firms did so very year. On average, the ten firms' high recommendation portfolios outperformed the index by 0.1 percent (2002) to 1.2 percent (2003) per month.

It is even more interesting, perhaps, to examine the returns of the medium and low recommendation portfolios. Just to emphasize, savvy institutional investors indicated in polls that they understood even before the settlement that a medium recommendation from analysts—regardless of the actual naming convention—meant to hold, not to buy, more of the stocks, while a low recommendation meant to sell the stocks. And regardless of how many categories a firm used before or after settlement, analysts are indicating their *relative* ratings of expected investment value through their use of high, medium, and low categories. Interestingly, as shown in table 5-3, the ten-firm averages for the medium and low recommendation portfolios also outperformed the S&P 500 every year. And disturbingly, they also outperformed the high recommendation portfolio more often than not. For most of the individual firms, their "low" recommendation portfolios outperformed their high recommendation portfolios. Those findings are generally the same for the value-weighted portfolios, as shown in table 5-5. Remarkably, nothing in tables 5-4 or 5-5 suggests that the high recommendation portfolios on average did a better job of outperforming the S&P 500 index after the Global Settlement than before. And perhaps more disturbingly, nothing suggests that on average, stocks ranked "high" outperformed those ranked "medium" or "low," either before or after the Global Settlement.

Of course, one might ask why most of the recommendation portfolios, whether "high," "medium," or "low," outperformed the S&P 500 index. Jegadeesh and others document that part of the explanation of the value of analyst recommendations is that analysts tend to issue positive recommendations for stocks that prior research shows had higher historical returns but that are riskier.[23] For example, over long periods of time, all else being equal, stocks of small-market-cap companies have outperformed stocks of large-market-cap companies. But the returns of the small company stocks often are considered riskier because historically they have also been more volatile. To examine to what extent increased risk explains the excess returns in tables 5-3 and 5-4, I estimated monthly time series regressions for each portfolio using the Fama and French

23. Jegadeesh and others (2004).

four-factor model, as in Barber and others.[24] Specifically, the portfolio one-month return is regressed on three factors in the Fama and French model:

—the excess market return $(R_m - R_f)$

—the return from a value-weighted, self-financing portfolio, which is long small-cap stocks and short large-cap stocks (SMB)

—the return from a value-weighted, self-financing portfolio, which is long value stocks and short growth stocks (HML).[25]

The fourth factor in the regression is an equal-weighted momentum portfolio return (MOM). This momentum portfolio is a Jegadeesh and Titman–type portfolio, with $J = 11$ and a one-month skip. It is long for the best 30 percent and short for the worst 30 percent of stocks.[26] I performed the regressions for the time series of portfolio returns from each firm for each category of stock recommendation level for the equal-weighted as well as the value-weighted portfolios. A positive loading on any of these four factors means that the portfolio takes on more of that type of risk. A negative loading in the regression indicates less risk.

Results from the regressions (they are not shown here for the sake of brevity, but they are available upon request) indicate that many portfolios outperformed the S&P index because they did load positively (that is, they carried more risk) for the three Fama and French risk factors. Interestingly, the medium and low portfolios outperformed the high portfolio more often than not because they loaded less heavily (and sometime negatively) on the momentum risk factor during periods when momentum portfolio returns were negative or low relative to historic performance.

Conclusions

At the Global Settlement press conference on April 28, 2003, U.S. Securities and Exchange Commission chairman William H. Donaldson stated:

> To provide the public with the tools necessary to assess the usefulness of an analyst's research, each firm must disclose quarterly the price targets, ratings, and earnings per share forecasted in its research reports. I expect that these disclosures will fuel development of private services to transform such

---

24. Barber, Lehavy, McNichols, and Trueman (2001), page 543.
25. Fama and French (1993).
26. See Jegadeesh and Titman (1993). We are grateful to Ken French for providing us with these data through his website (http://mba.tuck.dartmouth.edu/pages/faculty/ken.french/data_library.html [March 2006]). Further details on these factors also are available at his website.

Table 5-5. *Investment Value of Recommendations by the Ten Global Settlement Firms, Pre- and Post-Settlement (Value-Weighted Portfolios)*

Firm and recommendations	1999	2000	2001	2002	2003	2004
Average of all ten firms						
High recommendations	3.3	1.7	−0.7	−1.3	2.8	0.4
High recommendations minus S&P 500 index	2.5	1.7	0.7	0.8	0.4	0.4
Medium recommendations	2.5	2.3	0.0	−0.9	3.2	0.7
Medium recommendations minus S&P 500 index	1.7	2.4	1.5	1.2	0.8	0.7
Low recommendations	1.4	2.8	0.1	−0.8	4.0	0.4
Low recommendations minus S&P 500 index	0.6	2.9	1.5	1.3	1.6	0.4
High minus low recommendations	1.9	−1.2	−0.8	−0.5	−1.1	0.0
Firm 1						
High recommendations	3.0	1.5	−0.7	−1.5	3.0	0.3
High recommendations minus S&P 500 index	2.2	1.5	0.8	0.6	0.6	0.3
Medium recommendations	2.2	2.2	0.0	−0.4	3.5	0.7
Medium recommendations minus S&P 500 index	1.4	2.3	1.4	1.7	1.1	0.7
Low recommendations	1.4	2.5	0.3	−0.9	3.4	1.4
Low recommendations minus S&P 500 index	0.6	2.5	1.7	1.3	1.0	1.4
High minus low recommendations	1.6	−1.0	−0.9	−0.6	−0.5	−1.1
Firm 2						
High recommendations	4.1	1.1	−1.6	−1.2	2.9	0.1
High recommendations minus S&P 500 index	3.3	1.1	−0.2	1.0	0.5	0.1
Medium recommendations	3.2	2.1	−0.3	−1.1	3.0	0.9
Medium recommendations minus S&P 500 index	2.4	2.2	1.1	1.1	0.6	0.9
Low recommendations	1.0	2.9	0.6	−0.7	4.0	0.2
Low recommendations minus S&P 500 index	0.2	3.0	2.1	1.4	1.6	0.1
High minus low recommendations	3.2	−1.9	−2.3	−0.5	−1.0	0.0

(continued)

Table 5-5. *Investment Value of Recommendations by the Ten Global Settlement Firms, Pre- and Post-Settlement (Value-Weighted Portfolios) (continued)*

Firm and recommendations	1999	2000	2001	2002	2003	2004
Firm 3						
High recommendations	3.4	2.0	−0.6	−1.5	2.7	0.4
High recommendations minus						
S&P 500 index	2.6	2.0	0.8	0.6	0.3	0.4
Medium recommendations	2.3	2.1	0.2	−0.3	3.3	0.5
Medium recommendations minus						
S&P 500 index	1.5	2.1	1.6	1.9	0.9	0.5
Low recommendations	1.2	2.8	0.3	−0.4	5.0	0.6
Low recommendations minus						
S&P 500 index	0.4	2.9	1.8	1.8	2.6	0.6
High minus low recommendations	2.2	−0.8	−0.9	−1.2	−2.3	−0.2
Firm 4						
High recommendations	2.5	1.3	−0.7	−1.5	2.8	0.9
High recommendations minus						
S&P 500 index	1.7	1.4	0.8	0.6	0.4	0.9
Medium recommendations	2.4	2.2	0.2	−1.0	3.0	0.1
Medium recommendations minus						
S&P 500 index	1.6	2.2	1.7	1.1	0.6	0.1
Low recommendations	2.4	3.0	−0.4	−0.8	3.9	0.8
Low recommendations minus						
S&P 500 index	1.6	3.0	1.1	1.3	1.5	0.8
High minus low recommendations	0.1	−1.7	−0.3	−0.7	−1.0	0.1
Firm 5						
High recommendations	2.9	1.6	−1.0	−1.5	2.7	0.4
High recommendations minus						
S&P 500 index	2.1	1.7	0.4	0.7	0.3	0.4
Medium recommendations	2.6	2.5	0.3	−0.6	3.0	0.6
Medium recommendations minus						
S&P 500 index	1.8	2.6	1.7	1.5	0.6	0.6
Low recommendations	1.6	3.3	0.5	−1.0	3.8	0.5
Low recommendations minus						
S&P 500 index	0.8	3.3	2.0	1.1	1.4	0.4
High minus low recommendations	1.3	−1.6	−1.5	−0.5	−1.1	0.0

(continued)

Table 5-5. *Investment Value of Recommendations by the Ten Global Settlement Firms, Pre- and Post-Settlement (Value-Weighted Portfolios) (continued)*

Firm and recommendations	1999	2000	2001	2002	2003	2004
Firm 6						
High recommendations	3.0	2.0	−0.2	−1.6	2.7	0.5
High recommendations minus S&P 500 index	2.2	2.1	1.2	0.5	0.3	0.5
Medium recommendations	2.5	2.3	−0.5	−1.0	3.1	0.7
Medium recommendations minus S&P 500 index	1.7	2.4	0.9	1.1	0.7	0.7
Low recommendations	1.7	2.3	−0.4	−0.1	2.9	0.4
Low recommendations minus S&P 500 index	0.9	2.4	1.0	2.0	0.5	0.4
High minus low recommendations	1.3	−0.3	0.2	−1.5	−0.2	0.2
Firm 7						
High recommendations	5.7	1.3	−0.4	−0.8	3.0	0.4
High recommendations minus S&P 500 index	4.9	1.4	1.0	1.3	0.6	0.4
Medium recommendations	3.7	3.4	0.3	−1.6	3.1	0.8
Medium recommendations minus S&P 500 index	2.9	3.5	1.7	0.5	0.7	0.8
Low recommendations	3.2	2.1	0.8	−1.1	4.5	−1.4
Low recommendations minus S&P 500 index	2.4	2.2	2.2	1.0	2.1	−1.4
High minus low recommendations	2.5	−0.8	−1.2	0.3	−1.5	1.8
Firm 8						
High recommendations	2.5	2.0	−0.7	−1.2	2.8	0.5
High recommendations minus S&P 500 index	1.7	2.0	0.7	0.9	0.4	0.5
Medium recommendations	2.3	1.2	0.3	−1.7	3.2	0.8
Medium recommendations minus S&P 500 index	1.5	1.3	1.7	0.5	0.8	0.8
Low recommendations	1.2	3.1	0.6	−0.4	4.3	1.2
Low recommendations minus S&P 500 index	0.4	3.1	2.1	1.7	1.9	1.2
High minus low recommendations	1.2	−1.1	−1.3	−0.8	−1.5	−0.7

(continued)

Table 5-5. *Investment Value of Recommendations by the Ten Global Settlement Firms, Pre- and Post-Settlement (Value-Weighted Portfolios) (continued)*

Firm and recommendations	1999	2000	2001	2002	2003	2004
Firm 9						
High recommendations	3.2	1.9	−0.6	−1.3	2.8	0.2
High recommendations minus S&P 500 index	2.4	1.9	0.8	0.8	0.4	0.2
Medium recommendations	2.5	2.7	−0.2	−1.0	3.4	0.9
Medium recommendations minus S&P 500 index	1.8	2.8	1.3	1.1	1.0	0.9
Low recommendations	1.5	1.7	0.2	−1.2	3.6	1.2
Low recommendations minus S&P 500 index	0.7	1.8	1.7	0.9	1.2	1.2
High minus low recommendations	1.7	0.2	−0.8	−0.1	−0.8	−1.0
Firm 10						
High recommendations	2.5	1.9	−0.4	−1.1	2.9	0.2
High recommendations minus S&P 500 index	1.7	1.9	1.0	1.0	0.5	0.2
Medium recommendations	1.2	2.2	0.2	−0.7	3.0	1.0
Medium recommendations minus S&P 500 index	0.4	2.2	1.7	1.4	0.6	1.0
Low recommendations	−1.5	4.7	−1.6	−1.5	4.3	−0.5
Low recommendations minus S&P 500 index	−2.3	4.7	−0.2	0.6	1.9	−0.5
High minus low recommendations	3.9	−2.8	1.2	0.4	−1.4	0.7

This table reports the investment value of recommendations of the ten Global Settlement firms. Individual firms' identities are masked, with firms randomly assigned a number of one through ten. Each firm's three most frequently used recommendation levels are divided into "high" (most favorable recommendation), "medium" (next most favorable), and "low" (least favorable). Standing recommendations are calculated at the end of each month, and then portfolios are formed as shown below. Stocks are "value weighted" within portfolios (that is, stocks are weighted according to their market capitalization). Portfolios are rebalanced monthly. This table reports the mean monthly return each year (percent) from these investment portfolio strategies. Results are shown separately for each firm's recommendations along with the results equally averaged across all ten firms. Portfolio performance compared with the Standard and Poor's (S&P) 500 index provides a measure of the recommendations' relative investment value compared with investing in a mutual fund that replicates the S&P 500 index. The last line ("High minus low recommendations") provides a measure of how well analysts' high-ranked stocks performed compared with their low-ranked stocks.

raw data into investor-friendly report cards on the accuracy of the firms' research.[27]

In addition, NYSE and NASD analyst rules, effective 2002 and applicable to all brokerage analysts, require that along with the current recommendation rating of the stock, sell-side analysts publish the historical price performance of recommendations that they have made for that stock. It is unclear why individual investors should have to purchase private services to make sell-side research user friendly. The empirical findings presented here suggest that determining the investment value to be gained from standing (often "stale") recommendations of the ten Global Settlement firms is complicated in the sense that data need to be drawn across the aggregate of the firm's recommendations and compared against meaningful benchmarks, such as all the stocks for which the firm issued its other rankings. In addition, as higher returns are expected if investors take on higher risks, reporting higher returns without disclosing the risks those investments carry is misleading at best.

In the introduction to this chapter, I recommend disclosure on an ongoing basis of the performance of each firm's aggregate analyst recommendations. Because it is unlikely that the firms will provide these aggregate comparative reports voluntarily, we recommend that the statistics be calculated and provided by regulators on their websites for the Global Settlement firms. Furthermore, it is unclear why regulators could not also provide aggregate statistics for brokerage firms that were not part of the Global Settlement as those firms also are now required by the 2002 analyst rules to disclose historical price performance for each individual recommendation.

References

Barber, Brad, and others. 2001. "Can Investors Profit from the Prophets? Security Analyst Recommendations and Stock Returns." *Journal of Finance* 56, no. 2 (April): 531–63.

Boni, Leslie, and Kent Womack. 2002a. "Wall Street's Credibility Problem: Misaligned Incentives and Dubious Fixes?" *Brookings-Wharton Papers on Financial Services* (Brookings): 93–130.

———. 2002b. "Solving the Sell-Side Research Problem: Insights from Buy-Side Professionals." University of New Mexico and Dartmouth College.

———. 2006. "Analysts, Industries, and Price Momentum." *Journal of Financial and Quantitative Analysis,* forthcoming.

27. William H. Donaldson, speech prepared for SEC press conference regarding Global Settlement (www.sec.gov/news/speech/spch042803whd.htm [March 3, 2006]).

Busse, Jeffrey A., and T. Clifton Green. 2002. "Market Efficiency in Real Time." *Journal of Financial Economics* 65, no.3: 415–37.

Fama, Eugene, and Ken French. 1993. "Common Risk Factors in the Returns on Stocks and Bonds." *Journal of Financial Economics* 33, no. 1: 3–56.

Green, T. Clifton. 2004. "The Value of Client Access to Analyst Recommendations." Working Paper. Atlanta: Emory University, Goizueta Business School (February).

Hong, Harrison, Terence Lim, and Jeremy C. Stein. 2000. "Bad News Travels Slowly: Size, Analyst Coverage, and Profitability of Momentum Strategies." *Journal of Finance* 55, no.1: 265–96.

Ivkovic, Zoran, and Narasimhan Jegadeesh. 2004. "The Timing and the Value of Forecast and Recommendation Revisions." *Journal of Financial Economics* 73, no. 3: 433–63.

Jegadeesh, Narasimhan, and Woojin Kim. 2004. "Value of Analyst Recommendations: International Evidence." Atlanta: Emory University (March).

Jegadeesh, Narasimhan, and Sheridan Titman. 1993. "Returns to Buying Winners and Selling Losers: Implications for Stock Market Efficiency." *Journal of Finance* 48, no. 1: 65–91.

Jegadeesh, Narasimhan, and others. 2004. "Analyzing the Analysts: When Do Recommendations Add Value?" *Journal of Finance* 59, no. 3: 1083–124.

Madureira, Leonardo. 2004. "Conflicts of Interest, Regulations, and Stock Recommendations." University of Pennsylvania, Wharton School (October).

Stickel, Scott E. 1995. "The Anatomy of the Performance of Buy and Sell Recommendations." *Financial Analysts Journal* 51, no. 5 (September–October): 25–39.

Womack, Kent L. 1996. "Do Brokerage Analysts' Recommendations Have Investment Value?" *Journal of Finance* 51, no. 1: 137–67.

COMMENT BY
George Perry

LESLIE BONI ADDRESSES a number of useful and interesting topics in this chapter, and she provides a lot of evidence on the performance of sell-side analysts. Since I had no priors, all the results were news to me. What more can you ask?

I want to comment on just a few of the results. I will refer to "pre-settlement" and "post-settlement" data, and I will refer to the different stock categories as "buys," "holds" and "sells," since that is what I am used to doing. They also could be referred to as high, medium, and low recommendations.

Averaging across firms, table 5-1 shows a substantial reduction in sell recommendations in the post-settlement years, along with little change in the buys. On the face of it, that is not what you might expect if, as Leslie correctly notes, the concern was that analysts had been guilty of pumping up stocks for their investment bankers in the pre-settlement years. As for individual firms, table 5-1 also shows that analysts at seven of the ten firms reduced their buys by a noticeable amount (though one of these changed to abruptly more buys in the last year), a change that would be consistent with addressing the concerns that the chapter describes and that may provide some evidence that the firms' behavior had changed. Of course, a reduction in the number of buys may reflect a change of opinion about the overall market rather than presage an end to bias in recommendations. But if that is true, then the pattern over time of the buy recommendations is hardly evidence of good market timing, because buy recommendations were being reduced at the wrong time.

Table 5-1 provides a measure of clustering of firms' recommendations for individual stocks that shows how many of the ten firms shared the same recommendation—buy, sell, or hold—for any individual stock. That is an interesting question, and Leslie finds a small increase in clustering, on average, in the post-settlement period, and that result holds across individual firms. But if I understand correctly, the measure doesn't distinguish two very different things: how many firms covered the stock and how much those firms agreed. For example, a cluster value of 3 for a buy, which is in the neighborhood of the average that Leslie shows us, could mean that three firms covered the stock and all of them agreed that it was a buy. Or it could mean that ten firms covered that stock but that seven of them gave it a sell or a hold recommendation and only three called it a buy. Those are two very different stories.

Tables 5-3 and 5-4 present the most intriguing and puzzling results in the chapter. To keep it brief, I refer only to table 5-4, in which the results are based on value-weighted recommendations. There are two striking results here. First, the buy recommendations outperformed the S&P index in every year, surely a sign that clients were being well-served. And second, the sell recommendations outperformed the buys in all years but one, surely a sign that clients should look elsewhere for their advice.

In a comparison of the pre- and post-settlement years, the buy recommendations did relatively worse in the post-settlement years measured against either the S&P index or the sell recommendations. Leslie suggests that the good performance against the S&P index may be explained by a preponderance of small-cap stocks in the recommendations and the greater risk that investors take when they buy such stocks. She also reports that regressions using various measures of risk support that sensible thought. To further explore that and some of the other results in table 5-4, I put together a table (see table 5-6) that compares the analysts' performance with two indexes that give more weight to small-cap stocks than the S&P 500 does. One is the Wilshire 5000 index, which includes large- and small-cap stocks, more or less appropriately weighted. The second is the S&P Small Cap 600 index, which is confined to small-cap stocks.

My table, by the way, converts Leslie's data to annual rather than monthly returns. The numbers are the same, but it is much more exciting to make the comparisons based on what we all are accustomed to, which is the annual rate of return. Also, I omitted 2002 in comparing the pre- and post-settlement periods, which are shown in the last two columns of my table on the right. Since regulatory

Table 5-6. *Various Measures of Equity Returns, 1999–2004*

Measure	1999	2000	2001	2002	2003	2004	1999–2004 average	1999–2001 average	2003–04 average
Table 5-4									
Annual percentage returns, value weighted									
Buy recommendation	47.6	22.4	−8.1	−14.5	39.3	4.9	15.3	20.7	22.1
Sell recommendation	18.2	39.3	1.2	−9.2	60.1	4.9	19.1	19.6	32.5
Buy less sell	29.5	−16.9	−9.3	−5.3	−20.8	0.0	−3.8	1.1	−10.4
S&P Small-Cap 600 Index									
Annual percentage returns excluding dividends, value weighted	11.5	13.0	5.7	−15.3	37.5	21.6	12.3	10.1	29.6
Buy less small cap	36.1	9.4	−13.8	0.8	1.7	−16.7	2.9	10.6	−7.5
Sell less small cap	6.6	26.3	−4.5	6.1	22.6	−16.7	6.7	9.5	2.9
Wilshire 5000 Index									
Annual percentage returns including dividends, value weighted	23.6	−10.9	−11.0	−20.9	31.6	12.6	4.2	0.6	22.1
Buy less Wilshire	24.1	33.3	2.9	6.3	7.6	−7.7	11.1	20.1	0.0
Sell less Wilshire	−5.4	50.2	12.2	11.7	28.5	−7.7	14.9	19.0	10.4

changes were instituted during 2002, if I put 2002 in the pre-settlement period, there would be no qualitative change in the results of the comparisons.

A few points in my table are worth highlighting. One is that the performance of buys relative to sells deteriorates sharply in the post-settlement years. In the presettlement years, the buys outperformed the sells by 1.1 percent a year, whereas in the post-settlement years, they underperformed the sells by 10.4 percent a year. The underperformance of the buys, therefore, is concentrated in the second period. What explanation could there be for this? One that occurred to me is that the stocks that interested investment bankers were in fact stocks that were worth investing in (at least for a time), and that in the pre-settlement years, their forced entry onto the buy lists overcame relatively poor independent stock-picking by analysts. This was exposed in the post-settlement years, when we saw the analysts' own best views of the stocks. That is a cynical interpretation of analysts' capacities, but it is consistent with the story that we are trying to examine and to change.

However, that explanation does not really address the biggest surprise in the data. The Wilshire 5000 index should resemble the universe from which the recommendations were drawn, yet when we compare the numbers in the bottom panel, the *sell* recommendations strongly outperformed the Wilshire index in both the pre- and post-settlement years. On average, the sells outperformed the Wilshire index by 19 percent a year in the pre-settlement years and by 10.4 percent a year in the post-settlement years.

And the puzzle deepens when we look at the comparison with the small-cap index. That index outperformed the Wilshire in both the pre- and post-settlement periods. Yet despite the large weight of large-caps in recommendations, the sell recommendations outperformed the small-cap index in both the pre- and post-settlement years.

The only conjecture that I can come up with for this result is awfully cynical. Leslie's data come from IBES, which gets them from the individual firms. The result is so strange that it is hard to believe that the data are not somehow corrupted. Is it possible that when a rating goes bad, coverage is dropped before the reporting period, so that you never observe outlier bad news? Or is there some other way in which big mistakes go unreported in the IBES data? These possibilities make me wonder how accurate those data are. And if accuracy is a problem, then some of the recommendations that Leslie offers—for example, that regulators use those data to provide the information that investors like to have—may not be so useful.

Finally, let me turn to what most concerned investors and regulators, which was, of course, that firms with investment banking ties pushed certain stocks on their customers, a practice that surely existed and that concentrated on larger stocks, which is where the money was. Those stocks are in the average figures for everything that was recommended, but their performance would be better detected if we could look specifically at the stocks of large-cap companies that have made use of investment banking firms.

I assume that with a lot of work, that could be done using this dataset, though it raises the problem of where to assign a stock whose market value changes sharply. Many companies grew from small-cap to large-cap companies during the boom, and quite a few went from large-cap to no-cap after the bubble burst. So, off the top of my head, if I had to do that I would include a stock in a larger category when it got there and then keep it there for some period—say, perhaps, half a year after it got small again—just to reflect the actual behavior that we are trying to identify to see whether it has changed.

In any case, if it were possible to analyze one of these subsets of the data, it might bring the influence of investment banking on analysts' recommendations into sharper focus. Evidence of different behavior in the pre- and post-settlement analysis would suggest that the separation of investment banking from stock recommending accomplished its purpose, at least for now. I hasten to add that one can always ask for more, and it might be very difficult and perhaps impossible to actually accomplish that with these data. Leslie's work, using all the data, provides a useful first look at this issue. Even if the analysts' data prove to have some upward bias—and even if my suspicion that the data may be unreliable or biased proves true—as long as that bias is always present, it need not detract from the comparison of pre- and post-settlement performance that this chapter presents.

JOHN COFFEE

6

Conclusion

To analyze the role of gatekeepers intelligently, one must begin by defining what the term *gatekeeper* means. Two definitions are often used in the literature. The first and broader definition simply describes anyone who must give a necessary consent for a transaction or activity, literally or metaphorically, as a gatekeeper. Thus, a gatekeeper is one who possesses blocking or veto authority—that is, one who can close the gate. This broad definition encompasses a wide range of people and institutions. For example, under this definition, a board of directors is a gatekeeper.

A second and narrower definition of *gatekeeper* focuses on a professional's status as a reputational intermediary whose job is to assure investors and others of the reliability of representations made by the intermediary's client. This type of gatekeeper pledges its own reputational capital—which was likely built up over hundreds of clients and maybe a century or more of operations—because the client itself is not perceived as sufficiently trustworthy. For example, investors may not initially trust a young company's financial results, but if PricewaterhouseCoopers pledges its reputational capital that it has accumulated over 150 years on the company's behalf, then investors are more likely to consider those numbers reliable. This enables the young company to market its securities when otherwise it might not be able to do so or could do so only at a significant discount. On the other hand, if the financial results prove false, the professional reputation of the auditor will be damaged.

Who qualifies as a gatekeeper depends on which of these two definitions we use. Under the second and stricter definition of *gatekeeper*, well-established auditors and securities analysts may function as reputational intermediaries, but most boards of directors probably would not. This is because directors do not have well-known personal reputations. Nor can they pledge their reputations in the way that a professional firm does. Thus, boards of directors can be gatekeepers in the first sense of possessing a veto power, but not in the second sense of serving as a reputational intermediary.

This second definition hinges on the concept of reputational capital, and that concept has some problematic features. First, observers have recognized that competition is often lacking in many markets for gatekeeping services (for example, there are only four major accounting firms and only two major credit rating agencies). This should not come as a surprise, because reputational capital cannot be developed overnight. Even if a new entrant could assemble enough assets to challenge the Big Four auditors, investors would not immediately trust the newcomer. A reputation for integrity cannot simply be purchased. But, as a result, in concentrated markets firms may implicitly collude so as not to compete on the basis of their reputational capital.

Second, a more pervasive problem with reputational capital is that the gatekeeper may wish to present itself in different ways to different audiences. To investors, the gatekeeper wants to be viewed as reliable, totally honest, unbending, and principled, someone who will not tolerate fraud or deception. But to corporate managements, the gatekeeper may want to have a reputation for flexibility and creative problem solving, someone who can help them achieve their goals and knows all the tricks. The result can be "reputational schizophrenia"—as the gatekeeper tries to maintain inconsistent reputations with different audiences. In turn, this makes critical who hires and monitors the gatekeepers.

What is the social utility of gatekeepers? A typical entrepreneur about to do an IPO is often under pressure and faced with difficult decisions, the results of which could make the difference between going bankrupt or making millions of dollars. Investors understandably will be reluctant to trust someone subject to that kind of pressure, particularly when it has a strong incentive to overstate its financial results. In contrast, a third-party gatekeeper can be more easily trusted because the gatekeeper does not have as direct a stake in the success of a company that it evaluates. Also, the gatekeeper has a greater interest in its reputation for integrity, because it serves many clients and obtains business based on that reputation. The gatekeeper also is more likely to be deterred by the threat of legal liability than is its principal, because it has less to gain. Gatekeeping, therefore, is a law-compliance strategy with proven effectiveness. Long before there were securities laws, there were stock markets that relied upon auditors.

Who are the gatekeepers? The most familiar example of auditors has already been mentioned, but there are newer examples that play a functionally similar role. Securities analysts, investment banking firms, law firms, and credit rating agencies are other obvious examples that sometimes vouch for a company's statements. But there are newer and more novel examples. For example, lead plaintiffs in class action suits, such as Calpers or TIAA/CREF, may represent a new type of gatekeeper. Essentially, they choose the class counsel who prosecutes the class action. When a class action is filed, the first question for all the other class members is whether to opt out or to stay in the class. If they trust the ability and reputation of the lead plaintiff, they are less likely to opt out.

Another interesting new type of gatekeeper is the nominated adviser, or Nomad. Nomads have been increasingly relied upon in the Alternative Investment Market (AIM), a part of the London Stock Exchange that was launched in 1995 and has grown substantially since then. AIM is a market for emerging companies, set up to compete with the German Neuer Markt and, to a lesser extent, with NASDAQ. It lists companies that are emerging high-tech companies, which typically lack their own reputations and often have no real operating history. In particular, AIM has a lot of mining and exploration companies, and in the past the stocks of such companies have been exploited and manipulated.

The attraction to many issuers of AIM is that is has practically no regulation. Its main rule is that for a company to list and do an offering, a Nomad has to approve the appropriateness of the offering, its terms, and all related disclosures. The nominated adviser decides what the company is required to disclose. To become a Nomad, an applicant must be approved by the exchange. There are now approximately seventy-five Nomads; they are principally major underwriting firms, but they also include major accounting firms and one or two law firms. These Nomads are gatekeepers under both our earlier definitions because they have a veto power and they are relied-upon investors who would not necessarily trust the issuer. A Nomad possesses probably the greatest discretionary authority given to any gatekeeper: someone who oversees all of the terms and disclosure decisions for client companies that lack the experience or reputation to be trusted to make such decisions themselves. In turn, a Nomad is monitored by the stock exchange that approved it. But its success is still unproven.

A better known and more controversial gatekeeper is the securities analyst. Following the "dot.com bubble" of 2000–01, securities analysts fell into some disrespect because of their apparent optimistic bias and reluctance to ever recommend that a client's stock be sold. An investigation by New York Attorney General Eliot Spitzer revealed that many individual analysts had been pressured by their employers at broker-dealer firms to inflate their recommendations of firm clients. As a result, recent reforms have attempted to create an impenetrable Chinese Wall between analysts and underwriters in order to protect them from pressure. Unfortunately, these reforms have come at a high price; they have made these analysts relatively more independent, but also less prevalent. The irony is that we have less bias, but possibly also less market transparency. Prior to these reforms, the typical company listed on the New York Stock Exchange was covered by perhaps a half dozen analysts. Indeed, the SEC recently found that well-known, seasoned issuers had, on average, twelve analysts. But today, the bottom half of firms listed on the NASDAQ often may not have a single full-time analyst. The reason is that the analysts are no longer being subsidized by the underwriters, who are no longer allowed to communicate with, or determine the compensation of, the analyst in order to reduce pressure that previously influenced analyst research. The consequence has been a reduction in both the number of analysts and the number of firms covered by research. Because securities analysts do not directly charge investors a fee for their services, some indirect means must be found to subsidize their efforts. Reforms that simply barred underwriters from any attempt to influence analysts produced greater independence, but reduced transparency. The result is a Pyrrhic victory and shows the difficulty in regulatory attempts to improve gatekeeper performance. For the long term, the goal must be to find a way to subsidize research without thereby biasing it.

Currently, some new start-up firms, such as the National Research Exchange (NRE) and the Independent Research Exchange (IRE), are seeking to develop a new business model, something called "intermediated" research. Under this model, a "marriage broker" firm would be hired by companies to find and to select an objective securities analyst for the company. As with any other gatekeeper, the success of this marriage broker depends on whether investors will trust the reputation of the intermediary. Both of these new entities have grown out of NASDAQ. The NRE was formed by the former senior executives of NASDAQ, and the IRE is a joint venture between NASDAQ and Reuters. Although the success of these new entities is uncertain, they show that the market may be able to create new gatekeepers in response to new problems.

Recent experience with various types of gatekeepers underscores the growing impact of conflicts of interest across a broad variety of contexts. What explains these newly intensified problems? A good place to begin is with a 2002 Government Accountability Office (GAO) study on the number of financial statements

Figure 6-1. *Number of Restatement Announcements Identified, 1997–2002*

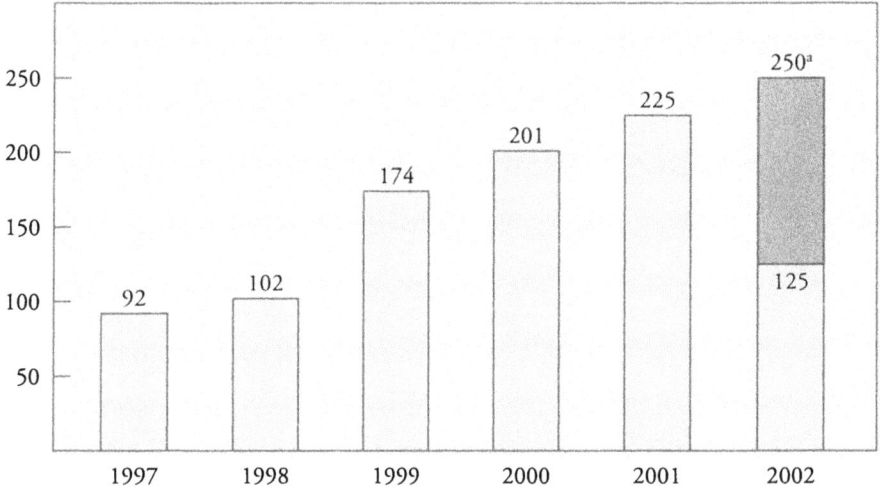

Source: Government Accountability Office.
a. Projected year end.

and restatements (see figure 6-1).[1] If we go back to the early 1990s, several studies have shown that on average, only about forty to fifty public companies a year announced financial restatements. By 2002, however, this number had increased hyperbolically to 250, and over the five-year period between 1997 and 2002, more than 10 percent of all the publicly traded companies on the stock exchange restated their financial statements at least once. More recently, by some accounts, the number has soared to over 1,000 in 2005. This suggests that Enron and WorldCom were not isolated examples but representative of a general decline in the reliability of financial reporting.

This hypothesis of a decline in the reliability of financial reporting is corroborated by more recent data from Huron Consulting (see figure 6-2). In fact, Huron calculated an even larger number of restatements than the GAO. It found that about one in eight companies, or 12.5 percent, restated their financial statements over the same five-year period.[2]

1. Government Accountability Office (2002).
2. See Huron Consulting Group, "2003 Annual Review of Financial Reporting Matters" at 4 (finding 330 restatements in 2002).

Figure 6-2. *Huron Consulting Restatements, by Year Filed*

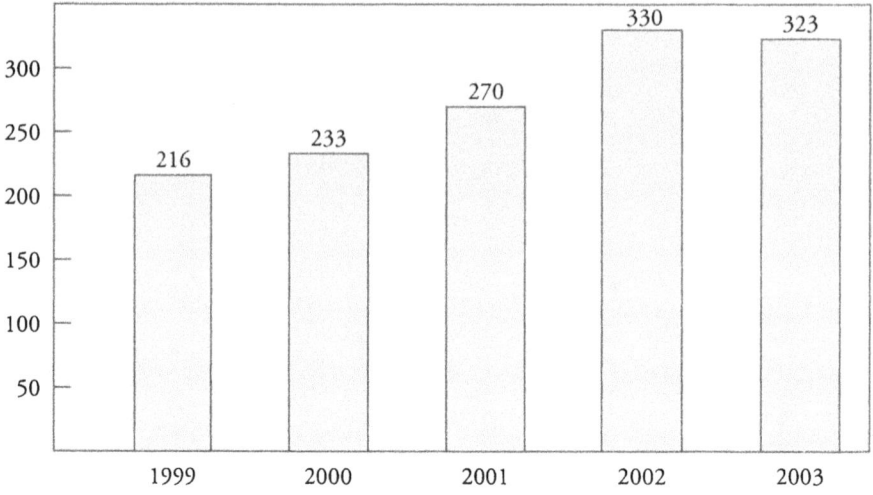

Source: Huron Consulting Group.

Restatements often have significant adverse impacts. The GAO study found that the average restating firm in its study lost 10 percent of its market capitalization over a three-day trading period surrounding the restatement's announcement, for a total loss across all companies studied of about $100 billion.

If the average restatement causes a 10 percent decline over a three-day trading period, this means that the stock market was surprised. Overall, a significant number of such surprises implies a real loss of investor confidence. One of the primary goals of reforms, such as the Sarbanes-Oxley Act, was to increase the predictability and certainty of financial reporting and thus to reduce the cost of equity capital. Lowering the cost of equity capital is an important social objective; it benefits not only investors, but the entire economy. To the extent that the cost of equity capital rises because of a lack of confidence in the accuracy of financial statements, a country's gross national product (GNP) will be adversely affected, and unemployment could rise.

Still, what underlay this sudden rise in restatements? Studies have reported that the most negative market reactions were those associated with restatements involving revenue recognition issues, such as prematurely recognizing income or treating consignments as sales. The GAO study found that revenue recognition issues were also the most common cause of restatements, accounting for about 38 percent of them. This trend toward premature revenue recognition was a symptom of a "disease" that began to spread over the financial markets in the 1990s.

Companies have always faced revenue recognition issues, but, until recently, managers typically reacted very differently to discretionary opportunities to recognize income. In the past, managers often "smoothed," or understated, earnings by deferring recognition, because they feared that the market would not give sufficient credit to significant earnings growth during a particular period. By hiding earnings in reserves and spreading them out later over time, managers could create the impression of smoother, more consistent earnings and avoid any suggestion of earnings volatility, which suggested higher risk and discouraged investors.

In the 1990s, however, the pattern of managerial behavior changed abruptly. Managers wanted to maximize current earnings, holding nothing back for the future. Accordingly, they pressured their auditors for premature recognition of income and used aggressive tactics, such as "channel stuffing," to maximize current earnings at the expense of later periods. What explains the change?

The most likely explanation for this change lies in a major transition in executive compensation during the 1990s. In 1990, the total compensation of a CEO of a large public corporation was composed of 92 percent cash and 8 percent equity. In 2001, its composition had shifted to two-thirds equity and one-third cash.[3] During the 1990s, without the fact being fully recognized, the U.S. system of executive compensation shifted, almost overnight, from cash to equity (figure 6-3). Equity compensation in itself is certainly not necessarily bad. All compensation systems have some perverse incentives. But this was a very rapid change, and as often happens, the market moved quickly, while corporate governance lagged behind.

What happened to the gatekeepers over the course of this shift? They came under intense pressure from managers, who now wished to inflate corporate earnings to maximize the value of their stock options. Moreover, there were no safeguards or other compensatory changes in corporate governance to counter this new pressure and protect the reliability of financial reporting.

In fairness, cash compensation also has its own set of problems. It creates incentives for what Michael Jensen calls "empire building": namely, the inefficient expansion of firms and the hoarding of "free cash flow" to justify higher cash salaries. That is the principal reason why institutional investors encouraged the shift from cash to equity-based compensation. They wanted managers to be more sensitive to the market. But they did not fully realize that at some point increased equity compensation could result in too much of a good thing.

3. See Hall (2003).

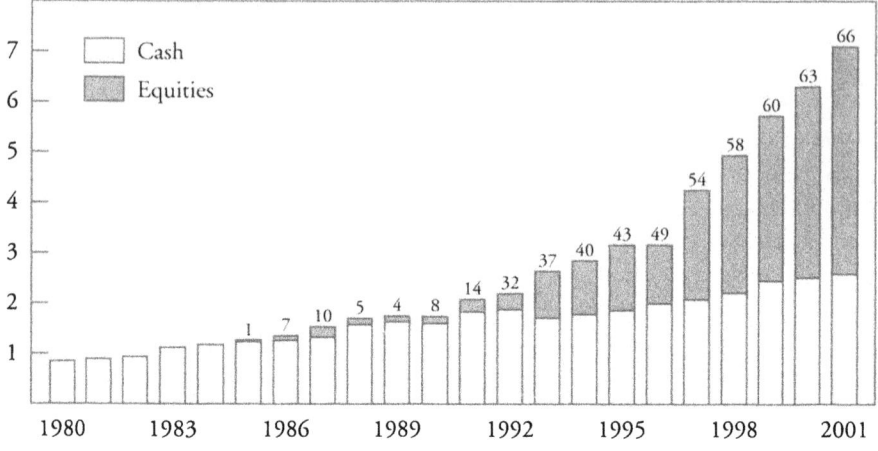

Figure 6-3. *Executive Compensation in Cash and Equities, 1980–2001*[a]

Source: Brian J. Hall, Harvard Business School.
a. Numbers indicate percentage of compensation in equities.

This problem is best illustrated by a simple example. Assume that a CEO has stock options covering two million shares, and his company has a 30:1 price-earnings ratio. If he can create just one dollar of additional earnings that the market does not anticipate, then he effectively becomes $60 million richer. This creates a powerful incentive to push the auditors to accept more aggressive accounting policies.

Under a system of predominantly equity compensation, an incentive arises to inflate earnings and take greater risk, even if the claimed growth in earnings is unsustainable. Although the stock price will eventually fall when the market belatedly discovers the inflation, managers can exploit non-public information and bail out before the crash. Once they sense the inevitable downturn, they can sell off their own stake months before the market realizes the truth. If they do this, it may be hard to demonstrate that they possessed inside information at that earlier point. This may explain what happened with the CEO of Global Crossing, who sold several hundred million dollars' worth of his firm's shares, and, months later, his firm spiraled down into bankruptcy. Using creative tactics, a share price spike can be maintained until there is a safe distance between the insider's sale and the collapse in the stock price.

Several studies offer some evidence to support this hypothesis. One, by Efendi and others, used a sample group of ninety-seven firms that restated their

CONCLUSION

financial statements over a given period. To match this group, they created a control group of a similar number of companies with the same market capitalization and same industrial classifications, but that did not restate their financial results.[4] They found that the primary difference between the restating and nonrestating companies was the amount of "in-the-money" stock options held by the chief executive officer. The restating firms' CEOs held, on average, options worth slightly over $50 million while the nonrestating firms' CEOs held, on average, $8.8 million—a nearly six to one ratio. Such studies show the dark side of equity compensation. They do not imply that equity compensation should not be used, but that stronger controls are necessary when it is heavily relied upon to motivate managers.

Auditors were not the only gatekeeper that came under increased pressure during this period. Securities analysts show even clearer evidence of increased pressure. The ratio of buy recommendations to sell recommendations rose, between 1991 and 2000, from 6:1 to 100:1. Part of this change can be attributed to the bull market, but it is still a very abrupt increase and an unrealistic ratio. Financial economists have studied the securities analyst profession and identified the factors that most predicted success for a securities analyst in the 1990s. Revealingly, they found that the factor that most predicted career success was above-average optimism in the analyst's forecasts. To be successful during this period, optimism was a necessity.

Barber and others present data that more fully illustrate what happened to the analyst as gatekeeper (see table 6-1).[5] When they examined analysts' stock recommendations from 1996 to 2000, they found two things. First, by the end of 2000, the year in which the market hit its high point, 98.4 percent of all recommendations were either buys or holds, while only 1.6 percent were sells. Again, this suggests that analysts were subject to some of the same distorting influences and pressures that also affected auditors.

Secondly, their study also shows a significant increase over this period in the number of recommendations made. Although the number of analysts cannot substantially increase year to year, as there are barriers to entry, such as licensing requirements, the number of recommendations jumped by about 30 percent or so over a period of two years. Seemingly, the prior system under which analysts prepared a limited number of carefully researched reports deteriorated into an assembly line system, as analysts came under pressure from underwriters (and others) to put out more recommendations. Quantity became as important as quality.

4. Jap Efendi, Anup Srivastava, and Ed Swanson, "Why Do Corporate Managers Misstate Financial Statements? The Role of In-the-Money Options and Other Incentives" (http://ssrn.com/abstract=547322) (2004).

5. Barber and others (2003).

Table 6-1. *Analyst Stock Recommendations, 1996–2000*

Year	Number of recommendations	Number of companies	Percent		
			Strong Buy/ Buy	Hold	Sell/ Strong sell
1996	22,409	5,480	65.2	31.3	3.5
1997	29,647	6,390	66.4	30.1	3.5
1998	42,321	6,783	66.4	30.1	3.5
1999	43,248	6,806	70.1	27.1	2.8
2000	41,965	6,666	72.1	26.3	1.6

Source: Barber and others (2003).

Multiple hypotheses can explain these trends, and they are complementary. First, as earlier mentioned, managers likely placed increased pressure on gatekeepers to acquiesce in risk accounting and issue optimistic forecasts because of the shift to equity compensation. Second, the threat of litigation declined over this period because of the Private Securities Litigation Reform Act (PSLRA), which passed over President Clinton's veto in 1995. This reduced litigation threat shows up strikingly in the greatly reduced number of lawsuits brought in the late 1990s against gatekeepers. In a study mandated by Congress, the SEC's Office of General Counsel found that before the PSLRA there had been around 200 lawsuits a years against auditors, but in the year after the PSLRA's passage, only a small handful of cases was filed against either auditors or law firms. The PSLRA was not the only cause of this reduced threat; the Supreme Court in the *Central Bank of Denver* case eliminated "aiding and abetting" liability in 1994.[6] Such "aiding and abetting" litigation had almost uniquely focused on the gatekeepers, and such litigation disappeared after 1994.

Put these two influences together: increased pressure for optimistic forecasts (because of equity compensation) and a reduced litigation threat (because of the PSLRA and *Central Bank*). If the benefits go up and the costs go down, an increase in output is inevitable. Here, the increased output came in the form of increased acquiescence by gatekeepers in risky or misleading accounting policies.

Other factors also were relevant. As noted earlier, reputational capital is the defining prerequisite for an effective gatekeeper. However, in a bull market as overheated as that of the late 1990s, investors may grow euphoric and became less interested in the quality of accounting. When investors are enjoying unprece-

6. *Central Bank of Denver, N.A. v. First Interstate Bank of Denver, N.A.*, 511 U.S. 164 (1994) (Rule 10b-5 held not to reach aiding and abetting a securities fraud).

dented growth in the stock market year after year (as they were in the late 1990s), auditors (and the risk of fraud) are probably not much on their minds. With less public concern about fraud, the importance of reputational capital went down, and gatekeepers had less incentive to protect it at the cost of losing clients.

Lastly, conflicts of interest arose and intensified across a variety of gatekeeper markets. Beginning in a major way in the 1990s, audit firms marketed consulting services to their audit clients. Arguably, the desire to market such consulting compromised auditor independence. Audit firms perceived that consulting revenues could rise exponentially, but audit fees were likely to remain flat or experience only low growth. Thus, they shifted their business model and decided to become full-service consulting firms.

The empirical evidence in this area is in some dispute. A number of studies have examined audit firms that offered both auditing and nonauditing services to determine whether clients who purchased a higher proportion of nonaudit services were more likely to restate their earnings later. The results have been mixed, but, generally speaking, they have not established that companies with higher ratios of nonaudit to audit fees restated more frequently than those with lower ratios.

However, this finding does not resolve the issue. Even if clients that purchased nonaudit services from auditors fared no worse than those clients that did not, the overall independence of the auditor could still be compromised by the desire to market these services. If the audit firms view the consulting market as a vast new area of expansion, they may be tempted to loosen auditing standards on all clients in order to encourage the purchase of these new, more lucrative services. In short, the real conflict arises because all audit clients become potential purchasers to whom the audit partner will defer in order to market consulting services. This possibility is consistent with the significant rise in restatements over this period.

In summary, for the various reasons discussed, managers appeared to gain substantial leverage over gatekeepers through the 1990s. That was the problem that the Sarbanes-Oxley Act sought to address. Controversy continues over whether it has been successful, but the more interesting question is what other options are available for the future for improving gatekeeper performance.

One avenue for reform is increasing gatekeeping liability. Restoring auditors' liability for aiding and abetting, which was eliminated by the *Central Bank* case, could help improve the quality of their oversight. This is clearly not a popular option with accountants themselves, and it should be pursued only with caution, because there is a legitimate threat that one or another of the major firms could ultimately become insolvent if liability costs are raised too high. Therefore, liability reform should be only part of the solution.

A second means of gatekeeping reform is to increase regulatory oversight. The Public Company Accounting Oversight Board (PCAOB) was created in 2002 to help oversee the accounting industry. As with any regulatory body, there is a risk that it will be captured by the industry, but PCAOB has done a good job so far and hopefully will continue to do so under its incoming (but still not chosen) new chairman. Yet, at present, its constitutionality has been challenged in court, and its future is uncertain.

Another goal for reform should be to empower gatekeepers. As earlier discussed, gatekeepers, as agents, lost leverage vis-à-vis their clients, the principals, during the 1990s. The empowerment approach to reform is illustrated by an existing SEC rule, which requires that, whenever an auditor is fired or resigns, specific disclosure must be made of any disagreements between the auditor and its client over the preceding two years. While the company initially files this disclosure, the auditor is asked to comment on its accuracy. This rule creates an embarrassment cost and makes it more difficult to fire an auditor. It is a good example of a means by which to empower auditors so that client companies cannot unduly influence their work.

Section 307 of the Sarbanes-Oxley Act, which requires securities attorneys under certain conditions to report any crime or related misconduct to top executives or the board, or both, is a similar example of an appropriate power shift toward gatekeepers. Although Section 307 imposes a mandatory duty on the securities attorney, it thereby empowers the attorney, increasing the attorney's ability to discourage corporate misconduct. The attorney can remind corporate officials that if they persist in certain conduct, the attorney would be compelled to report them to the board. As with the previous example, this adds to the gatekeeper's leverage.

Another form of gatekeeper empowerment is Regulation Analyst Certification, which the SEC adopted in the wake of the Spitzer investigation and which requires every analyst to personally sign his or her stock recommendations—buy or sell—and confirm that they represent the analyst's personal judgment. This regulation was a by-product of Eliot Spitzer's investigation of Merrill Lynch, which revealed that many analysts were putting out inflated recommendations under pressure, while writing private e-mails mocking them. Under this rule, the individual analyst's leverage is enhanced because only he or she can release a report.

These leverage-enhancing changes are helpful, but their impact is still relatively minor. Although they permit the gatekeeper to resist, such resistance may still be career endangering. A more substantial reform would be to revise the principal-agent relationship altogether. Once, investors hired gatekeepers directly, but later that power gradually shifted to managers, thereby weakening the independence of gatekeepers. The Sarbanes-Oxley Act improved this situation marginally by requiring the auditor to report to the audit committee, rather than to the chief financial officer. But by this same token, the securities attorney could also be instructed to report directly to the audit committee.

More radical proposals have been proposed for reforming our gatekeeper system. One calls for financial statement insurance.[7] This proposal would make the auditor an agent of a major insurance company that would in turn guarantee that issuer's financial statements to investors. Before writing such an insurance policy, the insurer would hire an auditor to audit the corporation's financial statements and verify their accuracy. Because the auditor's real client would now be the insurer, the auditor would have an increased incentive to be accurate and less incentive to defer to corporate management. Similarly, there have also been proposals to reform securities analysts through a voucher system, under which shareholders receive vouchers and choose their own securities analyst.

In common, both proposals seek to identify a new principal for the gatekeeper. Both these proposals are problematic for reasons that are beyond the scope of this discussion. Yet, their desire to shift control over the gatekeepers away from managers and to shareholders is well placed. Similar reforms may be needed for the credit rating agencies. Until the 1970s, they offered their services directly to investors on a subscription basis; this approach was less conflict ridden than the current system under which the rating agencies are paid by the corporations that they rate. In all these cases, the ideal system would be for the gatekeeper to be compensated by investors, not by the client that it rates or examines.

Lastly, the ultimate reform involves the prospect of antitrust divestiture. It is not beyond the power of Congress to break up the auditing industry or any other concentrated industry. In a concentrated market, reputational capital has less importance, and so the gatekeeper may be more easily seduced into deferring to corporate managers. Because significant barriers to entry exist in many gatekeeper markets, there is little prospect that increased competition will develop in the absence of governmental intervention.

The bottom line is that our gatekeeper system of oversight was weakened by developments in the 1990s and earlier. The reforms most likely to work are those that shift the selection and control of the gatekeepers from managers to investors and that encourage competition within gatekeeper markets. Only then will reputational capital play its proper role and in turn restore to gatekeepers the ability to perform their critical social and economic function.

7. Ronen (2002).

References

Barber, Brad, Reuven Lehavy, Maureen McNichols, and Brett Trueman. 2003. "Reassessing the Returns to Analysts' Stock Recommendations." *Financial Analysts Journal* 59 (March/April): 88–90.

Government Accountability Office. 2002. *Financial Statement Restatements: Trends, Market Impacts, Regulatory Responses, and Remaining Challenges.* Report to the chairman of the Committee on Banking, Housing, and Urban Affairs, U.S. Senate. GAO-03-138.

Hall, Brian J. 2003. "The Six Challenges of Equity-Based Pay Design." *Journal of Applied Corporate Finance* 15, no. 3 (spring): 49–70.

Ronen, Joshua. 2002. "Post-Enron Reform: Financial Statement Insurance and GAAP Revisited." *Stanford Journal of Law, Business, and Finance* 8: 39–68.

Contributors

Leslie Boni
University of New Mexico

John Coffee
Columbia Law School

Yasuyuki Fuchita
Nomura Institute of Capital Markets Research

Robert E. Litan
Kauffmann Foundation and Brookings Institution

Zoe-Vonna Palmrose
University of Southern California–Los Angeles

Frank Partnoy
University of San Diego Law School

George Perry
Brookings Institution

Justin Pettit
UBS

Paul Stevens
Investment Company Institute

Peter Wallison
American Enterprise Institute

Index

Abrams, Floyd, 94–95
Accounting Standards Board of Japan (ASBJ), 24
Accounting system, comparison of U.S. and Japan: continuity of engagement, 24–25; fees of auditors, 28, 30f; governance of CPAs, 23–24, 45, 49; liability issues, 25–26; number of accountants, 26–27, 27t; PCAOB vs. CPAAOB, 25, 49; reform measures, 4, 23–26; time spent for audits, 27
Accounting system in Japan, 16–29; amendment to Certified Public Accountants Law (*2003*), 3, 20–21, 26; and continuity of engagement, 20; fees of auditors, 4, 19, 28–29; initial efforts to reform, 18–19; insufficient time for audits, 27–28; post-Enron reform, 19–20; recent problems and further reforms, 5, 21–23; remaining issues for, 26–29; shortage of accountants, 4, 26–27
Accounting system in U.S.: antitrust approach to regulating, 189; and client misrepresentation, 7; competition among auditors, 57–58; consultant work performed by, 14, 52; and continuity of engagement, 24; decline in profitability of, 66; effect of reforms on, 6–8, 103–35; and engagement risk, 7–8, 109–13, 121–22; and fees, 8, 25, 28, 30f, 113; and fraudulent reporting of clients, 105, 123, 124–29, 136–37; and gatekeeper role of auditors, 106–09; generally accepted accounting principles (GAAP), effect of use of, 47, 105, 107, 111–12; governance of profession at state and federal levels, 23–24; and liability issues, 7, 11, 25–26, 106; number of and shortage of accountants, 26, 27t, 50–51; recommendations for effective oversight of, 8; Sarbanes-Oxley Act, effect on, 103–35, 189; scandals of, 1–2, 11, 13, 66, 137; and securities law and regulation, 107; types of risk of auditors, 110, 111f; Wallison comment on, 136–38. *See also* Public Company Accounting Oversight Board (PCAOB)

193

AICPA. *See* American Institute of Certified Public Accountants
Aiding and abetting liability of auditors, 186, 187
Alternative Investment Market (AIM), 179
American Assembly recommendations on PCAOB liability for audit failure, 128–29, 138
American Institute of Certified Public Accountants (AICPA), 7, 24, 25, 26
American Savings Bank v. *UBS PaineWebber (2002)*, 87
Analysis of Railroad Investments (Moody), 63
Analysts in Japan: comparison with U.S., 4, 36–38, 45, 49, 51; consideration of proper agency to regulate, 44–45; future implications of regulations on, 42–43; lessons from Japan's financial gatekeeping, 45–54; regulation of, 4–5, 38–42
Analysts in U.S., 8–10; compensation basis for, 2, 9; competition among, 58; conflicts of interest of, 57, 140; data used in study to determine effect of Global Settlement, 144–46; distortions in market due to (*1996–2000*), 185–86, 186t; effect of Global Settlement, 9–10, 43, 139–70; gains/losses from trading on analyst recommendations post-settlement, 157–65, 160–63t, 166–69t, 173–76, 174t; gatekeeper role of, 140, 179–80; ineffectual regulation of, 57, 180; investigation of compensation system of, 2, 9; investor reactions to analyst recommendations post-settlement, 155–57, 158t; nature of analyst recommendations post-settlement, 146–55, 148–53t; optimism of, effect of, 11, 13, 154, 186; Perry comment on, 172–76; recommended disclosure requirements for, 10, 143, 154, 170; reduction in number of, 180. *See also* Global Settlement

Ancillary services. *See* consultant work
Arbitrage. *See* collateralized debt obligations (CDOs)
Arthur Andersen, 13, 66, 137
ASBJ (Accounting Standards Board of Japan), 24
Attorneys: duty to report corporate misconduct under SOX, 188; positions within PCAOB, 118
Auditors. *See headings starting with* "accounting system"

Bank for International Settlements on CDO risk, 78
Banking Bureau of the Ministry of Finance, 17
Banking issues in Japan, 15–16, 17, 38–39, 44
Bankruptcy: in Japan, 4, 17; of U.S. auditing firms, 126
Barber, Brad, 185
Basel II and credit ratings, 35, 48, 83
Bear Stearns Cos., 65
Benston, G., 52
Big Five international accounting firms in dealings with Japanese accounting firms, 18
Bond market in Japan, 29, 31–32; and Mycal failure, 33–34
Bond market in U.S. *See* credit rating agencies in U.S.
Business Accounting Council (Japan), 22–23, 24
Busse, J. A., 155

CDOs. *See* collateralized debt obligations
CDSs. *See* credit default swaps
Central Bank of Denver v. *First Interstate Bank of Denver (1994)*, 186, 187
Certified Public Accountant Examination and Investigation Board (CPAEIB; Japan), 18–19, 21

INDEX

Certified Public Accountants and Auditing Oversight Board (CPAAOB; Japan): compared to U.S. PCAOB, 25, 49; creation of, 3, 20; influences on and impartiality of, 53; role and structure of, 21, 22

Certified Public Accountants Law (Japan): *2003* amendments to, 3, 20–21, 26; fee schedule of accountants under, 28; initial passage and scope of, 24; Ministry of Finance role under, 19

ChuoAoyama PricewaterhouseCoopers, 23, 26

Class actions against auditors, 124–27, 125t

Coffee, J. C., Jr., 96

Collateralized debt obligations (CDOs), 5, 60, 74–80, 93, 96

Commercial Code (Japan), 25–26

Commercial Financial Services v. Arthur Andersen (*2004*), 87

Commercial speech, regulation of, 85

Compensation: of analysts in Japan, 43; of analysts in U.S., 2, 9, 43; of CEOs and effect on revenue recognition, 11, 183–85, 184f; from consultant work, 14; effect on independence of gatekeeper, 52. *See also* fees of auditors; fees of credit rating agencies

Competition among gatekeepers, 50–52, 57–58

Conflicts of interest: of analysts in Japan, 40–42; of analysts in U.S., 57, 140; of credit rating agencies, 5–6, 14, 60, 68–73; of gatekeepers (generally), 14–15, 52, 56, 180; of monitors of gatekeepers, 53

Connecticut Resources Recovery Authority, 86

Constitutional protection of credit rating agencies. *See* First Amendment protections and credit rating agencies

Consultant work: by accounting firms in Japan, 19, 20; by accounting firms in U.S., 14, 52, 187; by credit rating agencies, 69–71

Continuity of engagement: comparison of U.S. and Japanese reforms, 24–25; in Japan, 20

Corporate and accounting scandals, 1–2, 11, 13, 66, 137. *See also names of companies*

CPAAOB. *See* Certified Public Accountants and Auditing Oversight Board (Japan)

CPAEIB. *See* Certified Public Accountant Examination and Investigation Board (Japan)

Credit default swaps (CDSs), 73–74, 91, 93

Credit rating agencies in Japan, 4, 29–36; comparison with U.S. credit rating agency regulation, 4, 45; oligopolization, 32–33; proposal for regulation of, 4–5, 36; ratings gap and changes since *2004*, 34–35, 35t; ratings lag, 4, 33–34; regulatory use of credit ratings, 32

Credit rating agencies in U.S., 5–6, 59–99; ancillary services offered by, 69–71; and CDOs, 5, 60, 74–80; certification of, 3, 4; comparison to other gatekeepers, 60, 61, 62–89; conflicts of interest of, 5–6, 14, 60, 68–73; fees of, 62, 63, 66, 69; historical background of, 62–66; need to regulate, 36, 48; oligopolization, 5–6, 60–61; Pettit comment on, 100–02; profitability of, 5, 62–68; prophylactic or empowerment rules proposed for, 96–97; reform proposals for, 6, 61, 89–96, 189; regulatory licenses provided to issuers by, 81–83, 89–95; role of, 59–60; and structured finance issues, 73–80; success and profitability of, 64–68, 65t, 67f, 67t, 100; tension in roles of, 56; unsolicited ratings from, 71–73; value of ratings to business community, 101–02. *See also* First Amendment protections and credit rating agencies; Nationally Recognized Statistical Rating Organizations

(NRSROs); *specific agencies (for example, Moody's)*
Credit Rating Agency Duopoly Relief Act of 2005 (U.S.), 36
Credit spreads, proposal to replace NRSROs with, 91–94

Daiwa Bank, 38–39
Deutsche Bank's settlement, 143
Disclosure: by analysts in Japan, 39–40, 42, 49; by analysts in U.S., recommendations for, 10, 143, 154, 170; corporate governance disclosure in Japan, 22; importance in securities regulation, 46–47
Donaldson, William H., 165
Dow Jones, 66
Dun & Bradstreet v. Greenmoss Builders (1985), 85

Earnings outlooks, disclosure of, 49
Efendi, J., 184
Engagement risk of auditors, 7–8, 109–13; PCAOB consideration of, 121–22
Enron scandal, 1, 13, 14, 19, 86, 105, 181
Equity analysts. *See* analysts in Japan; analysts in U.S.
Equity ownership in U.S., 56, 57. *See also* mutual funds
European Commission's Forum Group on Financial Analysts on conflicts of interest, 42
Executive compensation, effect on revenue recognition, 11, 183–85, 184f

FASB. *See* Financial Accounting Standards Board (U.S.)
FASF. *See* Financial Accounting Standards Foundation (Japan)
Fees of auditors: effect on independence of auditor, 52; in Japan, 4, 19, 25, 28–29, 30f; and risk management, 113; in U.S., 8, 25, 28, 30f

Fees of credit rating agencies, 62, 63, 66, 69
Financial Accounting Standards Board (FASB; U.S.), 25, 55
Financial Accounting Standards Foundation (FASF; Japan), 24, 25, 55
Financial gatekeepers (generally): in bull market when less concern about fraud, 186–87; conflicts of interest of, 14–15, 52; defined, 10–11, 177–78; in Japan, 15–16, 45–54, 56; monitoring of, 2, 53; need to regulate, 45–49, 47f, 188; organizations best suited to regulate, 53–54; reforms, 187–89; role of, 11, 14–15, 178; Stevens comment on, 55–58; types of, 11, 55, 179; types of regulations, 49–52. *See also specific types (for example, accounting systems, credit rating agencies, and analysts)*
Financial Services Agency (FSA; Japan): and credit ratings, 35, 36; criticism on IMF for relying on market analyst reports on Japan's bad debts, 44; goal to increase number of CPAs, 27; investigation of Daiwa Bank complaint against ING analyst reports, 39; relationship with CPAAOB, 21, 22, 53; role of, 4, 15; sanctions available to, 25–26
Financial statement insurance, proposal for, 189
Financial System Council (Japan): Subcommittee on the Certified Public Accountant System report, 20, 27; Working Group on Disclosure on Regulation Fair Disclosure (FD), 43
Financial Times on accounting system in Japan, 17
First Amendment protections and credit rating agencies: journalistic protections claimed by rating agencies, 6, 61, 66, 81, 83–89; legislation to change "recognized" to "registered" in NRSRO, challenge to, 94–95; and unsolicited ratings, 72, 73

Fitch: historical background of, 63; in Japan, 32; liability and journalistic privilege, 87; on market-based measures, 93–94; as NRSRO, 61; risk management consulting services of, 70; unsolicited ratings from, 71

Fraudulent reporting of clients, effect on auditors, 105, 123, 124–29, 136–37. *See also* liability of and lawsuits against auditors

Freedom to provide information as market principle, 46, 51

FSA. *See* Financial Services Agency (Japan)

Gatekeepers. *See* financial gatekeepers (generally)

Generally accepted accounting principles (GAAP), effect of use of, 47, 105, 107, 111–12

Global Crossing scandal, 184

Global Settlement: distribution of reports by independent research firms under, 43; effect of, 9–10, 37, 139–71; investor education as part of, 141; terms of, 2, 9, 37, 143, 144t. *See also* analysts in U.S.

Governance of CPAs, comparison of U.S. and Japanese reforms, 23–24

Government Accountability Office (GAO) study on financial statements and restatements, 180–82, 181f

Green, T. C., 155

Huron Consulting study on restatements, 181, 182f

IMF. *See* International Monetary Fund
Independent Research Exchange (IRE), 180
Influence on trades as reason to regulate financial gatekeepers, 46–47
ING Baring Securities Japan Ltd. report on Daiwa Bank, 38–39, 44

Insurance of audit firms, 106, 109–10; financial statement insurance, proposal for, 189

International Monetary Fund (IMF): on Japan's bad debt situation, 44; treatment of Asian countries following currency crisis, 18

International Organization of Securities Organizations (IOSCO): on accounting fraud, 20; on analysts, 40, 43; on regulation of credit rating agencies, 36

Investment Advisers Act of *1940* (U.S.), 49

Investment analysts. *See* analysts in Japan; analysts in U.S.

Investment Company Act of *1940* (U.S.), 82–83

Investment Company Institute and Securities Industry Association survey on equity ownership, 56

Japan Bond Research Institute (JBRI), 31, 33. *See now* Rating and Investment Information, Inc. (R&I)

Japan Credit Rating Agency, Ltd. (JCR), 31–32, 33–34, 35

Japanese Institute of Certified Public Accountants (JICPA): on continuity of engagement, 24–25; CPAAOB oversight of, 21; creation of, 24; fee setting by, 28; on internal controls of auditing firms, 22; recommended role in insuring independence of auditors, 18–19; rule changes to enforce accounting firm staff rotation, 20; on time spent on audits, 28

Japanese Securities Dealers Association (JSDA) regulation of analysts, 4, 36, 38–40; *2002* rules, 39–40; *2003* rules, 40; *2004* rules, 41

Japan's scandals and resulting regulation, 2, 3–5, 13–54; accounting system, 16–29; bad debt problems and stock market slump, 15; credit rating agencies, 29–36;

U.S. reform's effect on, 16. *See also* banking issues in Japan; *specific companies and business types*

Japan-U.S. Yen-Dollar Committee on credit rating system, 31

JCR. *See* Japan Credit Rating Agency, Ltd.

Jefferson County (Colorado) school district bond issues, 71–72, 87

Journalistic privilege and credit rating agencies. *See* First Amendment protections and credit rating agencies

Kanebo's reporting fraud, 16, 23, 26

Kinney, William R., Jr., 109

Koizumi government, 15, 19

KPMG, 137

Land Revaluation Law (Japan), 18

Liability of and lawsuits against auditors: aiding and abetting liability, 186, 187; class actions against auditors, 124–27, 125t; comparison of U.S. and Japanese systems, 25–26; jury vs. judge trials, 127–28; proposed auditing master's office report, effect of, 8; protection of Private Securities Litigation Reform Act of *1995* against, 11, 127; reforms recommended for, 105–06, 129–32, 137–38, 187, 189; shortcomings of system, 7, 106; theory behind, 109

Liability of credit rating agencies, 6, 61, 66, 72, 73, 81, 83–89, 94–96

Litan, R. E., 53

Lowe v. SEC (1985), 85

Mega-settlements in class actions against auditors, 124, 126–27, 128

Merrill Lynch, 188

Mikuni & Co., 33, 34

Ministry of Finance (MOF; Japan): Japan-U.S. Yen-Dollar Committee on credit rating system, 31; recommended role in regulating accountants and auditors, 19; regulation of capital adequacy of banks, 17

Mizuho, sanctions against, 26

Moody, John, 63

Moody's Investors Service, 34, 35; conflicts of interest by, 69; historical background of, 61, 63; in Japan, 32, 34, 35; lawsuits against, 85, 87, 88; market-based ratings of, 91, 102; nature of business of, 84; risk management consulting services of, 70; success and profitability of, 64–68, 65t, 67f, 67t, 100; support for proposed opening market to new NRSROs, 90; unsolicited ratings from, 71, 72

Mutual funds: comparison of U.S. and Japan, 4, 56; growth of, as factor requiring regulation of gatekeepers, 14; and investment advisers' role, 57

Mycal (Japanese supermarket) bankruptcy and bond default, 4, 33–34

National Association of Securities Dealers (NASD) regulation of stock analysts, 10, 37, 40, 147, 170. *See also* Global Settlement

Nationally Recognized Statistical Rating Organizations (NRSROs): change to Nationally Registered Statistical Rating Organizations, 36, 94–95; creation and importance of, 62, 64; First Amendment rights of, 88–89; and oligopolization of credit rating agency business, 5–6, 60–61; proposed elimination or reform of, 89–95; proposed opening market to new NRSROs, 90–91; proposed replacement with market-based measures, 91–94; regulation of, 36, 48. *See also specific NRSROs*

National Research Exchange (NRE), 180

Negligence of auditors. *See* liability of and lawsuits against auditors

INDEX 199

Net capital rules for broker-dealers, 64
Newby v. Enron Corp. (2005), 86
New York State Attorney General's Office investigations into financial industry. *See* Spitzer, Eliot
New York Stock Exchange (NYSE): registration requirements of, 1; rules governing stock analysts, 10, 37, 40, 147, 170
Nihon Keizai Shimbun surveys: on auditing staff rotation, 20; on fees paid to auditors, 28–29
Nippon Investors Service, Inc. (NIS), 31–32, 33
Nominated advisers (Nomads), 179
Nonperforming loans by Japanese banks, 15, 16
NRE (National Research Exchange), 180
NRSROs. *See* Nationally Recognized Statistical Rating Organizations
NYSE. *See* New York Stock Exchange

Organizations best suited to regulate financial gatekeepers, 53–54

Panel on Audit Effectiveness on disclosures by SEC and POB, 119
PCAOB. *See* Public Company Accounting Oversight Board (U.S.)
Perry, G., comment on analyst recommendations, 172–76
Pettit, J., comment on credit rating agencies, 100–02
POB. *See* Public Oversight Board (U.S.)
Private Securities Litigation Reform Act of 1995, 11, 127, 186
Profitability of credit rating agencies in U.S., 5, 62–68
Promotional activities of analysts: restrictions in Europe on, 42; restrictions in Japan on, 41–42; restrictions in U.S. on, 42–43

Public Company Accounting Oversight Board (PCAOB; U.S.), 113–19; attorney positions within, 118; budget and funding of, 123; challenges to, 53, 188; compared to Japan's CPAAOB, 25, 49; creation and role of, 1, 7, 24, 103, 114, 188; expertise issues within, 116–19; liability for audit failure, sharing of responsibility with auditors for, 128–29, 137; Office of Chief Auditor, 117; recommended creation of auditing master's office in, 8, 105–06, 129–32, 137–38; risk management by, 119–23; Standing Advisory Group (SAG), 117; statutory authority of, 114–16; transparency issues of, 118, 119
Public Oversight Board (POB; U.S.): compared with PCAOB, 117–18; Quality Control Inquiry Committee (QCIC), 131

"Quiet periods" after listing or registration of share offerings, 40
Quinn v. McGraw-Hill Cos. (1999), 87

Rating and Investment Information, Inc. (R&I), 31, 33, 35
Regulation AC (Analyst Certification), 37, 188
Regulation FD (Fair Disclosure), 43, 84, 96
Regulatory organizations best suited to oversee financial gatekeepers, 53–54
Research reports: and demand for independent research, 51; investigation of, 2; Japanese prohibition on misleading reports, 4; need to regulate, 46; uncertainty and subjectivity of information provided in, 47–49, 47f. *See also* analysts in Japan; analysts in U.S.
Restatements, importance of, 11, 180–82, 181f, 182f
Risk management: consulting services of credit rating agencies on, 70; engagement

risk of auditors, 7–8, 109–13; of PCAOB, 119–23; types of risk of auditors, 110, 111f

Sanctions against accounting firms: comparison of U.S. and Japan, 25–26. *See also* Global Settlement
S&P. *See* Standard and Poor's
Sarbanes-Oxley Act (SOX): auditor oversight under, 7, 107; backlash against, 104; and conflicts of interest, 52; effect on auditors, 103–35, 189; enactment of, 1, 40; incentives for auditors to detect and disclose reporting problems, 108–09; profits of accounting firms after, 66; section 307, 188; section 404, 82, 83, 137; theory behind, 2, 19–20, 52, 182, 187. *See also* Public Company Accounting Oversight Board (PCAOB)
Scandals. *See* corporate and accounting scandals; Japan's scandals and resulting regulation
SEC. *See* Securities and Exchange Commission (U.S.)
Securities Act of *1933* (U.S.), 23, 82, 84, 96
Securities analysts. *See* analysts in Japan; analysts in U.S.
Securities and Exchange Commission (SEC; U.S.): auditor oversight by, 6–7, 23, 53; authority over PCAOB, 116; on conflicts of interest of credit rating agencies, 68, 70; following "access theory," 55; investigation of NRSROs by, 88–89; investigation of stock analysts by, 40; net capital rules for broker-dealers, 64; proposed regulation of auditing function, 14; proposed regulation of credit rating agencies, 36, 61; proposed regulation of NRSROs, 90–91; and Regulation AC (Analyst Certification), 37, 188; and Regulation FD (Fair Disclosure) for analysts, 43, 84, 96. *See also* Global Settlement
Securities and Exchange Law (Japan), amendment to require internal control reports, 23
Securities and Exchange Surveillance Commission (SESC; Japan), 41
Securities Exchange Act of *1934* (U.S.), 82
Securities regulation: failure of, 13; registration statement and prospectus requirements in Japan, 32. *See also specific agencies regulating*
Seibu Railway's fraud, 4, 16, 22
Self-regulating organizations: of accounting profession, 24; role of, 53. *See also specific organizations in Japan and U.S.*
Sell-side analysts in U.S. *See* analysts in U.S.
SESC (Securities and Exchange Surveillance Commission; Japan), 41
Soft-dollar rules, 43
SOX. *See* Sarbanes-Oxley Act
Spitzer, Eliot, 1–2, 9, 139, 180, 188
Standard and Poor's (S&P): CDO Evaluator, use of, 76–78, 78t; historical background of, 62–63, 64; in Japan, 32, 33, 34, 35; journalistic privilege alleged by, 85, 86, 87–88; as NRSRO, 61; protections against conflicts of interest by, 69; risk management consulting services of, 70; on structured finance, 75; success and profitability of, 65–66; unsolicited ratings from, 71
Stevens, P., comment on comparison of financial gatekeepers in U.S. and Japan, 55–58
Stock market analysts. *See* analysts in Japan; analysts in U.S.
Stock market crash of 1929, 63
Subjectivity of information provided as reason to regulate financial gatekeepers, 47–49, 47f

Supreme Court, U.S.: on commercial speech, 85; on credit reports and First Amendment rights, 85

Thomas Weisel Partners' settlement, 143

Uncertainty of information provided as reason to regulate financial gatekeepers, 47–49, 47f

Unsolicited ratings from U.S. credit rating agencies, 71–73

Wallison, P., comment on risk management of auditors, 136–38
Warnings in annual reports in Japan, 18
WorldCom scandal, 1, 69, 105, 136, 181

Yamaichi Securities, 17

Brookings Institution

The Brookings Institution is a private nonprofit organization devoted to research, education, and publication on important issues of domestic and foreign policy. Its principal purpose is to bring the highest quality independent research and analysis to bear on current and emerging policy problems. The Institution was founded on December 8, 1927, to merge the activities of the Institute for Government Research, founded in 1916, the Institute of Economics, founded in 1922, and the Robert Brookings Graduate School of Economics and Government, founded in 1924. Interpretations or conclusions in Brookings publications should be understood to be solely those of the authors.

Nomura Institute of Capital Markets Research

Established in April 2004 as a subsidiary of Nomura Holdings, Nomura Institute of Capital Markets Research (NICMR) offers original, neutral studies of Japanese and Western financial markets and policy proposals aimed at establishing a market-structured financial system in Japan and contributing to the healthy development of capital markets in China and other emerging markets. NICMR disseminates its research among Nomura Group companies and to a wider audience through regular publications in English and Japanese.

Tokyo Club Foundation for Global Studies

The Tokyo Club Foundation for Global Studies was established by Nomura Securities Co., Ltd., in 1987 as a nonprofit organization for promoting studies in the management of the global economy. It sponsors research, symposiums, and publications on global economic issues. The Tokyo Club has developed a network of institutions from Europe, the United States, and Asia that assists in organizing specific research programs and identifying appropriate expertise. In recent years, the research agenda has strongly focused on emerging trends in global capital markets as well as current issues in macro-economic stability and growth. Information about past and future programs may be viewed on the Foundation's website, www.tcf.or.jp/.

www.ingramcontent.com/pod-product-compliance
Ingram Content Group UK Ltd.
Pitfield, Milton Keynes, MK11 3LW, UK
UKHW040203230326
469204UK00001B/12